Implementing international environmental agreements in Russia

MANCHESTER
UNIVERSITY PRESS

Issues in Environmental Politics

Series editors Mikael Skou Andersen and Duncan Liefferink

At the start of the twenty-first century, the environment has come to stay as a central concern of global politics. This series takes key problems for environmental policy and examines the politics behind their cause and possible resolution. Accessible and eloquent, the books make available for a non-specialist readership some of the best research and most provocative thinking on humanity's relationship with the planet.

already published in the series

Science and politics in international environmental regimes
Steinar Andresen, Tora Skodvin, Arild Underdal and Jørgen Wettestad

Congress and air pollution: environmental politics in the US
Christopher J. Bailey

Sustaining Amazonia: grassroots action for productive conservation
Anthony Hall

The protest business? Mobilizing campaign groups
Grant Jordan and William Maloney

Implementing EU environmental policy Christoph Knill and Andrea Lenschow (eds)

Environment and the nation state: the Netherlands, the European Union and acid rain Duncan Liefferink

Valuing the environment Raino Malnes

Life on a modern planet: a manifesto for progress Richard North

Public purpose or private benefit? The politics of energy conservation
Gill Owen

Environmental pressure groups Peter Rawcliffe

North Sea cooperation: linking international and domestic pollution control Jon Birger Skjærseth

Governance by green taxes Mikael Skou Andersen

European environmental policy: the pioneers
Mikael Skou Andersen and Duncan Liefferink (eds)

The new politics of pollution Albert Weale

Environmental policy-making in Britain, Germany and the European Union
Rüdiger K. W. Wurzel

Implementing international environmental agreements in Russia

Geir Hønneland
and
Anne-Kristin Jørgensen

Manchester University Press
Manchester and New York

distributed exclusively in the USA by Palgrave

Published by Manchester University Press
Oxford Road, Manchester M13 9NR, UK
and Room 400, 175 Fifth Avenue, New York, NY 10010, USA
www.manchesteruniversitypress.co.uk

Distributed exclusively in the USA by
Palgrave, 175 Fifth Avenue, New York,
NY 10010, USA

Distributed exclusively in Canada by
UBC Press, University of British Columbia, 2029 West Mall,
Vancouver, BC, Canada V6T 1Z2

British Library Cataloguing-in-Publication Data
A catalogue record for this book is available from the British Library.

Library of Congress Cataloging-in-Publication Data applied for

ISBN 0 7190 6386 8 *hardback*

First published 2003

10 09 08 07 06 05 04 03 10 9 8 7 6 5 4 3 2 1

Typeset in Sabon
by Northern Phototypesetting Co. Ltd, Bolton
Printed in Great Britain
by Bell & Bain Ltd, Glasgow

Contents

Figures

Tables

Preface

The research underlying this book was made possible by two different grants. First, studies of the implementation of international environmental agreements in Russia constituted part of the Fridtjof Nansen Institute's (FNI) strategic institute programme 'International Environmental and Natural Resources Regimes: Implementation, Conflict and Synergy'. The programme was financed by the Norwegian Research Council and carried out during the period 1999–2001. Second, the empirical data needed for the book were mainly collected under the project 'Northwestern Russia as a Non-Military Threat to Norway: Mechanisms for Problem Solving at the International, National and Sub-National Level', financed by the Norwegian Ministry of Defence for the years 2000–2001. The book also partly builds on our previous research on Northwest Russian politics, particularly in the spheres of fisheries management, nuclear safety, federalism and civil–military relations.

We are indebted to a number of colleagues and partners for input to and feedback on our research. Our work on Russian fisheries management has been carried out together with Frode Nilssen at the Norwegian Institute of Fisheries and Aquaculture. Likewise, we have worked closely together with our colleagues Arild Moe and Steven Sawhill on the study of nuclear safety issues in Russia. Our more generalised focus on Russian politics has in recent years benefited from collaboration with the Centre for Russian Studies at the Norwegian Institute of International Affairs, and, in particular, with its director Helge Blakkisrud. Olav Schram Stokke, research director of the FNI and project leader of the above-mentioned strategic institute programme, helped formulate the book's research topic and has offered valuable advice and comments on parts of the manuscript. Thanks are also due to Christel Elvestad, Arild Moe, Elena Nikitina, Frode Nilssen, Ivan Safranchuk, Steven Sawhill, Jørgen Wettestad and an anonymous reviewer for comments. The standard phrase that the authors take full responsibility for the contents of the book applies here too, naturally.

Thanks also to Boris Alekseyev, Sergey Filippov, Lyudmila Ivanova, Frode Johansen, Igor Lebedev, Ernst Lukmanov, Christen Mordal, Lyubov Nikiforova, Aleksandr Ruzankin, Irina Sokolova, Anatoliy Vasilyev, Anatoliy Yevenko, Aleksandr Zelentsov, Vyacheslav Zilanov and Andrey Zolotkov for helpful advice, to Claes Lykke Ragner for cartography, Chris Saunders for language editing and Maryanne Rygg for the final editing of the text.

In the transcription of Russian words into Latin characters, we have tried to pay attention both to general practice and consistency. Although we wanted to give consistency the upper hand, we have occasionally allowed exceptions in order not to depart from what might be considered general practice. While the Russian *ë* is generally transcribed as *yo*, we maintain customary English transcriptions – such as Gorbachev, for instance. Russian *e* is written as *ye* at the beginning of words and after vowels. Nevertheless, we skip the *y* in proper names that already have a common spelling in English, e.g. Karelia. The Russian hard and soft signs are not transcribed.

The names of Russian organisations are generally rendered in English translation rather than by their Russian acronyms, which would probably bring little meaning to readers without any Russian. Exceptions are made in the case of organisations whose full names are seldom used in Russian. For instance, we write the State Committee for Fisheries (instead of the more colloquial Goskomryba), but maintain acronyms such as Sevryba and Murmanrybvod. All translations from the Russian and Norwegian are by the authors.

Abbreviations and acronyms

Abbreviations

ACFM	Advisory Committee for Fisheries Management
AEPS	Arctic Environmental Protection Strategy
AMAP	Arctic Monitoring and Assessment Programme
AMEC	Arctic Military Environmental Co-operation
BEAR	Barents Euro-Arctic Region
CAFF	Conservation of Arctic flora and fauna
CTR	Co-operative Threat Reduction Programme
EEZ	Exclusive Economic Zone
EPPR	Emergency preparedness, prevention and response
FAO	UN Food and Agriculture Organisation
IAEA	International Atomic Energy Agency
ICES	International Council for the Exploration of the Sea
IMO	International Maritime Organisation
INES	International Nuclear Event Scale
LOSC	Law of the Sea Convention
LRTAP	UN Economic Commission for Europe Convention on Long-range Transboundary Air Pollution
MNEPR	Multilateral Nuclear Environmental Programme in the Russian Federation
MSY	Maximum sustainable yield
NAFO	Northwest Atlantic Fisheries Organisation
NEAFC	Northeast Atlantic Fisheries Commission
NEFCO	Nordic Environmental Finance Corporation
NGO	Non-governmental organisation
NUSS	Nuclear Safety Standards

PAME	Protection of the Arctic Marine Environment
POP	Persistent organic pollutant
RSFSR	Russian Soviet Federative Socialist Republic
SSBN	Ballistic missile-firing submarine
TAC	Total allowable catch

Russian acronyms

Gosatomnadzor	Federal Inspectorate for Nuclear and Radiation Safety
Goskomgidromet	State Committee for Hydrometeorology and Environmental Monitoring
Kolkhoz	Collective farm (here: fishing fleet)
Minatom	Russian Ministry of Atomic Energy
Murmanrybprom	Murmansk Fishery Enterprise
Murmanrybvod	Murmansk Fishery Inspection Service
PINRO	Knipovich Scientific Polar Institute for Marine Fisheries and Oceanograph
Rosenergoatom	Russian Atomic Energy Enterprise
Roskomgidromet	Russian Committee for Hydrometerorology and Environmental Monitoring
Sevrao	Northern Enterprise for the Treatment of Nuclear Waste
Sevryba	Association of enterprises in the Russian Northern fishery basin
VNIRO	All-Russian Scientific Institute for Fisheries and Oceanography

See preface for a note on translation/acronymisation of the names of Russian organisations.

1
Introduction

How do Russian authorities go about implementing their international environmental obligations? This question, indicating the present book's main topic of study, implies that implementation is here understood as the political processes taking place at the national, and possibly the sub-national, level after the conclusion of agreements or establishment of regimes at the international level. In the literature on international environmental agreements, processes at the domestic level are receiving increased attention.[1] After an initial main focus on regime *formation*,[2] the literature has in recent years come to be dominated by studies of regime *effectiveness* and the *implementation*, including processes at the domestic level, of provisions laid down by international regimes.[3] Moreover, the issue of regime *linkages* is also gradually coming to the fore,[4] i.e., how various regimes are linked to each other normatively and structurally,[5] and how national authorities economise efforts by giving the same agency responsibility for implementing the provisions of various international agreements. While the questions of regime effectiveness and linkages at the regime level are not explicitly discussed in this book, the study does aim at providing an in-depth analysis of implementation processes at the national and sub-national level in Russia, including the linkage of issues by agencies at these levels.

Why focus on Russia? To answer with a cliché, Russia is a former superpower, and still the world's largest country, and hence deserves attention in all matters involving Russian interests or possible implications for the outside world of policy choices made in Russia. In the realm of environmental politics, this is particularly true: the outside world cannot simply fence itself off from transboundary environmental problems originating in Russia. This leads us to a second reason for the choice of focus: post-Soviet Russia is, in an international context, particularly hard hit by environmental degradation and resource depletion. The plan economy of the Soviet Union did not pay sufficient attention to the sustainability of the environment and natural resources and large parts of the country's natural environment were in a dire state when the Union was dissolved in 1991. Several of these problems, in particular air pollution and the danger of nuclear radiation, are of a transboundary character and of such gravity that they pose serious threats to the outside world.[6] Moreover, post-Soviet Russian politics have more than anything been characterised by chaos and unpredictability; all the more interesting is it then to see whether relatively stable policy patterns can be found across various cases in Russian environmental politics.

Finally, although there has been a certain amount of attention in the literature on the implementation of international environmental agreements in so-called transition economies,[7] there has been little systematic study of such implementation processes in Russia that covers more than a few areas and analyses of more overarching political development trends in the country.[8] While students of international environmental politics have tended to concentrate on Western states and countries in the third world, observers of Russian politics have generally been preoccupied by following the day-to-day political battle in Moscow and the Russian regions, and have only to a very limited extent delved into specific areas of politics such as environmental issues.[9] Hence, the present study seeks to fill a gap in the existing literature by providing both a systematic in-depth analysis of various cases from the management of natural resources and the environment and linking the discussion closely to general trends in contemporary Russian politics.

The book includes case studies from the fields of fisheries management,[10] nuclear safety and air pollution control in Northwestern Russia,[11] here understood as Murmansk and Arkhangelsk Oblasts, and, to some extent, also the Nenets Autonomous Okrug (see Figure 1.1).[12] The Russian Federation inherited the federal structure of the Soviet Union and the Russian Soviet Federative Socialist Republic (RSFSR) and today consists of 89 federal subjects. The relationship between Moscow and the federal subjects has been a main issue of contention in Russian politics since the establishment of the Federation in 1991.[13] Hence, the division of responsibility between federal and regional authorities will necessarily be a major concern in a study of the implementation of international environmental obligations in the regions of Russia, as will co-ordination of work between various agencies at both the federal and the regional level. Northwestern Russia is a good case in point for an in-depth analysis since it in many respects represents a microcosm of the Russian Federation. Most important in this context, it epitomises an 'exaggerated' version of Russia as a whole with its abundant natural resources and extremely grave environmental conditions.

Figure 1.1 *Northwestern Russia*

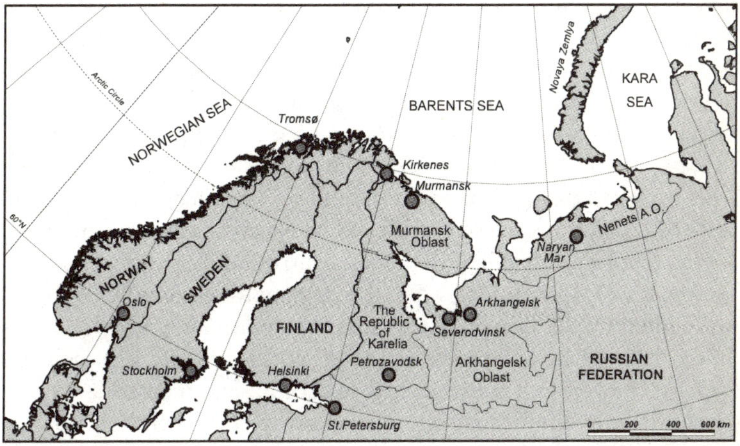

What is the problem?

If asked to characterise the northwestern part of the Russian Federation in one or two phrases, it would be difficult to avoid a depiction of the region as both blessed with extremely bountiful natural resources and, at the same time, bedevilled by grave environmental problems. The region, a northern periphery partly located north of the Arctic Circle, owes the existence of its human settlements largely to the presence of natural resources. In the southern parts of the region, mainly in today's Arkhangelsk Oblast, forestry has for centuries constituted the foundation for life.[14] In the more barren Murmansk Oblast, which geographically corresponds to the Kola Peninsula, fisheries and mining provided the industrial foundation for the creation of large human settlements after World War I, rendering the region the most densely populated area of the Circumpolar Arctic during the last half of the twentieth century.[15] The fishing grounds of the adjacent Barents Sea are among the most productive in the world, and the mineral deposits of the Kola Peninsula, mainly iron ore, nickel and apatite, are remarkable for their richness.[16] From the 1920s onwards, massive fishing fleets were built up in the region and, at the time of the break-up of the Soviet Union, Murmansk had the largest fish-processing plant in the entire Union.[17] Town names such as Nikel and Apatity, for their part, indicate the importance of the mining and metallurgical complex in the region.

The extraction of natural resources and the accompanying military build-up have, however, taken place at the expense of environmental considerations. Since the 1990s, Northwestern Russia has been more renowned for its environmental degradation than for its abundant resources.[18] Since Western journalists were gradually given easier access to this heavily militarised region from the mid-1980s, the black tree stumps of the dying forests around Nikel and Monchegorsk have come to symbolise the sullen environmental state of Russia to many in the West. The nickel smelters of these two towns had virtually killed the forests surrounding them and served as sources of pollution also for the neighbouring Nordic countries and other parts of Russia. 'Stop the death clouds!' became the slogan of environmental organisations in the Nordic countries in the early 1990s. The Nordic countries had plans for gigantic assistance programmes to reduce the pollution spewing out of the production plants of the mining and metallurgical complex of Northwestern Russia, but nothing has come of these plans so far.[19] Financial hardship has forced the plants to cut back on activities in recent years, though without affecting the alarming rate of air pollution in the European Arctic to any significant extent.

Throughout the 1990s, another environmental threat in the region upstaged air pollution as a focus of public concern, namely the danger of radiation from nuclear installations, discarded nuclear vessels, radioactive waste and spent nuclear fuel. The fire on board and subsequent sinking of the nuclear submarine *Komsomolets* of the Russian Northern Fleet southwest of Bear Island in the Barents Sea in April 1989 was a further wake-up call for the European public to the danger of nuclear radiation from nuclear-powered vessels stationed in Northwestern Russia.[20] Towards the end of 1990, rumours emerged that the Soviet Union had been dumping radioactive material in the

Barents and Kara Seas.[21] The rumours were officially confirmed in a Russian parliamentary report a few years later (Yablokov *et al.* 1993). A major problem in the latter half of the 1990s was the build-up of radioactive waste and spent nuclear fuel in Northwestern Russia. Existing storage facilities were full, and there were no safe vehicles to transport the radioactive material out of the region for reprocessing or permanent storage. Moreover, financial constraints have forced the Northern Fleet to decommission large quantities of nuclear-powered vessels in recent years.[22] Rumours are also circulating about the unsafe functioning of vessels still in service (Hønneland and Jørgensen 1999a). The *Kursk* accident of August 2000, albeit mainly a human tragedy, functioned as a reminder of the potential dangers residing in the Northern Fleet's nuclear-powered vessels, not least to the environment. Although radiation levels in the region are at present low, there are considerable risks connected with the unsatisfactory storage of radioactive waste, decommissioned nuclear submarines awaiting dismantling and the continued operation of unsafe nuclear power installations, notably the Kola Nuclear Power Plant at Polyarnye Zori.

Finally, signs of resource depletion have recently been emerging in the region, most notably in the Barents Sea fisheries.[23] These fisheries, managed bilaterally by Russia and Norway since the mid-1970s, had for many years been seen as a management success. At the turn of the millennium, however, the Norwegian–Arctic cod stock, by far the most commercially important species in the area, appeared to be in severe crisis. Some would have it that the situation is similar for the management system itself due to the dire state of its main object of regulation. There are indeed reasons for such an allegation: scientists are uncertain as to the size of the stock; managers do not follow the advice of the scientists in the establishment of quotas; and the enforcement system, at least on the Russian side, seems poorly fit to keep track of actual catch levels and avoid fishing of juvenile specimens. As will follow from Chapter 4, many of these problems can be directly related to more general developments in Russian society and politics.

What is to be implemented?

The environmental problems of Northwestern Russia are directly or indirectly addressed by a number of international treaties, agreements, regimes and other co-operative arrangements. Some of these are global instruments that happen to have implications for the particular problems of the region; others are specifically aimed at solving them. In some cases, specific arrangements are linked to more general instruments at the global level. Moreover, some are 'hard', legally binding arrangements and others 'softer' approaches of a more programmatic character. Both legally binding and non-binding instruments are included in the present study.[24]

An overview is given below of the international agreements and regimes whose implementation is studied in the cases used in this book. It differentiates between arrangements at the global, regional and bilateral levels.[25] The list is not meant to be exhaustive, but rather to include those instruments considered of most importance to the problems at hand. The main selection criterion is that the arrangements must have provisions that require attempts at influencing the behaviour of target groups located in Northwestern Russia.

Fisheries management

The major global instrument underlying systems for marine fisheries management throughout the world is the 1982 Law of the Sea Convention (LOSC) (United Nations 1982), which entered into force on 16 November 1994. The Convention, with its 320 articles and 9 appendices, deals with a range of issues related to the use and management of the world's ocean areas.[26] Most important for fisheries management is the introduction of the principle of 200-mile exclusive economic zones (EEZ). This implies that coastal states are given 'sovereign rights for the purpose of exploring and exploiting, conserving and managing the natural resources' in these zones (United Nations 1982, Article 56[1]). With the rights follows the *obligation* to secure reasonable exploration, exploitation, conservation and management of the resources. For instance, fish stocks are to be maintained at a level that can produce *maximum sustainable yield* (MSY), i.e. the level at which the greatest quantity of fish can be caught annually without the total size of the stock being reduced. Moreover, coastal states are required to promote the objective of optimum utilisation of the living resources of its EEZ, and to establish total allowable catches (TACs) for each fish stock within its EEZ. Finally, coastal states are obliged to co-operate in the management of shared stocks.

More recent global fisheries agreements tend to focus mainly on the management of fisheries taking place in high seas areas, i.e. beyond 200 miles from shore. They include the 1995 Fish Stocks

Agreement (United Nations 1995), which, *inter alia*, foresees the establishment of regional or sub-regional organisations or arrangements for the management of marine resources on the high seas[27] – and two FAO documents: the FAO Compliance Agreement of 1993 (Food and Agriculture Organization 1993) and the FAO Code of Conduct for Responsible Fisheries of 1995 (Food and Agriculture Organization 1996). The Compliance Agreement sets out the responsibility of the flag state and includes provisions on the maximisation of information about high-seas fishing activities. The Code of Conduct is a non-binding instrument which promotes a responsible approach to all aspects of fishing.

In the Barents Sea, both Norway and Russia established their EEZs in 1977. This led to a transition from multilateral negotiations for the Barents Sea fisheries under the auspices of the Northeast Atlantic Fisheries Commission (NEAFC) to bilateral negotiations between coastal states with sovereign rights to fish stocks. To formalise these mutual fishing rights and, more importantly, to establish a common management regime suitable to secure the fish stocks of the area, Norway and the Soviet Union entered into several bilateral fishery co-operation agreements in the mid-1970s. The most important agreements on the establishment of the management regime are the mutual agreements of 11 April 1975 (Stortinget 1975) on co-operation in the fisheries sector and of 15 October 1976 (Stortinget 1976) on mutual fisheries relations, the so-called framework agreements.

The Norwegian–Russian management regime for the Barents Sea fish stocks defines objectives and practices for co-operative management between the two states within the fields of research and regulations, and, since 1993, also enforcement. The co-operation between Russian/Soviet and Norwegian scientists in the mapping of the Barents Sea fish resources dates back to the 1950s.[28] It is now institutionalised within the framework of the International Council for the Exploration of the Sea (ICES). The Joint Norwegian–Russian Fisheries Commission, consisting of bureaucrats, scientists and representatives of the fishing industries of the two countries, convenes at least once a year to establish TACs for the joint fish stocks of the Barents Sea: cod, haddock and capelin. Cod and haddock are shared on a 50–50 basis, while the capelin quota is shared 60–40 in Norway's favour. In addition, quotas of the parties' exclusive stocks are exchanged. After the sessions in the Joint

Commission, the two parties conduct further quota exchanges in bilateral negotiations with third countries. An enforcement co-operation between Norway and Russia in the Barents Sea fisheries has been in operation since 1993.[29] A Permanent Russian–Norwegian Committee for Management and Enforcement Co-operation within the Fisheries Sector was established under the Joint Commission that year. In addition to administering enforcement co-operation, it has undertaken several more comprehensive tasks, such as elaborating a uniform system of conversion factors, joint routines for the closing and opening of fishing grounds, and a co-ordinated introduction of obligatory use of selection grids in the cod fishery. Moreover, the Permanent Committee functions as a forum for discussion and clarifications between the parties in the periods between sessions in the Joint Commission.

Several regional fisheries regimes and agreements are also of relevance for Northwestern Russia. Although NEAFC lost much of its significance after the introduction of the EEZs and coastal state management authority to within 200 miles, it still exerts a certain regulation responsibility in high seas areas in the Northeast Atlantic.[30] Moreover, Northwest Russian fishers occasionally participate in fisheries in the Northwest Atlantic, or the NAFO area (Northwest Atlantic Fisheries Organization 1978). In these 'convention areas', Russian authorities are obliged to ensure that convention obligations are complied with by Russian fishers. Finally, Russian participation in ICES obliges Russian scientists to contribute to the estimates of size and state of the fish stocks of the Northeast Atlantic, in particular in the Barents Sea.

Nuclear safety

As follows from the above description of environmental problems of Northwestern Russia, the threats of nuclear radiation emerge from several different sources in the region: dumped radioactive materials, decommissioned nuclear submarines, nuclear waste and spent nuclear fuel, as well as the unsafe functioning of nuclear installations. Hence, the handling of these various problem complexes is regulated by different instruments at different levels. The most important arrangements at the global level are found in attempts to secure the safe functioning of nuclear installations, mainly under the auspices of the International Atomic Energy Agency (IAEA).[31] The statute of IAEA entered into force in 1957 and authorises the

Agency 'to establish or adopt [. . .] standards for protection of health and minimisation of danger to life and property (including such standards for labour conditions), and to provide for the application of these standards' (International Atomic Energy Agency 1957, Article III.A.6). The development of practical international co-operation in nuclear safety began in the early 1960s and reached its present wide-ranging scale in the 1980s and 1990s after the accidents at Chernobyl and Three Mile Island (Timerbaev and Iorysh 1999). The present IAEA regime on safe development of nuclear energy is based on a range of international legal instruments. Major elements of the regime are, *inter alia*: the 1963 Vienna Convention on Civil Liability for Nuclear Damage (International Atomic Energy Agency 1963);[32] the 1974 Nuclear Safety Standards (International Atomic Energy Agency 1974);[33] the 1986 Notification Convention (International Atomic Energy Agency 1986a);[34] the 1986 Assistance Convention (International Atomic Energy Agency 1986b);[35] the 1994 Convention on Nuclear Safety (International Atomic Energy Agency 1994)[36] and the 1997 Joint Convention on the Safety of Radioactive Waste Management (International Atomic Energy Agency 1997).[37]

The 1972 London Convention (International Maritime Organization 1972)[38] is the main instrument of the global dumping regime, banning the disposal at sea of hazardous waste, defined in terms of toxicity, persistence and tendency to bioaccumulate in marine organisms. Radioactive waste has been the most politicised of the issues involved (Stokke 1998, 2000b). Some items may not be dumped at all whereas others require special permits. Members of the regime are obliged to monitor and record their dumping activities and report them to the secretariat of the Convention, located with the International Maritime Organisation (IMO). The regime also includes provisions for enforcement and dispute settlement.

Four regional instruments stand out as relevant for nuclear safety issues in Northwestern Russia: the AMEC and CTR programmes in connection with discarded nuclear submarines and storage of spent nuclear fuel and other nuclear wastes; the MNEPR as a planned initiative to secure satisfactory framework conditions for foreign states engaged in nuclear safety projects in Russia; and BEAR as a more general co-operative framework aimed partly at environmental issues.

The Declaration on Arctic Military Environmental Co-operation (AMEC) (Ministry of Foreign Affairs 1996) was signed in 1996 by Norway, the Russian Federation and the USA.[39] The parties stated their mutual interest in reducing the deleterious effects of military operations to the Arctic environment, including the ecological risks associated with nuclear waste in the Arctic. Norway and the USA pledged their support in providing the Russians with technological and other assistance to help them de-fuel nuclear submarines removed from service, and to develop safe storage facilities for spent nuclear fuel and other nuclear wastes. The AMEC Declaration establishes an institutional framework for contact and co-operation between military authorities in the three states. By 1998, however, the agreement had little to show for itself in terms of practical results.

In the spring of 1998, US authorities decided to link AMEC with the Nunn–Lugar Co-operative Threat Reduction Programme (US Department of State 1992, 1993; Sawhill 2000). The CTR Programme was created by the US Congress in 1991 as a mechanism to assist the Soviet Union in complying with its obligations of arms reductions with the START I Agreement, and hopefully also new commitments under START II. It has provided more than USD 2,000 million to former Soviet states since 1991. One of the goals of the CTR Programme is to scrap 30 Russian ballistic missile submarines by 2001. The Russians currently have the capacity to scrap only a handful of submarines per year, the major obstacle being the de-fuelling process and dealing with the resulting waste and spent nuclear fuel. By linking AMEC and CTR, US authorities were able to provide a ready source of cash (USD 5 million for 1998) and indemnification from liability.

Finally, it can be discussed whether the Barents Euro-Arctic Region (BEAR) (Ministry of Foreign Affairs 1993) should be perceived as a regional regime of relevance to nuclear safety in Northwestern Russia. This co-operative arrangement between Norway, Sweden, Finland and Russia was established in 1993 and has both a national and regional component.[40] It includes co-operation in a range of functional areas, but environmental issues are supposed to permeate the regime as a whole. A separate working group on the environment is also part of the regime. Stokke (2000a) argues that the BEAR co-operation is closely linked to other regimes at global, regional and bilateral level of relevance to the environment of the European Arctic.

Various bilateral activities of a programmatic character exist in the field of nuclear safety between Russia and other countries. The most comprehensive bilateral co-operation programme is the one with

Norway. In 1995, the Norwegian Government introduced a Plan of Action on nuclear safety in neighbouring countries (Ministry of Foreign Affairs 1995), aimed primarily at combating threats from Northwestern Russia.[41] In the period 1995–99, NOK 343 million was allocated to activities supported under the Plan of Action. The activities have been categorised into four priority areas: (1) safety measures at nuclear facilities; (2) management, storage and disposal of radioactive waste and spent nuclear fuel; (3) radioactive pollution in northern areas; and (4) arms-related environmental hazards. In May 1998, a Framework Agreement was signed between Norway and Russia, stating that Norway shall render free technical assistance in the stated areas, and that Russia shall exempt the delivery of such assistance from taxes, customs duties and other fees and provide nuclear liability protections to Norway in ten projects identified as covered by the Agreement (Ministry of Foreign Affairs 1998). The Framework Agreement foresees the establishment of a Joint Russian–Norwegian Commission to co-ordinate and control its implementation. The Commission has so far convened once every year since 1998 and devoted most of its work to the implementation of the ten projects identified in the Framework Agreement. Finally, it should be mentioned that an expert group on investigations of radioactive pollution in the northern areas was established under the Joint Russian–Norwegian Environmental Commission (see next section) as early as in 1992.

Norway has taken a leading role in endeavours to create a Multilateral Nuclear Environmental Programme in the Russian Federation (MNEPR). The aim of this initiative is to secure satisfactory conditions for all participating countries in nuclear safety projects in Russia, e.g. related to indemnity against nuclear liability, access and oversight and exemption from taxes, customs and other fees. The current draft agreement is stricter than the Russian–Norwegian Framework Agreement as it includes provisions on personnel immunity, access and oversight. A Declaration of Principles was signed in March 1999 (Ministry of Foreign Affairs 1999), but a binding legal framework is still not in sight.

Air pollution control

International efforts to regulate emissions of environmentally hazardous substances into the air include instruments aimed at solving the problems of acid rain, depletion of the ozone layer and climate change, of which only the former will be discussed here. Related to the air pollution of Northwestern Russia, by far the most important international instrument[42] is the 1979 UN Economic Commission for Europe Convention on Long-range Transboundary Air Pollution (LRTAP) (UN Economic Commission for Europe 1979).[43] It addresses problems in Europe and North America concerning airborne pollutants, notably acid rain, and establishes a framework for co-ordinating pollution control measures and common emission standards.[44] The contracting parties are to take into account the precautionary approach as set forth in the 1992 Rio Declaration. They must reduce annual emissions from a reference year, and emission limits are established for some selected sources. A monitoring system has been set up, and five substantive protocols have been negotiated under the regime: on NO_X (1988) (UN Economic Commission for Europe 1988a);[45] volatile organic compounds (1991) (UN Economic Commission for Europe 1991);[46] sulphur (1994) (UN Economic Commission for Europe 1994);[47] heavy metals (1998) (UN Economic Commission for Europe 1998a);[48] and persistent organic pollutants (1998) (UN Economic Commission for Europe 1998b).[49] The Soviet Union/Russian Federation has been an active partner in the LTRAP regime. Traditionally rather reserved towards co-operation with the West during the Cold War, in the late 1970s the Soviet Union was enthusiastic in its support of the LRTAP process, regarding it more in terms of 'high politics' than from an environmental point of view (Kotov and Nikitina 1998a). At present, Russia has ratified the Convention itself and the NO_X Protocol and signed, but not ratified, the Sulphur Protocol.

The Arctic Environmental Protection Strategy (AEPS), a programmatic, legally non-binding document and process initiated by Finland in 1991, commits the eight Arctic states (Russia, Canada, the United States and the five Nordic countries) to undertake research and develop strategies for six priority environmental problems. A number of co-operative programmes have been established: (1) Arctic Monitoring and Assessment Programme (AMAP); (2) Protection of the Arctic Marine Environment (PAME); (3) Conservation of Arctic Flora and Fauna (CAFF); and (4) Emergency Preparedness, Prevention and Response (EPPR) programme. These programmes reported to the Ministers of the Environment of the Arctic countries, who, in turn, identified priority areas for further action. Four ministerial conferences were held under the AEPS framework between 1991 and

1997. The AEPS programmes have now been subsumed under the Arctic Council, a forum established by the Arctic states in 1996 (Arctic Council Declaration 1996). At the first meeting of the Arctic Council, a Regional Programme of Action for the Protection of the Arctic Marine Environment (RPA), developed by the PAME working group, was adopted. VanderZwaag (2000, p. 192) describes the adoption of the RPA as 'small, soft steps in addressing land-based pollution in the Arctic', observing at the same time that detailed actions are only recommended for persistent organic pollutants (POPs) and heavy metals, and that financial and technical commitments are left uncertain, although the need to assist the Russian Federation in taking pollution prevention actions is stressed.

Environmental co-operation between Russia and the Nordic states in the Barents Euro-Arctic Region (BEAR) (see previous section) and bilaterally is also of relevance for air pollution control in Northwestern Russia. Of particular importance is the Joint Russian–Norwegian Environmental Commission, which was established in 1988. Under the Joint Commission, comprising leading environmental agencies in the two states, several working groups have been established, including the Working Group on Airborne Pollution. The latter has developed an environmental monitoring and modelling programme for the border areas. The focus of capacity-enhancement efforts has been on the question of the modernisation of the Pechenganickel smelter, which was brought up at governmental level when the Environmental Commission was established.

The 'clusters' of agreements to be implemented

The various agreements to be implemented are listed in Table 1.1. In the management of the Northwest Russian fisheries, Russia has a rather clear set of international commitments. From the global instruments come obligations to manage the fish stocks with a view to maintaining Maximum Sustainable Yield (MSY), to establish TACs for the fish stocks in the Russian EEZ, to co-operate with Norway in the management of shared stocks, and to take responsibility for the activities of vessels under Russian flag in high seas areas. Regional arrangements demand participation by Russian scientists in ICES and enforcement of international standards in 'convention areas' such as NAFO and NEAFC. The obligations from the global, and partly regional level, are confirmed and specified in the bilateral regime with Norway. The framework agreements provide basic guidelines for the co-operation. Decisions by the Joint Commission, partly interpreted, specified and adjusted in the Permanent Committee, give concrete obligations that are binding for the parties. This includes the obligation that joint decisions are enforced in due manner by Russian authorities and complied with by target groups.

Table 1.1 *International obligations of the Russian Federation requiring implementation in its northwestern region*[a]

Level/case	*Fisheries management*	*Nuclear safety*	*Air pollution control*
Global	LOSC Fish Stocks Agreement Compliance Agreement Code of Conduct	(IAEA) London Convention	
Regional	ICES (NEAFC) (NAFO)	AMEC CTR (MNEPR) (BEAR)	LRTAP (BEAR) (AEPS/Arctic Council)
Bilateral	Joint Russian–Norwegian Fisheries Commission[b] Bilateral quota-sharing agreements with other states	Joint Russian–Norwegian Commission on Nuclear Safety[b] Various programmatic activities with other states	Joint Russian–Norwegian Environmental Commission[b] Various programmatic activities with other states

[a] The agreements/regimes in parenthesis are not explicitly discussed in this book. Others are mentioned only sporadically in the case studies since their commitments are specified in agreements at lower levels. For instance, this is the case with the global fisheries agreements.
[b] The Commissions are here used to denote the entire bilateral regimes, including obligations issuing from levels higher (framework agreements) and lower (committees subordinate to them) than the Commissions themselves.

There is a rather uniform set of international commitments also in the case of air pollution control. Binding standards for emission reduction are provided by the LRTAP regime, and more programmatic instruments at the regional and bilateral level, such as BEAR, AEPS/Arctic Council and the Joint Russian–Norwegian

Environmental Commission, seek to assist Russia in fulfilling these obligations. A difference between the regimes for fisheries management and air pollution control is the relative weight of the different levels and the way in which commitments at various levels are linked. While the 'lower' levels of the air pollution control regime serve mainly to assist in the implementation of obligations from 'higher' levels, new and more concrete obligations follow from the 'lower' levels of the fisheries management regime. The global regime provides general principles which are given concrete contents at the regional, and primarily bilateral level. Hence, the bilateral level emerges with heavier weight in the fisheries management regime, or, alternatively, the global/regional level is more specific in the case of air pollution control than in fisheries management.

What are here grouped together as the 'nuclear safety regime' for Northwestern Russia, provide a far more loosely coupled set of obligations than is the case with fisheries management and air pollution control. This follows partly from the fact that nuclear hazards come from highly different sources, such as dumping of radioactive materials, stored nuclear waste and spent fuel and the unsafe functioning of nuclear installations. Various global and regional instruments are aimed at different problem areas: the IAEA at safety at nuclear installations, the London Convention at dumping activities and AMEC and CTR mainly at decommissioned nuclear vessels. Again, programmatic activities under BEAR and the Joint Russian–Norwegian Commission on Nuclear Safety supplement the global and other regional initiatives, mainly in terms of financial assistance. Concrete commitments come primarily from the 'higher' levels, but with the conclusion of the 1998 Framework Agreement between Russia and Norway, more specific international obligations emerge also from the bilateral level.

What is the wavelength?

Chapter 2 gives a more detailed account of the questions we seek to answer. One could at this point, however, ask why we have selected that particular set of questions. Is this primarily a book about the implementation of international environmental agreements or of particular sectors of Russian politics? What readership do we want to address and what body of scholarly literature do we want to make our findings relevant to? What's the 'wavelength' of the book?

Despite its explicit theoretical focus on implementation of international obligations, we would claim that this is primarily a book about the peculiarities of Russian politics. It is our aim to extend the description and discussion of political processes beyond the point at which most accounts of Russian politics tend to stop. For instance, a common theme in studies of Russian politics in recent years has been the relationship between authorities at the federal and regional level. Such studies normally concentrate on legal, political and economic aspects of these relations. How much autonomy does the Constitution give to the Russian federal subjects? How 'authoritative' do the governors emerge before federal authorities? How much financial resources do the different regions manage to extract from the federal budget? Seldom are such discussions followed up by analyses of consequences for different sectors of politics: do the recent changes in the formal status of governors have any influence on fisheries management in the region? Does the bilateral agreement between a federal subject and Moscow have any impact on environmental politics in the region? In addition to these questions, it is our aim to provide detail and nuances to the debate about the relationship between various agencies at the same political level. How 'federal' are actually federal agencies located in the regions? Do the old Soviet industrial complexes in the region come through as allies of regional or federal authorities? Do some federal agencies appear to stand closer to regional authorities than to other agencies at the same level? The comparison of three different cases from one and the same region will hopefully reveal patterns that can serve as useful supplements to the more general literature on Russian politics.

On the other hand, we are still convinced that our discussion will prove relevant also to the theoretical implementation debate. While the described events must be 'seen through the glasses' of Russian politics – having a logic not necessarily applicable to political processes in other countries – the results are intended to add up to the accumulating knowledge on implementation of environmental agreements. Among the questions asked that are of relevance to the overarching theoretical debate are the following: how does the nature of the problem influence implementation? To what extent can implementation performance be explained by the nature of the international agreement? Is it decisive which national agencies are given responsibility for implementation? Does the inclusion of target groups or NGOs make implementation more effective?

How does financial support from other countries affect the implementation process?

At a somewhat less ambitious level theoretically – focusing on implementation in Russian regions rather than on implementation in general – one can compare the three cases of the book in a quest to reveal what kind of international agreements stand the best chance of being successfully implemented in the regions of the Russian Federation. Can differences between the cases be ascribed to the nature of the problems at hand or to the character of the international agreements? To the extent that the latter appears to be the case: is implementation improved by the existence of a 'heavy' global or regional commitment (securing, for instance, support from federal authorities that might view the implementation of such agreements as a national prestige)? Or would it prove easier to influence the behaviour of target groups in the region by use of more flexible programmatic initiatives at the bilateral level (hinging, as in the case of Northwestern Russia, on geographical proximity to foreign countries)? On the other hand: do non-binding arrangements at the global level have any effect at all? What about binding agreements at the bilateral level? And finally: can any lessons of a more general nature be drawn from the three cases about the linkage of binding and programmatic instruments and initiatives at the various political levels?

Hence, one can 'tune in' on our investigation from various points of departure: from a theoretical interest in implementation of international agreements or power constellations in Russian politics, or from a more practical interest in Russian politics or Arctic environmental affairs.

A note on methodology

The empirical data used in the case studies of the book are based on frequent field trips over several years to Murmansk and Arkhangelsk Oblasts and Moscow. A range of interviews have been conducted with representatives of federal and regional authorities, industries, NGOs and others.[50] Regional media have also been very useful. We have elsewhere elaborated the difficulties of conducting social science research in Northwestern Russia (Hønneland and Jørgensen 1999a, pp. 6–7): as one of the most heavily militarised areas in the world and rather 'conservative' politically,[51] the region is, in general, characterised by suspicion towards curious foreigners. Since Russia has no long-standing tradition of 'free' social science research, foreign researchers are often mistaken for journalists or even spies. Furthermore, foreign involvement in environmental affairs has, since the arrest of Aleksandr Nikitin in February 1996,[52] come to be closely linked to espionage in the minds of many inhabitants of Northwestern Russia.[53] In addition to a careful and gradual build-up of trust between us and potential sources of information, the well-known Russian method of using acquaintances has been indispensable also for this study.[54] When no other source of information is mentioned, the data are built on personal interviews. Such interviews have been more important in the case studies on fisheries management and nuclear safety; the study of air pollution control is to a larger extent based on secondary literature. In order to protect our interviewees from potential problems at home, we have chosen not to reveal their identity.

An issue with methodological implications is how the temporal aspect of implementation is perceived. As will follow from Chapter 2, an important question is how the emergence of international obligations influences policy issues at the national and regional level in Russia. Are the observed patterns of behaviour the result of these particular obligations, or would they have occurred anyway? The international agreements under investigation here were concluded at different times, nearly half of them with the Soviet Union as contracting partner. Do we want to study political processes initiated immediately after the establishment of an international regime, or how the Russian Federation in recent years has gone about fulfilling these obligations? The primary focus of the investigation is on political processes during the 1990s. For one thing, it has proven difficult to obtain information about earlier events.[55] Moreover, more than half of the agreements studied were concluded during this period. Our main argument for focusing on that decade is, however, the fact that major changes have taken place in Russian politics since 1990. First, a new state formation emerged in 1991, taking over most international obligations of the Soviet Union. Second, such a far-reaching restructuring of the political system of the state has taken place after its establishment that it becomes an interesting question in itself to investigate how these obligations have been handled along with the reorganisations.

Outline of the book

This chapter has given a preliminary introduction to the research questions addressed in the book and a brief overview of the international arrangements that are of most relevance to fisheries management, nuclear safety and air pollution control in Northwestern Russia. Chapter 2 provides more detail on the theoretical debate about the implementation of international environmental agreements, leading up to a more individualised approach to the issues under investigation here. Chapter 3 deals with recent developments in Russian politics at the federal and regional level, providing a backdrop to our subsequent discussion of the division of responsibilities in the implementation of international environmental commitments. The first part of this chapter focuses in particular on relations between Moscow and the regions. What does the 1993 Constitution say about these relations, and how have things developed in practice? Which legal, political and economic instruments do federal authorities have to influence development in the regions? The second part of Chapter 3 turns to political and economic developments in Northwestern Russia in recent years. In addition to providing background information about the history, economy and industry of the region, a major aim is to sketch the overarching power structures of Northwest Russian politics. What is the authority and power of the popularly elected governors (the regional executives), the oblast dumas (the regional legislative) and representatives of federal authorities in the region? Chapters 4, 5 and 6 constitute the main discussion of the book, addressing the Russian implementation of international agreements within fisheries management, nuclear safety and air pollution control, respectively. A similar set-up is followed in each of the three chapters, starting with a more detailed description of the problem at hand and the major target groups than has been provided in this introductory chapter. A discussion follows on the extent to which the particular international obligations are reflected in the existing legal basis of the Russian Federation. Next, attention is turned to the role of various actors in the implementation process: to what extent are federal authorities, regional authorities, the industrial complex, NGOs and others engaged in implementation activities? How is the power balance between various governmental bodies – representing, for instance, differing interests such as utilisation and conservation of resources and the environment – at the same level? The issues of implementation performance and target compliance are addressed in the concluding sections of each case study.

Chapter 7 sums up the major findings of the study. Experiences from the implementation process of the three cases are compared and lessons extracted for the theoretical implementation debate in general, and for the implementation of international environmental agreements in Russia in particular.

Notes

1 See, e.g., Hanf and Underdal (1998) and Underdal and Hanf (2000).
2 See, e.g., Young (1989, 1991), Haas (1990), Benedick (1991) and Young and Osherenko (1993).
3 See, e.g., Haas *et al.* (1993), Victor *et al.* (1998a), Wettestad (1999) and Young (1999). Another important volume is Weiss and Jacobson (1998), which focuses particularly on treaty compliance, but understands this concept as part of those processes we define as implementation (see Chapter 2).
4 See, e.g., Young (1996) and Stokke (2000a, 2001).
5 Normative linkages imply that norms developed within one regime affect the normative contents of another. By structural linkages we mean the transfer or imitation of components of one regime to or by another (Stokke 2000a).
6 For instance, Russia emits roughly as much carbon dioxide (CO_2) as all of Western Europe combined (Victor *et al.* 1998b, p. 3).
7 The concept of 'transition economy' – see, for instance, how Victor *et al.* (1998b, p. 3) speak of these countries' 'transition from central planning to a liberal, market-based society' – indicates a development optimism on behalf of these states' economy and politics that we find hard to apply to contemporary Russia. Instead, we speak of 'post-Soviet Russian economy and politics' to denote the period after the dissolution of the Soviet Union; whether recent developments will lead to a 'liberal, market-based society' remains to be seen.
8 A few cases of Russian implementation are compared in Victor *et al.* (1998a), but they are only to a limited extent considered in relation to major development trends in Russian politics. The works of Vladimir Kotov and Elena Nikitina deserve particular mention (Kotov 1994; Kotov and Nikitina 1996, 1998a, 1998b; Munton *et al.* 1999, Nikitina 1991, 1995; Zimmermann *et al.* 1998). See also Stokke (2000a, 2000b) for contributions dealing with implementation of international environmental agreements in Russia. International institutions for environmental aid to the former Soviet Union are discussed in Connolly

and List (1996) and Connolly *et al.* (1996). Darst (1997, 2001) provides detailed information on environmental management at the national level in Russia and on the country's co-operation in this field with other states, but does not focus explicitly on the implementation of Russia's international commitments.

9 It might, of course, be argued that this is an over-simplification; there is, for instance, a considerable literature on Russian nuclear safety politics. However, this literature is seldom linked in a systematic way to studies of overarching political processes in the country. Our point is that specialists on Russian politics tend to focus on political development trends of a more general nature than those found *within* different policy sectors.

10 Whether fisheries management can be classified as environmental politics, can of course be disputed. The management of natural resources and the environment are, however, often grouped together in policy studies. For the sake of language variation and simplicity, we occasionally speak of environmental politics in this book when we in fact have in mind the management of both the environment and natural resources.

11 The selection of cases for the study was based on a mixture of substantial and practical concerns. First, fisheries management, nuclear safety and air pollution control are among the most important environmental and resource issues for the region, as will be argued below. Second, the authors have prior in-depth knowledge on fisheries management (Hønneland 1998, 2000a, 2000b, 2001; Hønneland and Nilssen 2000, 2001; Jørgensen 1999) and nuclear safety (Hønneland and Jørgensen 1999a; Hønneland and Moe 2000; Sawhill and Jørgensen 2001), and to some extent also air pollution control (Hønneland *et al.* 1999), through earlier research projects on Northwest Russian politics.

12 See Chapter 3 for further elaboration on the geographical delimitation of the study.

13 For a discussion of centre–region relations in the Russian Federation, see, e.g., Shlapentokh *et al.* (1997), M. McAuley (1997), Blakkisrud (1997), Stavrakis *et al.* (1997), Alexseev (1999) and Hønneland and Blakkisrud (2001).

14 See, e.g., Hønneland and Blakkisrud (2001).

15 For brief overviews of the history of the Kola Peninsula, see, e.g., Hønneland and Jørgensen (1999a, 1999b) or Hønneland and Blakkisrud (2001).

16 *Ibid.*

17 For an overview of Northwest Russian fisheries, see Hønneland (1998, 2000a).

18 See AMAP (1997, 1998) for authoritative reviews of the environmental state of the Russian Arctic.

19 Previous schemes were finally buried in 1997, but a new agreement on the modernisation of the Pechenganickel smelter was concluded between Norway and Russia in June 2001. The new project is scheduled to be completed in 2006–7; see Chapter 6.

20 The Chernobyl accident in April 1986 was, of course, the first wake-up call for the European public to the dangers of nuclear radiation. The Komsomolets accident, for its part, served to remind the public that radiation could emanate from other sources than power plants, still by far the most serious threat to the general public.

21 See, e.g., Stokke (1998, 2000b).

22 See Nilsen *et al.* (1996) for an authoritative assessment of the risk of radioactive contamination from the Russian Northern Fleet.

23 As mentioned above, the extraction of stationary resources on the Kola Peninsula has decreased in recent years due to economic problems at company level.

24 There are good arguments for not focusing exclusively on legally binding arrangements. First, it can be assumed that non-binding agreements are also sought to be implemented by states. Second, states vary in their propensity to conclude binding agreements, and many tend to enter into such agreements only when they feel certain that they will be able to comply with their obligations, this being particularly true for the Soviet Union/Russian Federation (Victor *et al.* 1998a). Hence, it can be expected that 'implementation activities' – efforts to change the behaviour of target groups – are no less prevalent in Russia for non-binding than for binding agreements.

25 Clearly, the categorisation could have been done in other ways. The sub-regional level, comprising co-operative arrangements between parts of various countries, has been omitted here. Bilateral arrangements, often regarded as 'regional' instruments, are here separated out as a category of their own.

26 See Churchill and Lowe (1999) for an overview and evaluation of the LOSC.

27 See, e.g., Balton (1996) or Hayashi (1995, 1996) for discussions of the Fish Stocks Agreement.

28 See Stokke *et al.* (1999) for a discussion of the Russian–Norwegian fisheries research co-operation.

29 For a review of the enforcement co-operation between Russia and Norway, see Hønneland (2000b).

30 This authority is nested in a revised Convention of 1982 (Northeast Atlantic Fisheries Commission 1982). The signatory states can also choose to delegate management responsibility for certain species in their EEZs to NEAFC. See Churchill (2001) for a discussion of the NEAFC regime.

31 See Fisher (1997) for a history and overview of activities of IAEA.

32 The Convention entered into force on 12 November 1977. It is signed, but not ratified by the Russian Federation.

33 This is a series of codes and safety guidelines intended to ensure the safe design, siting and operation of nuclear power reactors.

34 The Convention entered into force on 27 October 1986. It is signed and ratified by the Russian Federation.

35 The Convention entered into force on 26 February 1987. It is signed and ratified by the Russian Federation.

36 The Convention entered into force on 24 October 1996. It is signed and ratified by the Russian Federation.

37 The Convention has not yet entered into force.

38 The Convention entered into force on 30 August 1975. It has been signed and ratified by the Russian Federation.

39 See Sawhill (2000) and Sawhill and Jørgensen (2001) for a description and assessment of the AMEC co-operation.

40 The Regional Council is composed of representatives of the three northernmost counties of Norway, the two northernmost counties of Sweden and Finland, Murmansk and Arkhangelsk Oblasts, and the Republic of Karelia and Nenets Autonomous Okrug in Russia, as well as a representative of the indigenous people of the region, the Saami. At the national level, the Barents Council consists of government representatives from Russia, the five Nordic countries and the European Commission. For discussions of the establishment and performance of BEAR, see Dellenbrant and Olsson (1994), Stokke and Tunander (1994), Dahlström *et al.* (1995), Dellenbrant and Wiberg (1997) and Flikke (1998).

41 See Hønneland and Moe (2000) for an evaluation of the Plan of Action.

42 No global convention exists on land-based pollution control; the main initiatives to date have shunned a strict precautionary approach to pollution control (VanderZwaag 2000).

43 The Convention entered into force on 16 March 1983. It is signed and ratified by the Russian Federation.

44 See, e.g., Hanf (2000) for an overview of how the acid rain regime evolved.

45 The Protocol entered into force on 14 February 1991. It is signed and ratified by the Russian Federation.

46 The Protocol entered into force on 29 September 1997. It has not been signed by the Russian Federation.

47 The Protocol entered into force on 5 August 1998. It is signed, but not ratified by the Russian Federation. The Protocol follows the former Sulphur Protocol adopted in Helsinki 8 July 1985, which entered into force 2 September 1987.

48 The Protocol has not yet entered into force. It has not been signed by the Russian Federation.

49 The Protocol has not yet entered into force. It has not been signed by the Russian Federation.

50 Since both of us speak Russian, all interviews have been conducted without interpreter. This is assumed to enhance the validity of the interview data.

51 Murmansk is one of the few Russian cities where a Lenin statue still dominates a main thoroughfare – in this case the Lenin Prospekt.

52 Former Northern Fleet officer Aleksandr Nikitin was accused of espionage while collecting data on the nuclear risk on the Kola Peninsula for the Norwegian environmental NGO Bellona. Charges were finally dropped in 2000.

53 Cf. a recent news bulletin from Radio Free Europe/Radio Liberty under the heading 'Murmansk a Hotbed of Foreign Spies': 'Foreign intelligence services have targeted Murmansk Oblast as a "priority" area for their activities, Nikolai Zharkov, head of the Federal Security Service (FSB) directorate in Murmansk Oblast, told Interfax North-West on 28 December [. . .] Zharkov also revealed that foreign governments frequently "pursue their own interests" under the cover of environmental organizations' (RFE/RL Newsline, 30 December 2000).

54 Even 'official figures' have agreed to talk to us only after being introduced to us by common acquaintances.

55 In practice, it has not been very difficult to relate to this temporal aspect of implementation notwithstanding missing historical data. When, for instance, it can be established that a 'department for convention areas' exists under the fisheries enforcement agency Murmanrybvod, the interesting point is not so much when it was established – it was obviously set up to take care of Soviet/Russian obligations under the NEAFC and NAFO Conventions – but *that* it exists, under whose political authority it is nested, and how it functions.

2

Theoretical background

The last two decades of the twentieth century saw a remarkable increase in the breadth and depth of international environmental co-operation.[1] Several explanations have been offered to account for this trend, among them the growing transborder implications of national environmental problems and the combination of a general rise in international transactions and governmental involvement in environmental affairs at the national level (Hanf and Underdal 1998, pp. 149–51). Co-operative arrangements show great variation in their degree of formalism and ambition as well as in their geographic and functional scope. Typically, co-operation in a given issue area will initially be accompanied by rather vague joint declarations on the need to address the problem in question. Subsequently, as the co-operative process gets under way and the understanding of the problem – as well as the consensus on its nature – grow deeper, the parties may agree on stricter and more specific obligations.[2] Moreover, environmental accords vary in scope, ranging from global via regional and sub-regional to bilateral arrangements. Global agreements tend to be of a framework character whereas more specific requirements are often found in accords at a lower level, typically nested in the more overarching global arrangements.

The aim of this chapter is to provide a theoretical backdrop to and elaborate a research design for the investigation. The chapter consists of four main parts. The first section seeks to place the implementation literature in a wider theoretical context, asking how the two major theoretical approaches to international relations, realism and liberalism, see the role of institutions in the implementation of international agreements. The 'whats', 'whys' and 'hows' of the implementation debate are addressed in the second section, focusing in particular on the interface between the concepts of 'implementation', 'effectiveness' and 'compliance'. Some major lessons from implementation of environmental agreements in post-Communist societies are summarised in the third section of the chapter. The theoretical background and the experience of implementation in post-Communist states are subsumed in the fourth section, which elaborates a specific research design for the study. The chapter should be read in conjunction with Chapter 1, which presents the overall focus of the investigation, and Chapter 3, which focuses more specifically on the legal, political and economic conditions for implementation in the Russian Federation.

Do institutions matter?

The question of whether international co-operative arrangements *in themselves* have any influence on national policies is a matter of dispute among students of international relations. This dispute originates from divergent views on the nature of the international system of states. Thus, to the hardcore realist, the anarchic nature of the world community is its most salient feature, and the states of which it is composed appear as rational unitary actors with maximisation of a fairly clear-cut set of national interests as the sole motivation for any action undertaken. In a purist-realist perspective, the fact that there is no such thing as international government necessarily implies that international agreements and other co-operative arrangements either simply reflect the national interests of participating states, or they reflect the specific preferences of the most powerful states. Consequently, such agreements have no independent influence on states' actions. In the realist perspective, state implementation of or compliance with international obligations is not considered a particularly interesting issue. For one thing, states are assumed to generally comply with such obligations. The argument is that: (1) states accept treaties only when their governments have concluded that they are in their interest; (2) they generally comply with treaties; and (3) when they do not, sanctions are employed both to punish offenders and to deter others from violating them (Weiss and Jacobson 1998). As asserted by the famous realist Morgenthau (1978), the great majority of the rules of international law are observed by most nations most of the time. For the realist, behaviour frequently conforms to treaty rules because both the behaviour and the rules reflect the interests of the powerful states. In essence, observed compliance merely reflects one of the following three situations: (1) a hegemonic state has forced or induced a less powerful state to comply; (2) the treaty rules only codify the parties' existing behaviour; or (3) the treaty resolves a co-ordination game in which no party has any incentive to violate the rules once a stable equilibrium has been established (Mitchell 1994a).

In the relative simplicity of the realist approach lie both its major strength and its greatest shortcomings. While allowing for coherent theorising and construction of elegant models, realist perspectives are criticised for ignoring the complexity of international relations. The main opposing camp – less coherent than the realist one, and alternately labelled pluralist and liberal[3] – tends to emphasise complex interdependence between states as opposed to international anarchy. It also emphasises the complexity of domestic decision-making as opposed to the rational unitary actor perspective of the realists. States' actions are seen as outcomes of complex policy processes at both the domestic and the international level, and international co-operative arrangements are viewed as one of many variables that may contribute to shaping these outcomes. This by no means implies that interests and power are considered insignificant in international relations. However, within the complex interdependence model, the role of non-state actors is drawn into the calculus, the concept of national interest is questioned, and the relevance of power is seen as highly dependent on the actual issue area. Specifically, many researchers have argued that the realist perspective may be most relevant where analyses of high politics – in particular security issues – are concerned, while more complex approaches may be called for when dealing with 'low politics', including environmental issues. In the realm of environmental policy, it will not always be clear what the 'national interest' of a state is. Various sub-groups of society may have highly diverging interests, while sharing common interests with sub-groups in other countries. Moreover, the 'value' of a clean environment compared to that of the continuation of a polluting activity is not easily determined. It may be tied to a given society's 'culture', and it may change over time, e.g. as a result of new knowledge (Hanf and Underdal 1998; Weiss and Jacobson 1998). Considering this, it may be argued that there is some room for institutions like international co-operative arrangements to actually influence states' policies. Such institutions may empower 'green' sub-groups in participating states, and they may contribute to the production and diffusion of new knowledge. Rather than forcing states to act against their own interests they may help 'to shift countries' perceptions of their self-interest and the possibilities for reaching it through joint actions' (Hanf 2000, p. 38, referring to Levy's argument (1995)).

A common trait of most literature on implementation and treaty compliance, reflecting its origin in the broader liberal camp, is the claim that institutions matter. Where realists view treaty compliance as 'coincidental' in the sense that they claim the observed behaviour would have occurred even in the absence of treaty rules, liberalists argue that compliance might be the result of the chosen form of organisation of the regime. Liberalists maintain that it might be right that most states comply with most treaty rules most of the time, but that this is not because enforcement is applied against non-compliers. Chayes and Chayes (1995, p. 32) claim that 'Sanctioning authority is rarely granted by treaty, rarely used when granted, and likely to be ineffective when used'. The lack of formal sanctions does not mean, however, that there are no penalties for non-compliance or rewards for compliance. In line with the theory of complex interdependence, liberalists argue that states have continuing relationships with each other over a range of issues, and that questions of compliance arise in an environment of diffuse reciprocity.

One important liberalist argument in the debate about implementation of and compliance with international agreements is that negotiations do not end with the conclusion of a treaty, but are a continuous aspect of living under the agreement (Chayes and Chayes 1991). Securing compliance with a treaty becomes a matter of 'bargaining in the shadow of the law' (Mnookin and Kornhauser 1979). This implies that disputes are sought to be resolved and compliance induced through negotiations after the treaty has been concluded. The procedures employed may range from simple bilateral negotiations to formal arbitration, either specifically provided by the treaty or evolving in response to need. Attempts have even been made to bridge the compliance literature and bargaining theory, introducing the concept of 'post-agreement bargaining' (Jönsson and Tallberg 1998). Moreover, liberalists claim that bureaucratic processes often favour compliance over non-compliance. In national bureaucracies, economy counts in decisions to comply with a treaty as a matter of standard operating procedure, rather than in weighing the costs and benefits each time an issue of compliance arises. Gathering information and securing inter-agency agreement are high-cost activities and can be performed only in relatively important questions (Chayes and Chayes 1991). The liberalist perspective includes two main types of prescriptions to increase compliance for participants in international regimes: first, to arrange the institutional setting of the regime to facilitate compliance; and second, to engage in argumentative efforts in order to persuade potential non-compliers to comply. In particular, it recommends *transparency* in the working of regimes or treaties, *mechanisms for dispute settlement* and *technical and financial assistance to states that have practical problems with complying* (Chayes and Chayes 1991, 1993; Mitchell 1994a, 1994b).

Implementation: the whats, whys and hows

So far, we have spoken rather loosely about the implementation of and compliance with international agreements, without defining the concepts. This section looks more thoroughly into how various authors have understood these concepts, and a definition of implementation is provided for further use in this study. Moreover, we ask which circumstances may require a particular focus on the implementation process, rather than on compliance performance, as far as international environmental agreements are concerned. Finally, some of the main hypotheses set forth by other authors in the field are reviewed.

What is implementation?

Whether vague and declaratory or explicit and binding, international commitments generally imply some sort of behavioural changes at the national level, which will ideally lead to the fulfilment of those commitments. Domestic implementation refers to the steps undertaken nationally in order to induce these changes. This process includes the translation of international commitments into national legislation, as well as administrative and other measures adopted by relevant authorities in order to induce target groups to comply. It may also include activities undertaken by NGOs or the target groups themselves. List and Rittberger (1998) thus identify several levels of implementation activity. Transformation of international agreements into national law takes place at the national *normative* level. *De facto* implementation by state activity and by private actors, as well as state supervision and stimulation of private actors, takes place at the national *factual* level. Sometimes, domestic implementation is conceived of as a much narrower concept. For instance, Weiss and Jacobson (1998) take implementation to refer only to national legislative activities (i.e. the national normative level), while subsequent activities are understood in terms of compliance or non-compliance. This understanding of implementation renders the concept a stylised and rather dull thing to study. Moreover, while accords between states are necessarily concluded at the international level, implementation primarily takes place within the individual states, i.e. at the national and sub-national levels. Hence, we understand by implementation the measures undertaken at the national and sub-national levels to bring the behaviour of target groups into accordance with the particular state's international commitments. We assume that national and sub-national authorities as well as NGOs and target groups can be involved in implementation activities. Moreover, we assume that implementation is sometimes carried out jointly by national groups and members of other states; this is referred to as joint implementation.[4]

The concept of implementation is intimately tied to that of effectiveness: if international commitments are not followed through at the national level, the agreement in question will have little effect, since the activities to be regulated are normally of a domestic character. The effectiveness of an international regime is often connected to either the achievements of the stated objectives of the regime or the solution of the problems that led to the establishment of the regime (see e.g. Weiss and Jacobson 1998). Effectiveness is sometimes seen as primarily related to compliance. However, as suggested by, e.g., Victor *et al.* (1998b), the degree of implementation may be a more trustworthy measure of effectiveness than the degree of compliance. In cases where commitments are less ambitious, states may achieve perfect compliance with the formal provisions of a given agreement with very little behavioural adaptation.[5] Compliance may also be accidental, while implementation is by definition instrumental. In accordance with this view, we are in this study interested in the *active* steps taken by authorities and other actors within the state in focus to bring the behaviour of target groups into line with the state's international commitments. We are less concerned with the degree of compliance by target groups, although compliance is considered relevant to the extent that it is believed to be the result of implementation efforts (see last section of this chapter). Nor are we primarily occupied with the solution of the problems in question or other aspects of regime effectiveness.

Why study implementation?

Implementation of international environmental regimes is surprisingly often a very difficult task. If our subject of study were, say, international co-operation in the field of disarmament, it might be argued that the process of attaining agreements would warrant more interest than their subsequent implementation, since the former could be expected to be the most difficult part of the process. Once an agreement on reducing, e.g., the number of nuclear warheads is in place, the state in question will usually have little difficulty in carrying out that commitment – providing, of course, that it intends to honour the agreement. In contrast to this, and in contrast to realist assumptions, recent studies indicate that failure on the part of states to implement *environmental* commitments is often unintentional, in the sense that it is a result of real and often unexpected difficulties encountered during the implementation process, rather than a conscious choice to refrain from implementation (Chayes and Chayes 1993, 1995; Mitchell 1994a, 1994b; Weiss and Jacobson 1998; Victor *et al.* 1998a).

Successful implementation of international commitments is contingent upon both the will and the ability of states to influence activities at the domestic level. Environmental problems are a side effect of legitimate activities, and environmental policies tend to penetrate deeply into other policy areas (Hanf 2000). Regulating the behaviour leading to, e.g., pollution often involves constraining the actions of many actors or groups of actors – from certain sectors of the economy down to the individual citizen. Moreover, precisely because of the 'intrusive' character of environmental politics, its implementation is seldom left to the environmental authorities alone. Just like the 'problem' activities, the regulative efforts typically involve many actors: environmental authorities as well as industrial ministries; agencies at the central, regional and local levels. Moreover, 'the *costs* of environmental protection tend to be certain, immediate, and concentrated to specific sectors of the economy, while the *benefits* will appear, by comparison, to be diffuse, uncertain, collective, and something that can be harvested only in a more or less distant future' (Hanf and Underdal 1998, p. 157).

Thus, successful implementation may be highly dependent on a given state's *capacity to govern*, and on its ability to design policies to overcome, for instance, the danger of *vertical disintegration*, whereby a vast number of micro-decisions lead to unexpected and contrary aggregate outcomes (1998).

Analysing implementation processes

Implementation is not necessarily a process in which the state in its various incarnations tries to modify the behaviour of certain target groups. Often, target groups (typically the industry in question) possess information and knowledge that may make implementation more effective, providing these actors are allowed to participate actively in the process. Non-state actors like NGOs may also play a role, although some studies have concluded that NGOs typically play a greater role during the regime formation phase than during the subsequent implementation stage (Victor *et al.* 1998a). External support may also be important, not least for states that have few bureaucratic or economic resources. This support may consist in anything from direct financial contributions to joint implementation of relevant projects.

Weiss and Jacobson (1998) have specified a number of variables that are believed to affect the chances of successful implementation of international environmental agreements. The characteristics of the activity to be governed imply that some activities are of greater economic value to the state than others, some are more easy to monitor than others, while the process of implementation has more side effects related to some activities than to others. Another important issue is the nature of the agreement. What is the scope of the agreement – in other words, how much behavioural adaptation does it require by states? Are its provisions precise or general? Are they binding or non-binding? Moreover, a state's implementation efforts are presumably affected by the encompassing international environment. Have other states taken action to implement the agreement in question? Is it possible to be a free rider under the accord? Finally, the social, cultural, political and economic characteristics of the implementing country are assumed to influence implementation and compliance.

Implementing international environmental commitments in post-Communist societies

From the initiation of large-scale industrialisation in the Soviet Union in the 1930s and until the fall of Communism, the environmental policy performance of that country – and of the whole Eastern Bloc – was notoriously poor. As international environmental co-operation developed and broadened during the 1970s and 1980s, the industrial countries at least to some extent recognised their responsibility as the largest contributors to global environmental degradation by accepting stricter commitments than they expected developing countries to take on. However, where the Eastern Bloc countries are concerned, there was a marked tendency for them to take on only commitments that would require little or no behavioural adjustments.

Today, all these countries are going through some sort of transition towards democracy and a market economy, although they differ with respect to aspirations as well as performance.[6] In principle, this ought to create some hope for improvement, since liberal states generally have a better environmental record than non-liberal states. However, the one study that has included a specific focus on post-Communist societies and implementation (Victor *et al.* 1998a), does not give much reason for optimism, particularly with respect to Russia.

Admittedly, polluting activities in the former Eastern Bloc countries have declined during transition, but closer scrutiny reveals that compliance with, e.g., the Long-range Transboundary Air Pollution (LRTAP) provisions is largely attributable to economic decline. Pollution per unit GDP has generally risen in post-Communist states, indicating that their industry is actually 'dirtier' than ever, and that a mechanism is at work which has been described as 'compliance without implementation' (Raustiala and Victor 1998, p. 670).

The post-Communist period has been marked by a growing inclusion of the East European countries, and, to a lesser extent, the former Soviet republics, into international co-operative arrangements of various kinds, including environmental ones. At the domestic level, the post-Communist states have tended to use Western models for environmental policy regulation, notably by adopting provisions relying on market mechanisms. However, as demonstrated by Victor *et al.* (1998a), such measures frequently have other (mostly unexpected and undesirable) consequences in post-

Communist states than in the more developed liberal market economies of the West. Moreover, the post-Communist states are characterised by certain developmental traits, some of which are conducive to implementation of environmental policies, but many of which have the opposite effect. These traits can be summed up as democratisation and decentralisation of political power, transition from a planned to a market economy and extensive changes in the legal sphere. A crucial factor that has exacerbated or impaired the impact of these processes, is the fact that in most cases they have been accompanied by considerable economic decline.

The political sphere

Several studies indicate that a state's political system may profoundly affect its performance in the area of environmental policy, both in the area of domestic politics and international co-operation. It would be a gross over-simplification to treat the relationship between the two variables ('political system' and 'environmental performance') as precisely defined. Nevertheless, there seems to be a tendency for democratic states to show greater will to give priority to environmental considerations, while totalitarian states, though less inclined to prioritise environmental issues, show greater ability to implement environmental commitments, once they are taken on.

Towards the end of the 1980s, in the heyday of glasnost and perestroika, democratic mobilisation in Eastern Europe and the Soviet republics frequently centred around environmental issues. As the veil of secrecy was partially lifted, serious ecological problems were revealed to a public formerly ignorant of their scale – in some cases even of their existence – and these issues swiftly moved to the top of the political agenda. However, while a democratic system may be associated with higher concern for the environment, economic decline tends to have the opposite effect, and this certainly seems to be confirmed by subsequent developments in the post-Communist countries. Most people soon became more concerned with their own economic well-being – indeed, with day-to-day survival – than with ecological problems, and, likewise, politicians increasingly focused on how to reverse the negative trend and achieve economic growth.

At the same time, to the extent that governments were willing to implement environmental policy goals (international commitments as well as nationally defined objectives), they found themselves increasingly unable to do so. While the Soviet Union, for instance, with its extremely centralised political system, actually may have come quite close to the realist conception of states as unitary actors, this image hardly applies to any of the post-Communist countries. Although the democratisation process cannot be viewed as fully completed in these countries, decentralisation and diffusion of power has lengthened the chain of implementation and thus decreased the governments' abilities to implement policy in general, not least in an area as complex as environmental politics. In the Russian case, this tendency is strengthened by the federal structure of the state. Moreover, the economic crisis combined with the particular trajectory of economic reform in Russia have greatly undermined the fiscal strength of the government, rendering its implementation capabilities even weaker. Thus, in the post-Communist countries in general, and in Russia in particular, economic decline has served as a counter-force to the tendency of democracy to enhance public environmental concern, while it has amplified its tendency to complicate the task of implementation.

The economic sphere

A functioning market economy is normally characterised by high economic efficiency, and thus the transition from plan to market in Russia and Eastern Europe ought ideally to have put a stop to the inefficient and environmentally unsound over-consumption of resources so typical of these countries' industries. It might also have been expected that the market forces' push towards efficiency would have caused industrial enterprises to invest in new technologies, which in turn would create considerable environmental dividends. On the other hand, the market transition could be expected to have some negative effects as well, since privatisation would result in weaker state control over target groups (e.g. industrial enterprises). Again, the negative predictions have been proven right, while the predicted positive outcomes (i.e. investments in cleaner technology) have largely failed to materialise. Adjustments of production modes and a shift to new technologies both require immediate investments, while the increased returns take some time to occur. The lack of a functioning system for credit blocked this option for many enterprises. Moreover, privatisation was largely carried out in a legal vacuum and in circumstances characterised by little transparency, poor oversight by the authorities and a general lack of certainty about the future. Thus, incentives were created for those controlling (not necessarily owning) the privatising enterprises to harvest great short-term profits in ways which were hardly conducive to the long-time profitability of the enterprises. Far from making investments in their enterprises, some directors and/or owners blatantly plundered them of their assets and pocketed the profits. At the same time, many highly inefficient enterprises were kept alive and not allowed to go bankrupt, as authorities feared the social consequences of their demise.

The legal sphere

The earliest phase of transition was characterised both by a strong focus on environmental matters and on intensive revision of old legislation, and in many of the post-Communist countries this resulted in relatively progressive laws in the area of environmental protection. However, gradually the initial momentum was lost, and in many cases this meant that strong framework legislation, e.g. as expressed in the constitution of a particular state, was not reflected in specific laws and regulations. Moreover, the belief in the efficiency of market mechanisms as a way of regulating target behaviour has not been quite justified by realities. The post-Communist states do not yet have functioning markets, and thus 'distortions' occur more often here than in mature market economies. Sanctions such as fines have been rendered inefficient due to inflation, which demonstrates how the legislative process has failed to keep pace with the general development of society. The court system has often proven unable to enforce regulations effectively, and it often takes a very long time before a case is brought to court. The independence of courts cannot be taken for granted, and the same goes for controlling agencies, which often have strong ties with regional or local executive authorities. The authorities, in turn, are often more concerned with an enterprise's role as an employer, taxpayer and/or provider of social services than with any adverse effect its activities may have on the environment.

The transition period has been less protracted and less difficult in the East European and Baltic States than in the former Soviet republics. Many of the former countries show signs of approaching the end of transition, while the future of the latter, the Russian Federation included, still seems highly uncertain.

An agenda for research

The study will focus on Russian implementation activities related to the international commitments outlined in Chapter 1. By implementation activities we understand the active steps initiated by Russian authorities, and presumably carried out in co-operative efforts between federal and regional authorities, target groups and other non-state actors (and sometimes also in co-operation with other states), in order to bring the behaviour of target groups in line with international commitments. Compliance with international agreements is here not seen as particularly interesting in itself, cf. the tendency referred to above of post-Communist states to show 'compliance without implementation'. However, compliance is viewed as relevant to the extent that the observed behaviour of target groups can be causally linked to implementation activities. Therefore, each case study will contain an overview of target group compliance related to the overall discussion of implementation performance.

A point of departure for the study is the lesson drawn in previous studies that implementation failure is often unintentional, the result of difficulties encountered during the implementation process rather than a conscious choice by the state in question to refrain from implementation. As pointed out in the previous section of this chapter, it can be assumed that this is particularly true for post-Communist states. During the so-called transition period, these states have experienced devolution of power – lengthening the previous chain of implementation – weakened fiscal strength and control over target group activities, a slow legislative process, a tendency for sanctions to be ineffective and have only a brief history of independent enforcement agencies. Hence, the study has a particular focus on Russia's 'capacity to govern', here: capacity to initiate and co-ordinate the necessary organisational and policy-related measures required to bring the actions of target groups into line with the country's international commitments.

By approaching each problem area in the same fashion and systematically asking the same questions, we will facilitate comparison between the three cases. First, factors will be identified that further/hamper implementation in each specific case. Second, cases will be compared in order to distinguish between factors that are case-specific and those that are common to all three cases. Third, these findings will be compared with findings from other relevant studies.

The first step to be carried out within each problem area is to examine the nature of the problem. This will have strong implications for our subsequent evaluation and comparison of implementation records in each of the cases. If the problem is related to activities of private actors, the implementation process is believed to be more difficult than if it relates to the working of state enterprises. Likewise, implementation is assumed to be more difficult the greater the significance of the regulated activity in economic terms, and the harder it is to monitor the activity and detect non-compliant behaviour by target groups.

Key questions related to the nature of the problem are:

- Is the activity controlled by private or public actors?
- How important is the activity in economic and other terms?
- How are costs and benefits associated with the activity, and with regulation, distributed?
- Is it easy or difficult to monitor the activity and detect non-compliance with regulations?

The next step of the investigation is to study the international commitments selected for examination in each issue area. The more demanding the commitments – binding rather than non-binding, containing specific provisions rather than vague ones, and requiring significant adjustments in the behaviour of target groups – the more difficult the implementation process can be expected to be.

Key questions related to the nature of the commitments include:

- How much adjustment in behaviour do the commitments require?
- Are the provisions of the commitments vague or precise?
- Are the commitments expressed through binding agreements or are they declaratory in nature?

The nature of the problem and the nature of the international commitments will be studied to the extent that they may offer alternative explanations for variation in compliance, i.e. variation that cannot be ascribed to characteristics of the domestic implementation process. By contrast, the domestic process is defined as our main object of scrutiny; thus, it will be studied in greater detail.

Usually, the first step in the domestic implementation process is to adjust national legislation to the requirements laid down by the international agreements in question, i.e. in those cases where such requirements exist. Consequently, we shall address the legislative issues first, asking whether the necessary laws and regulations have been passed at the national and sub-national level, what sanctions are prescribed and whether these are actually employed.

Key questions related to the incorporation of international commitments in national legislation are:

- Are international commitments reflected in domestic laws and regulations?
- Has new legislation been adopted to reflect these commitments?
- What kind of sanctions (if any) does the law provide for in case of non-compliance?

The further domestic process, whereby the intentions expressed in the international commitments and in domestic legislation are translated into action, can progress in different ways. Unless the target groups are already in compliance with the provisions of the commitments – which, indeed, would render implementation as we define it unnecessary – the authorities must try to influence target group behaviour. This may involve the use of various methods, from coercion (law enforcement by [threat of] sanctions), to positive incentives (e.g. material support) and communicative efforts (e.g. information campaigns), and it may involve a large number of actors. Due to the complexity of this process, we shall approach it in a stepwise fashion, studying the roles of various groups of actors separately: authorities at various levels, target groups and other actors like NGOs and research communities. The role of external actors, like international governmental organisations (IGOs) and foreign NGOs, in the domestic implementation process will also be addressed.

The main responsibility for policy implementation normally rests with the executive branch of government. The delimitation of responsibilities between various sectoral branches within the executive as well as between the federal and regional level will be studied. Of particular interest is the division of responsibility between governmental structures representing polluters and users of natural resources on the one hand and monitoring and enforcement bodies on the other. As far as target groups and other non-state actors are concerned, we are primarily interested in whether they are 'admitted' into the implementation process, their material capabilities to influence implementation and the degree of independence they enjoy *vis-à-vis* public authorities.

Key questions related to implementation activities of public authorities include:

- What are the roles of governmental structures representing polluters and users of natural resources (e.g. industry ministries) versus those responsible for environmental protection?
- Which are the 'strongest' in terms of formal status, budget, personnel resources etc.?
- To what extent is the responsibility for implementation delegated to regional and local authorities?
- To what extent are sanctions prescribed by legislation used in practice?

Key questions related to implementation activities of target groups are:

- Is the activity in question carried out by private or state actors?
- What kinds of capabilities do the target groups have at their disposal in terms of financial resources, relations with authorities and contacts to major 'financial–industrial groups'?
- To what extent is the responsibility for implementation delegated to the target groups?

Key questions related to implementation activities by other non-state actors include:

- Are these groups given any official role in the implementation process?
- What kind of capabilities do they have in terms of financing, knowledge, contacts etc.?

The latter two questions are relevant also with respect to external actors. It is necessary to keep in mind that the role of external actors is analytically somewhat ambiguous. They may be involved more or less directly in the domestic implementation process, but nevertheless it might be more correct to define their activities as an 'international', rather than 'domestic', variable.

Notes

1 For instance, Weiss and Jacobson (1998, p. 1) note that at the time of the United Nations Conference on the Human Environment in Stockholm in 1972 there were only a few dozen multilateral treaties dealing

with environmental issues. By the time of the United Nations Conference on Environment and Development in Rio in 1992 more than 900 international legal instruments wee either directed towards environmental protection or had more than one important component addressing the issue.

2 Thus, Hanf and Underdal (1998) point out how such policy processes typically run through a number of stages, where the identification of a problem is frequently followed by the adoption of a framework convention, which, at a later stage, is supplemented by protocols spelling out more specific measures.

3 Modern international relations theory claims that both realism and liberalism are *rationalist* perspectives as opposed to *reflectivist* approaches; see, e.g., Wæver (1996).

4 We are aware that the concept 'joint implementation' has a more limited meaning when speaking about, for instance, the global climate regime. Nevertheless, we have chosen to use it here referring to all kinds of joint initiatives between Russia and other states to facilitate implementation of Russia's international obligations.

5 This is, of course, very much a question of how effectiveness is defined. Underdal (1992) points out that effectiveness may be understood either in terms of relative improvement, or in terms of the distance to a defined optimal state of affairs. The scope of implementing activities carried out may give a better indication of relative improvement, while compliance rates may say rather more about the distance to the optimal state.

6 See note 7, Chapter 1, for our reservations against labelling the post-Comunist states 'transition economies'.

3
Northwestern Russia and the federative system

This chapter gives a presentation of Russia's federative system and of the political and economic situation in the northwestern regions of the country. The objective of the first part of the chapter is to describe the overarching political structures of the Russian Federation, particularly those pertaining to the centre–region dimension, thus providing a backdrop to the discussion of various agencies' involvement in the implementation of international environmental agreements. The second part of the chapter addresses the particular political and economic conditions under which implementation is supposed to take place in the case studies of the book.

The development of a Russian federation

The Russian Federation, in the form it has taken since the disintegration of the Soviet Union, is the direct successor of the Russian Soviet Federative Socialist Republic (RSFSR). Some central traits of this structure, particularly those concerning the formal arrangements of centre–periphery relations, have been retained in the new federation. However, the substance of these relations has undergone considerable changes since the Soviet era. After a brief outline of the Soviet legacy, the main features of the new Russian federalism, focusing on legal, political and economic aspects, will be presented in this section.

Federalism and regional self-government: the Soviet legacy[1]

Unlike its predecessor, the Russian empire, the Soviet Union was organised in a federal structure.[2] Originally, the rationale for establishing a federal state structure was partly tactical, partly a consequence of Bolshevik nationalist theory. From a tactical point of view, the organisation of the RSFSR as a federal unit in January 1918,[3] as well as the establishment of the Soviet Union four years later, can be regarded as a historical compromise between the Russian-dominated Bolshevik party and their non-Russian allies (Smith 1995). The Bolsheviks were facing pressures from civil war and dissolution tendencies within the previous empire, and the most important ethno-national groups were granted a certain degree of autonomy as a reward for signing up to the new federal state formation. Furthermore, the establishment of a federal structure partly follows from the prescriptions of Marxist ideology. Marx himself had characterised the Russian empire as the 'prison of nations', and his statement that 'no nation is free as long as it suppresses another nation' was frequently cited by Lenin (Kaiser 1994).

The Soviet federal structure that evolved under Stalin was a compromise between these ideological guidelines and the demands of practical politics. The result was a form of 'pro forma ethno-federalism organised according to the *matryoshka* principle' (Blakkisrud 1997, p. 13). Ethnic groups of more than one million people, living within a geographical region that could easily be demarcated, whose territory bordered on a third state, were allowed to create union republics. Groups failing to meet one or more of these requirements were granted a more limited autonomy within the borders of the union republics. Depending on various conditions, such as the size of the population and its level of development, these groups could establish autonomous republics, autonomous oblasts (regions) or autonomous okrugs (districts). The administrative division of the union was subject to frequent revisions under Stalin, and to a certain degree also under Khrushchev, but from the early 1960s to 1991, it consisted of 15 union republics, 20 autonomous republics, 8 autonomous oblasts and 10 autonomous okrugs.

Parallel to the ethno-federal structure, there existed a strictly administrative-territorial division in krays (territories) and oblasts within the greater union republics. These territorially defined units were directly subordinate to the union republics and were thus not part of the federal structure. On the other hand, krays and oblasts could themselves contain federal units, as an autonomous oblast could be included in a kray, and an autonomous okrug in either a kray or an oblast.

Despite the formal arrangement of both the Soviet Union and the RSFSR as federations, their power structure was extremely hierarchical and centralised.[4] In effect, a total subjection to central party organs was required. The Soviet system of government consisted of three parallel hierarchies: the representative or legislative organs (soviets); the executive organs (which were nominally subordinate to the soviets at each level); and the Communist Party of the Soviet Union (CPSU). At each administrative level (union, republic, oblast, okrug etc.), there was a soviet, an executive committee and a party organisation.[5] The party provided the vertical line of command that held the system together. The soviets were large, 'decorative' assemblies that met rarely, and did little more than rubber-stamp the decisions of the executive committees, which had usually been agreed with the party organisation at the relevant level. The soviets, on their part, worked according to the paradoxical principle of democratic centralism: deputies at each level were accountable both to their electorate and to the soviet at the next level up. In practice, however, *centralism* generally had the upper hand, and, as already described, party organs exercised a complete control over decisions in soviets and executive committees.

From RSFSR to the Russian Federation

Among the most dramatic results of Gorbachev's reforms was the nationalistic awakening that eventually led to the dismantling of the Soviet Union itself. After the 1991 August coup attempt failed, the very processes that the coup makers tried to prevent started to accelerate. Gorbachev's authority became even weaker than before the failed coup, and institutions at the union level lost most of their legitimacy, influence and, eventually, also financing. By December 1991, the actual decision-making authority in the Soviet Union had been transferred to the republic level. One republic after another declared itself sovereign, and when the leaders of the RSFSR, Ukraine and Belarus met in early December to create the Commonwealth of Independent States (CIS), the demise of the Soviet Union was formalised.

There seems to have been no disagreement among Russian leaders that a federal structure should be retained also in the new Russian state formation. There were, however, different opinions as to which *form* of federalism should be chosen.[6] The outcome of the debate was quite pragmatic: in the unstable political situation of the day, extensive administrative reforms were perceived as too hazardous, and it was agreed to preserve a slightly modified version of the old structure. The system of both ethnically and territorially defined federal subjects was retained. The latter were kept unchanged, while there was an upgrading in administrative status of the autonomous republics and four of the five autonomous oblasts, which were hereafter defined as republics.[7] The new Russian Federation consists of 89 federal subjects, of which 32 are ethnically defined (21 republics, 1 autonomous oblast and 10 autonomous okrugs) and 57 are territorially defined (6 krays, 49 oblasts and 2 cities with status as federal subjects). The federal subjects vary widely with respect to both population and territory. Whereas the autonomous areas comprise more than 50 per cent of the federation's territory, they contain only 18 per cent of its population.

The most controversial issue of Russian politics during the years 1992–93 was the elaboration of a new federal constitution. The primary controversy ran along the basic fault lines in Russian politics: the division of power between the President and the Parliament, and between federal authorities and the regions. The process of elaborating a new constitution was embarked upon already in 1990, but it was only with the dissolution of the Soviet Union and the establishment of the Russian Federation that the need for a new basic legal framework became urgent. Various drafts were presented during 1992 and the first half of 1993. Two of these became the object of serious discussion, one produced by President Yeltsin and one by the Constitutional Committee. As was to be expected, the President's proposal prescribed a strong presidential rule, while that of the Constitutional Committee implied a parliamentarian model. The federal subjects diverged in their view of the proposals. The vertical division of power, i.e. the federal structure, was more important to them than the horizontal organisation of the state. As the controversy sharpened, both the President and the Parliament made new concessions to the regions in an attempt to win their support. Several aspects of President Yeltsin's proposal are clearly designed to suit the interests of the ethnically defined federal subjects.

In June 1993, Yeltsin summoned a constitutional conference, which one month later launched a compromise between the two proposals. A working group was appointed in September to implement further co-ordination, but before it could present its result, political realities in Russia changed dramatically. On 21 September, Yeltsin dissolved the Parliament and ordered new elections. Fierce protests from the opposition immediately followed. The dispute culminated on 3 and 4 October when the protests of the parliamentarians and their supporters, who had barricaded themselves within the White House, were overcome by force. After these incidents, President Yeltsin had control of the parliamentary opposition, and his revised constitution draft represents a clear concentration of power with the presidential apparatus, as well as a centralist structure of decision-making.

As the Parliament was now eradicated as a political competitor, the President no longer depended on the same level of support from the federal subjects as before. Several of the privileges they had won in the course of the previous power struggle were now modified or even omitted from the constitution draft. The republics were, for instance, no longer described as sovereign entities. When the draft was voted on in a referendum on 12 December, more than half of the republics as well as 11 territorially defined federal subjects rejected it, either through low participation or by votes against it from more than 50 per cent of the electorate. Nevertheless, the new Constitution was adopted since it received support from 58.4 per cent of the electorate at the federal level, and since election turnout was above 50 per cent (54.8 per cent).

Evolving centre–region relations

The 1993 Constitution replaced the centralised administrative regime of the Soviet period with a system that grants the federal subjects a considerable degree of legal autonomy. Executive power of the regions is nested with the regional administration and its head of administration, or governor (in the republics: president). The large regional soviets (with 200–250 members) are replaced by smaller legislative bodies – most often named dumas[8] – at the regional level.

This section provides a brief overview of main aspects of the legal relationship between Moscow and the subjects of the Russian Federation. It also raises the question whether the formal rights of the federal subjects have been followed up in practice. First, have political realities in post-Soviet Russia allowed the devolution of power to ensue according to the legal stipulations of the Constitution? Second, has decentralisation been accompanied by sufficient sources of economic revenue at the regional level or been reduced to a judicial and/or political exercise of good intentions?

Legal aspects[9] The Constitution lays down a threefold framework for the distribution of jurisdiction between federal and regional authorities (see Figure 3.1). Article 71 lists all areas where federal authorities have exclusive competence, including foreign and security politics. Article 72 defines a comprehensive list of areas over which federal and regional authorities have joint jurisdiction. Article 73 states that except for the areas of jurisdiction mentioned in Articles 71 and 72 the federal subjects 'exercise the entire spectrum of state power'. The picture is completed by Article 76, Paragraph 4, which states that on matters of joint jurisdiction 'laws and other regulatory legal acts of the subjects of the Russian Federation may not contravene federal laws'.

In a discussion of centre–region relations, Article 72 is clearly of most interest since it involves both the federal and regional level. The Article lists 14 different areas in which the two levels share jurisdiction, among them 'issues of possession, use and management of the land, mineral resources, water and other natural resources' (Article 72, Paragraph 1(c)) and 'management of natural resources, protection of the environment and ecological safety' (Article 72, Paragraph 1(e)). In accordance with Article 76, Paragraph 5, the Constitution grants federal legislation priority over regional legislation in areas of joint jurisdiction. On the other hand, the scope of regional legislation is not limited by the areas covered by federal legislation. In practice, the federal legislature has so far failed to pass legislation on a variety of important issues under Article 72, leaving considerable room for regional legislators to freely draft regulations.[10]

In addition to working through the above-mentioned regional legal initiative, some federal subjects have tried to reduce the impact

Figure 3.1 *The legal hierarchy for distribution of competence between the federal and regional levels*

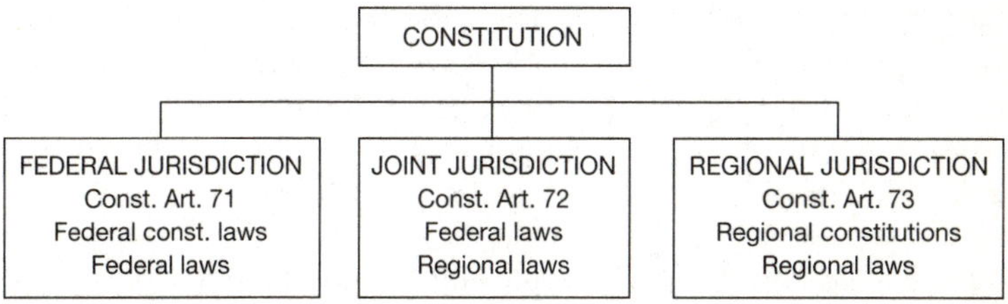

Source: Risnes (2001).

of the legislative vacuum by concluding bilateral agreements with the federal centre. These agreements normally contain declaratory provisions on co-operation between federal and regional authorities, but are followed by a number of sub-agreements regulating more practical questions of particular importance to the federal subject in question. Although initially conceived as a way to bring a reluctant Republic of Tatarstan back into the Federation, the bilateral treaties soon developed into a dynamic tool for regulating centre–region relations. By now, more than half of the federal subjects have adopted such agreements. On the one hand, the adoption of bilateral agreements strengthens the legal basis of centre–region relations; on the other, they increase the diversity and inconsistency of the legal system as a whole.

Finally, it should be noted that the centralised administrative structure of the Soviet period has not disappeared altogether. Compared to the significant changes in Russian law and politics since the early 1990s, the bureaucracy has changed surprisingly little. Most important spheres of politics are still the exclusive responsibility of federal authorities – ministries (23),[11] state committees (6), federal commissions (2), federal services (13), federal agencies (8) and supervisory agencies (2) – and these have a fine-meshed net of representations in the regions. The new legal status of regional authorities resulted in a need for co-operation between regional administrations and regional branches of federal authorities. The co-operation was often co-ordinated by the presidential representative in the region, a position introduced by President Yeltsin to oversee the implementation in the regions of decisions made at the federal level.[12] In general, the presence of federal authorities in the regions appears to have constituted a buffer against effective transferral of power to the federal subjects. On the other hand, it has been claimed that regional authorities in reality have enjoyed considerable influence over federal administration in the regions. As a result, President Putin in May 2000 introduced seven new federal administrative districts aimed at managing the work of federal agencies in the regions (see next section). At the same time, he took an initiative to bring all regional legislation into accordance with federal legislation and review the future of the bilateral agreements by the end of 2001.

Political aspects[13] The years prior to the adoption of the 1993 Constitution had been characterised by demands for increased sovereignty for political entities at all levels in the Soviet Union/Russian Federation, often referred to as the 'Parade of Sovereignties'.[14] As noted above, however, President Yeltsin no longer depended on the strong support of the regions after defeating the Supreme Soviet in the autumn of 1993. Already before that, he had secured for himself the right to personally appoint the heads of regional administrations (governors) although the Parliament – against the veto of the President – in the spring of 1991 had adopted a law which opened for direct election of heads of administration.[15] Combined with the introduction of presidential representatives in the regions (see previous section), the period 1993–96 is clearly characterised by Yeltsin tightening his grip on regional executives.[16] Moreover, the division of power emerging during this period developed along what has been called the 'executive vertical', replacing the Communist Party as the 'transmission belt' in relations between the regions and political centre of the state. At both the federal and regional level, the legislatures were considered subordinate political positions.

After 1996, the Russian regions have consolidated their position and to some extent also increased their autonomy. A major event in centre–region relations was the long awaited gubernatorial elections organised during the winter of 1996–97 (the 'Parade of Governors'). The heads of the regional administrations can now refer to a popular mandate rather than presidential decree as their source of legitimacy, clearly reducing their dependence on federal authorities. The centre can no longer rely on direct control over the executive vertical and has now to resort mainly to the budgetary process in its efforts to influence development in the regions (see next section).

Recent years have again been characterised by federal authorities attempting to stop the devolution of power from the centre. As mentioned above, giving the presidential representatives responsibility for overseeing the activities of federal agencies in the regions was no guarantee of these representatives' loyalty to federal authorities. In practice, the majority of presidential representatives appear to have 'gone native', ending up as allies of the governors or republican presidents. In the May 2000 reorganisation mentioned above, President Putin introduced a new administrative layer between the centre and the federal subjects, the federal okrugs. Seven federal okrugs were established, led by presidential representatives. The old system of presidential representatives in the federal subjects was abolished. It can be argued that the reorganisation represents a re-centralisation in itself. Simultaneously, the regional leaders lost the control they had acquired over federal agencies located on their territory. Shortly after, Putin also curbed the legal power of the regional heads of administration by depriving them of their representation in the Federation Council, the upper house of the Federal Parliament.

Economic aspects[17] In the period that followed the establishment of the Russian Federation, the economy of the country underwent radical economic reforms. The main elements were privatisation, price and tax liberalisation and the adoption of a number of laws to facilitate the introduction of a market economy. The economic aspect of Russian federalism rests on three main pillars: the division of responsibility between federal, regional and local authorities; the re-distributive effects of the tax system; and transfers between the federal and regional level. The division of responsibility between the different levels of government implies that the federal level is responsible for macro-economic stabilisation, inter-regional distribution and the provision of public goods of national interest, such as defence. Sub-regional authorities cover expenditures such as health, primary education and housing subsidies.[18] The Russian tax system consists of local, regional and federal taxes. The most important taxes are the VAT, the corporate profit tax and the personal income tax.[19] Eighty-five per cent, 81 per cent and 3 per cent, respectively, of these taxes is transferred to the federal budget. The tax system is generally considered to be complicated, and compliance is low. Transfers from federal authorities to the regions is the third instrument of fiscal federalism in Russia, constituting approximately 10–12 per cent of the total federal budget in recent years.[20] A. McAuley (1997)[21] finds that more support is transferred to regions that are poorer than the national average compared to other regions. Moreover, ethnically defined federal subjects are, almost without exception, net receivers of federal support.

Until the eve of the rouble crisis in August 1998, the Russian economy seemed to have stabilised and even embarked on a slightly positive trend. During the crisis – by Russians referred to only as *August* – Russia changed its exchange rate regime from a fixed exchange rate to a floating one. The devaluation was regarded as a major defeat for the Russian stabilisation policy,[22] but in hindsight it appears to have implied one step back in order later to take two steps forward. The rouble has stabilised, inflation did not accelerate, the trade balance has improved, and, most importantly, Russia had economic growth in 1999 and 2000.

Under the Soviet central planning system, political priorities, and not market mechanisms, determined which resources should be developed and where production should take place. The extremely centralised decision-making process, low perceived transportation costs and remote sources of raw materials contributed to a decentralised economic geography. A by-product of Soviet resource exploitation and industrial policy was the construction of a large number of mono-industrial towns in the resource-rich, formerly largely unpopulated northern peripheries of the Soviet Union.

During the Soviet period, the centripetal forces that have depopulated Western peripheral regions were not in operation in Russia. Paradoxically, the introduction of decentralised economic decision-making may reactivate these centripetal forces. Exposed to new demands for profitability and competitiveness, the transport-intensive Soviet-style economy faces severe structural problems. Depopulation may spark a negative spiral at the regional level: fewer people means a decreasing home market for local industries. This has two implications for a region's industrial potential. First, it reduces the market for local supply industries. Second, it reduces the incentives for the location of other industries to the region. Ironically, then, economic decentralisation in a post-Soviet Russian context thus might lead to depopulation and centralisation.

The economy and politics of Northwestern Russia

This section presents the northwestern periphery of the Russian Federation, providing an overview of the economic situation in the region and its most important political power structures. First, the geographical concept 'Northwestern Russia' is discussed and defined for further use in the book. Next, a brief historical background is provided along with some main characteristics of the region in terms of population, resources and industry. Finally, an overview is provided of the political system at the regional level in Northwestern Russia.

Northwestern Russia: a concept definition

In Russia, there are several 'official' definitions of the country's northwestern part. The Russian Northwestern Economic Region, for instance, is defined as the oblasts of Novgorod, Leningrad and

Pskov as well as the city of St Petersburg; whereas Murmansk, Arkhangelsk and Vologda Oblasts, the Republics of Karelia and Komi and Nenets Autonomous Okrug are defined as the Northern Economic Region.[23] The Northwestern Association, on its part, was established early in 1993 to facilitate co-ordination of the northern regions' relations with the federal centre and to draw Moscow's attention to its particular problems.[24] It includes the Republics of Karelia and Komi, as well as Arkhangelsk, Vologda, Kaliningrad, Kirov, Leningrad, Murmansk, Novgorod and Pskov Oblasts, Nenets Autonomous Okrug and the city of St Petersburg.

The Russian conceptions of 'Northwestern Russia' are all either significantly broader than – or totally different from – those found in the West, in particular in the Nordic countries. In the West, the term 'Northwestern Russia' is normally used when referring to the Russian part of the Barents Euro-Arctic Region, i.e. Murmansk and Arkhangelsk Oblasts, the Republic of Karelia and Nenets Autonomous Okrug. However, there is a tendency at least in Norway to understand the term even more narrowly; people occasionally speak of Northwestern Russia even if they primarily have in mind the Kola Peninsula or Murmansk Oblast. In this book, the subject matter of the discussion forces a compromise between the two latter definitions. In terms of implementation of international environmental agreements in the Barents Sea region, Murmansk and Arkhangelsk Oblasts, and, partly, also the Nenets Autonomous Okrug, are by far the most relevant federal subjects. Among these, focus is in particular on the former. For instance, although the 'northern fishery basin' of the Russian Federation is defined as including the fisheries of Murmansk and Arkhangelsk Oblasts, the Republic of Karelia and Nenets Autonomous Okrug, the majority of fishing enterprises are located in Murmansk Oblast.[25] Likewise, air pollution control is more urgently required on the Kola Peninsula than in the rest of the region, as are nuclear safety measures.

A brief historical background

Northwestern Russia represents a true microcosm of Soviet and Russian administrative-territorial engineering. The four federal subjects that are normally understood of as comprising 'Northwestern Russia' include the three main categories of Russian federal entities: Karelia is a republic, Nenets an autonomous okrug, and Arkhangelsk and Murmansk are oblasts.[26] A brief historical background to the two latter regions, covering the main geographical scope of the current study, is given in the following.

The history of Murmansk (see Figure 3.2) – both the administrative entity and the city itself – is a relatively short one. In the autumn of 1997, the inhabitants of Murmansk City celebrated the 80th anniversary of its founding. At the same time, those so inclined could celebrate the 80th anniversary of the Bolshevik Revolution, underscoring the relatively brief political and economic history of the region.

Figure 3.2 *Murmansk Oblast*

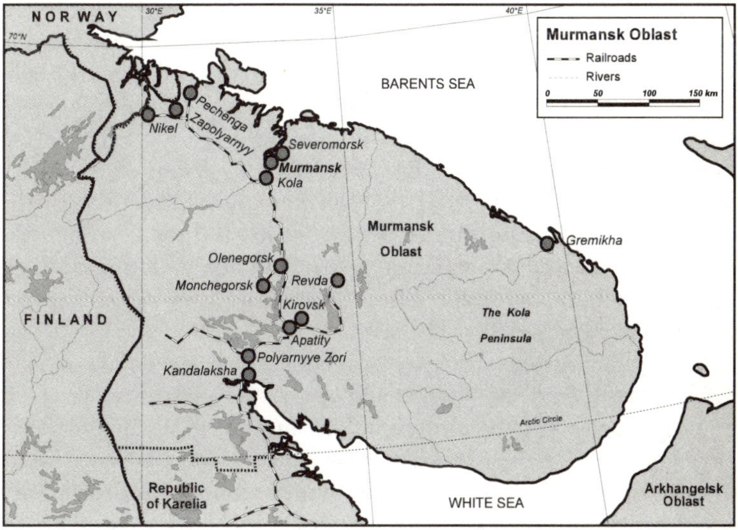

Until World War I, the vast territory of the Kola Peninsula was inhabited by only a few thousand people and was of practically no significance, military or otherwise, to the Russian empire.[27] Although the strategic potential of the ice-free Murman Coast had been recognised at least a half-century earlier, the Russian authorities did not move to develop this potential until they were forced to act by the vicissitudes of World War I. The lack of ice-free ports in European Russia, except for those in the Black and Baltic Seas where the Russian fleets could easily be cut off in narrow straits, prompted the construction of the Murman Railway, which reached the Kola

Fjord in 1916. The same year, the supply port Romanov-na-Murmane was founded at the end-stop of the railway line. In 1917, its name was changed to Murmansk.

During the Civil War of 1918–20, Murmansk was a base for British, French and American expeditionary forces against the Bolsheviks, and Soviet power was established only in 1920. The following year, Murmansk became the administrative centre of the newly formed Murmansk Guberniya. From 1927 through 1937, the region was administered as an okrug within Leningrad Oblast. As a result of the region's growing population and economic and political significance, Murmansk attained oblast status in 1938.[28]

During World War II, the strategic importance of Murmansk and the Kola Peninsula was proved again – both as a vital corridor for supplies during the siege of Leningrad and as the home base for the Northern Fleet, which had been founded in 1933. During the subsequent Cold War, Murmansk Oblast was one of the two regions within the Soviet Union that shared borders directly with a NATO member and was thus given high priority. The peninsula was heavily militarised, and by 1970 the Northern Fleet had become the largest and most important of the Soviet naval fleets. The military complex employed a significant part of the population and developed into a state within the state, endowed with its own infrastructure, generally superior to the civilian one.

The civilian sector of the post-war economy in the oblast came to be dominated by heavy industry. Entire towns and cities were built from scratch around enormous mining, metallurgical, and chemical enterprises (e.g. Nikel, Monchegorsk, Apatity and Kirovsk). Many of these industrial centres were constructed along the Murman Railway,[29] which still constitutes the infrastructural backbone of the Kola Peninsula. In coastal settlements, and especially in Murmansk City, the fisheries and fish processing industry also played a significant role. The fish processing industry in Murmansk gradually came to supply the USSR as a whole.

Murmansk is a typical Russian northern region in the sense that major population growth post-dated the Bolshevik Revolution and was based on the construction of a relatively small number of massive industrial enterprises and military complexes. The industrialisation policies of the 1920s ushered in a period of mass immigration to the Kola Peninsula, a trend that except for a temporary slump during World War II continued until 1991. The immigrants were attracted by a number of advantages granted to the inhabitants of the Soviet North, such as higher wages, a lower retirement age, and subsidised holidays at resorts at the Black Sea. Although the standard of living in Murmansk Oblast therefore was well above the Soviet average, many of its inhabitants still regarded it as a temporary place of residence rather than as their permanent home. Most workers returned to their former areas of residence upon retirement, if not before, to live on their generous pensions and the savings that the northern system of compensation had allowed them to accumulate. Those working in the military and fisheries sectors, where personnel turnover is generally high, had an even weaker sense of attachment to the region. The region's demographic profile has reflected this situation; the average age of the population was low, and young males were over-represented.

The two oblasts of the northwestern Russian periphery, Arkhangelsk and Murmansk, represent old and new Russia, respectively. Whereas Murmansk is a prime example of the Soviet industrial and military adventure, Arkhangelsk (see Figure 3.3) is a centre of traditional Russian cultural heritage. Zavolochya, which is the old name of the region where Arkhangelsk Oblast is now situated, was colonised by the Novgorodians in the Middle Ages. With the fall of Novgorod, the territories along the shores of the White Sea came under Moscow's control. The population was sparse, and settlement spearheaded by hermits and monks. At the site where Arkhangelsk City is located, the Monastery of Michael the Archangel was founded in 1136, and there were also a number of other important monasteries in the region, e.g. on the Solovets Islands.

The original administrative centre of the region was the city of Kholmogory, which in the late sixteenth century, at the time Arkhangelsk City was founded, had some 1,000 inhabitants. The immediate reason for the founding of Arkhangelsk was Russia's loss of the Baltic port of Narva in 1581, which cut Moscow's access to the Baltic Sea. Some thirty years earlier, the English seaman Richard Chancellor, in a failed attempt to find a northeast passage to China, had landed in the White Sea. Chancellor was received in Moscow by Tsar Ivan IV, who granted England favourable conditions for trade with Russia over the White Sea. Commerce developed rapidly, and after the loss of Narva Ivan the Terrible in 1584 decided to develop a new port to facilitate this trade at the shore of Northern Dvina, i.e. Arkhangelsk.

Figure 3.3 *Arkhangelsk Oblast and Nenets Autonomous Okrug*

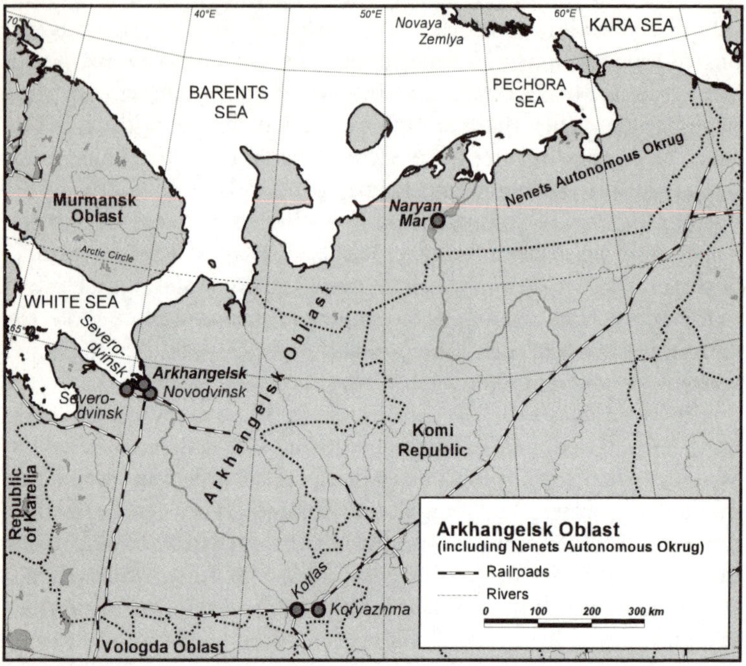

The new city soon became an important harbour for trade in grain, furs, leather, lard and wax. In 1693, the first state-run shipyard in Russia was established in Arkhangelsk – what has later been commemorated as the founding of the Russian navy. After Peter the Great opened his 'Window on Europe', St Petersburg, in 1703, however, exorbitant duties were introduced to redirect trade to this new town, and Arkhangelsk lost some of its importance. In 1708, Arkhangelsk Guberniya was founded. The guberniya was considerably larger than the present oblast, covering the Russian European North from the Danish–Norwegian border to the Urals. Although trade dwindled, Arkhangelsk remained by far the largest city in the Russian north. Moreover, the building of a railway from Moscow to Arkhangelsk in 1898 spurred industrial growth in the region.

In the Civil War that followed the October Revolution of 1917, Arkhangelsk became a centre of resistance against the Bolsheviks and headquarters of the White Army under General Miller's command.

In August 1918, British troops landed in the city, and although they were withdrawn in 1919, Arkhangelsk did not fall into Soviet hands until the following year. The Soviet development of the Far North led to new growth in Arkhangelsk. While the population of Arkhangelsk City was 45,000 at the end of the Civil War, it quadrupled over the next decade and peaked at over 425,000 at the end of the Soviet period. Soviet focus on industrialisation and urbanisation led not only to an increased share of urban population (from 39.6 per cent in 1939 to 73.4 per cent in 1989) but also to a fall in rural population in absolute numbers (from 641,800 in 1939 to 417,800 in 1989). Overall, the population of the oblast increased by almost half a million from 1,062,600 in 1939 to 1,515,800 in 1989.

In 1929, Soviet authorities established the Northern Kray, the administrative centre of which was Arkhangelsk City. In 1937, the kray was dissolved and replaced by two oblasts, Arkhangelsk and Vologda. Nenets Autonomous Okrug remained a constituent part of the oblast throughout the Soviet period. It is a subject of the Russian Federation, but still forms part of Arkhangelsk Oblast. Although the 1993 Constitution recognises all subjects of the federation as equal in relation to the federal centre, it maintains the system of autonomous districts forming a part of an oblast or a kray. The Constitution does not regulate the legal consequences of this, but merely states that the legal relations between an autonomous okrug and the oblast or kray which it forms part of can be regulated either through federal law or an agreement between the two federal subjects. Arkhangelsk Oblast and Nenets Autonomous Okrug concluded a preliminary agreement in 1994 and an extended agreement in 1996. These agreements did not solved all questions of formal relations between the two federal subjects, but at least provided a foundation for working relations between the two.[30]

Population and industry in the region[31]

Murmansk Oblast encompasses the geographic area of the Kola Peninsula, covering a land area of 144,900 km^2. Almost all the territory is situated north of the polar circle and the oblast covers two climatic zones – tundra and taiga. During the 1990s, immigration to the oblast slumped and Murmansk, like most other Russian northern regions, experienced a population decline (11.2 per cent from 1990 to 1999). At present, the population is around 1,034,500. In spite of the recent fall in population, this still makes Murmansk one of the most densely populated areas in the entire circumpolar north (7.1 people per km2). The overwhelming majority of the population (92 per cent) is concentrated in the region's widely scattered urban settlements. There are 16 cities in the oblast, the largest being Murmansk with 387,400 inhabitants (down from more than 468,000 at the end of the Soviet period), Apatity (70,600), Monchegorsk (59,800), Severomorsk (57,100) and Kandalaksha (46,900).

Although immigration to Murmansk came from all over the Soviet Union, the oblast is predominantly Russian with ethnic Russians making up 83.8 per cent of the total population. Other ethnic groups living in Murmansk are Ukrainians (8.3 per cent), Belorussians (3.5 per cent), Tatars (1 per cent), Mordvins (0.4 per cent) and Chuvashs (0.2 per cent). The aboriginal population, the Saami, today number approximately 1,600 (0.15 per cent of the total population), and are concentrated to the Lovozero Rayon.

The economic geography of Murmansk Oblast is typical of Soviet mono-industrial specialisation. Several of the largest towns in the oblast are dependent on a single or very few enterprises operating in the same type of industry. Table 3.1 shows that the 'dependency rate', defined as the ratio of the number of employees in the largest enterprise in each town to the number of inhabitants, is extremely high in the oblast (more than 20 per cent in all the listed towns).

Table 3.1 *Employment by main firm and population in some towns of Murmansk Oblast*

Town	*Employment in main company*	*Population in municipality*	*Main product*
Kovdor	5,000 + 2,500[a]	28,000	Iron concentrate, apatite
Apatity	18,000	82,000	Apatite concentrate
Olenegorsk	5,500	33,800	Iron concentrate
Lovozero	4,000	19,000	Loparthite
Polyarnye Zori	6,000	18,000	Nuclear power
Monchegorsk	10,000	65,500	Nickel
Pechenga	8,500	20,000 + 22,000[b]	Nickel

Source: Maurseth (1997, 2001).

[a] two firms.

[b] population in Nikel and Zapolyarnyy.

Although the industrial sector of Murmansk Oblast performed better than the Russian average during the economic hardships of the 1990s,[32] industrial production decreased significantly during the 1990s, as reflected in Figure 3.4. The figure shows a dramatic reduction in agricultural production and the fishing industry. The fish-processing plant in Murmansk City used to be one of the largest in Europe, but has operated at a fraction of its full potential since the mid-1990s. The production of raw materials like iron ore and concentrate has decreased less than the overall industrial production. There has even been an increase in the production of apatite. The high concentration of mono-industrial towns in the oblast makes Murmansk particularly vulnerable to economic fluctuations.

Arkhangelsk Oblast – including the archipelagos of Novaya Zemlya and Franz Josef Land, as well as Nenets Autonomous Okrug – covers a territory of 587,400 km^2. Even if the okrug is excluded on the basis of constituting a separate federal entity, Arkhangelsk, with a territory of 410,700 km^2, remains one of the larger federal

Figure 3.4 *Output of some industrial products in Murmansk Oblast in 1998 in % of 1993 output*

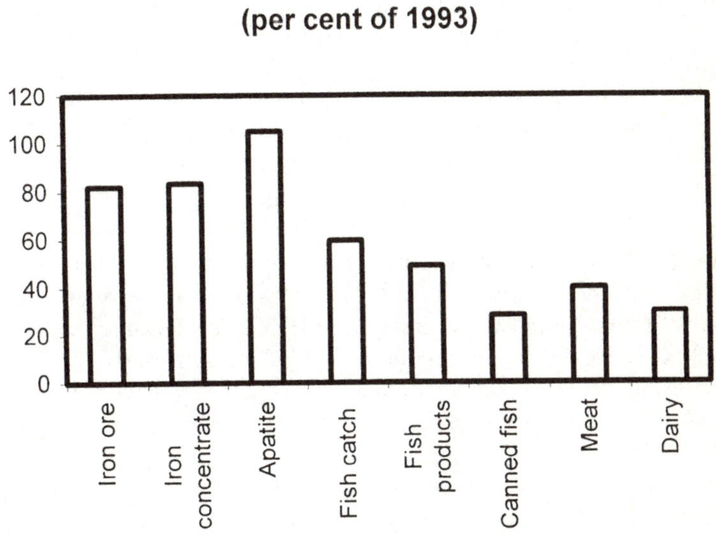

Source: Maurseth (2001) and Murmansk Regional Committee of State Statistics (1999).

subjects. The present population of the oblast (again excluding the okrug) is 1,491,900 people; 74.1 per cent of the population live in urban settlements. There are fourteen cities, the largest being Arkhangelsk City with 368,900 inhabitants. Other important cities are: Severodvinsk (239,000 inhabitans), Kotlas (66,800), Novodvinsk (48,700) and Koryazhma (44,500).[33]

Arkhangelsk is a thoroughly Russian oblast: 92.1 per cent of the population is ethnic Russian.The largest minority groups are made up by Ukrainians (3.4 per cent), Belorussians (1.3 per cent), and Komi (0.5 per cent). Local Russians were traditionally known as Pomors, a subgroup of the Russian ethnos. The Pomors distinguished themselves through their occupation (fishing), traditions, culture and distinct dialect. With the influx of newcomers to the region in the Soviet period, however, the Pomor culture has all but disappeared. The aboriginal population (ancient tribes such as the Chuds and Biarms, as well as the present day Nenets and Saami) have either been assimilated or pushed aside throughout the centuries of Russian domination and no longer compose distinct elements (altogether some 750 Nenets live in the oblast).

Historically, forestry has been the most important industry in the Arkhangelsk region. Until the 1970s, when it was surpassed by Irkutsk Oblast, Arkhangelsk was the leading producer of timber in the Soviet Union. Up to two-fifths of the industrial production is still related to forestry (saw-timber, furniture, paper, pulp etc.). Also shipbuilding has deep roots in Arkhangelsk. The Sevmash and Zvyozdochka shipyards in Severodvinsk serve the military sector (Sevmash builds and Zvyozdochka repairs and modifies nuclear submarines).

Also Arkhangelsk Oblast was hit by the economic crisis of the 1990s. Figure 3.5 demonstrates that, apart from the oil and gas industry mainly located in Nenets Autonomous Okrug,[34] there was a significant decrease in industrial output in the region. As in Murmansk Oblast, industries serving the domestic consumer market, such as the diary and meat industries, were particularly hard hit. 'Traditional' production of timber and paper nearly halved in the period. The fish-processing industry also experienced a serious decline as a result of lack of raw materials, the local industry unable to compete either in price, or in location in relation to fishing grounds and markets. Arkhangelsk Oblast has a more diversified industrial structure than Murmansk Oblast and is therefore better suited to meet the challenges of further economic hardships. So far,

Figure 3.5 *Output of some industrial products in Arkhangelsk Oblast in 1998 in % of 1993 output*

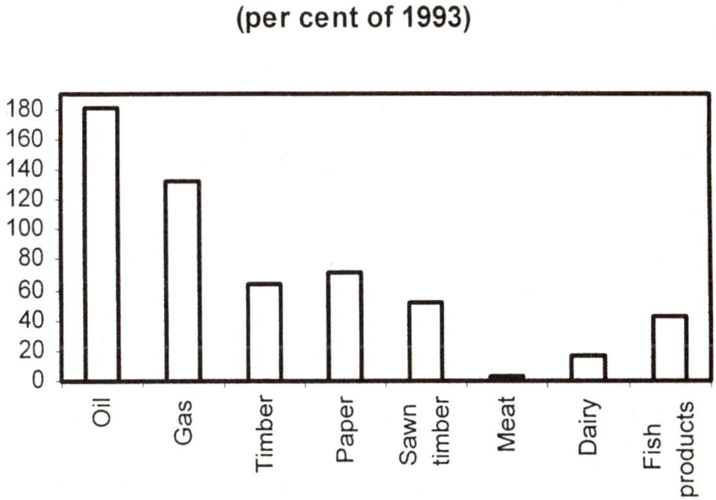

Source: Maurseth (2001) and Arkhangelsk Regional Committee of State Statistics (1999).

however, Arkhangelsk has been heavily dependent on federal transfers. Among the Northwest Russian federal subjects, only Murmansk has been a net donor to the federal budget.

Political organisation of the region

The regions of the Russian Federation are organised politically according to the same principle as the federal level: a sharing of responsibility between a legislative duma and a directly elected head of the executive power (a president at the federal level as well as in the republics, and governors in the other federal subjects). The latter is not answerable to the former.

The political organisation of Murmansk and Arkhangelsk Oblasts is laid out in their Regional Charters of 26 November 1997 and 23 May 1995, respectively. According to the Charters, the Head of Administration (Governor) is the leading political figure of both regions. The Governor is elected for four years and can only hold the post for two periods. The legislative body of Murmansk Oblast, the regional duma, consists of 25 deputies elected for a four-year period. In Arkhangelsk Oblast, there is a regional sobraniye consisting of 41 representatives (including one from Nenets Autonomous Okrug). The Governors have rather wide authority over the regional legislatures inasmuch as they have the right to summon extraordinary sessions of the duma/sobraniye and to reject laws adopted by it. Hence, political power in Northwestern Russia resides for all practical purposes with the Governors and their administration. The Arkhangelsk regional sobraniye is considered as rather co-operative *vis-à-vis* its regional administration, the Murmansk legislature more hostile (Blakkisrud 2001b, p. 74). In February 1998, a new political structure, the regional government, was introduced in Murmansk Oblast. It is appointed by the Governor and consists of the Deputy Governors, i.e. the leaders of all departments of the regional administration. The First Deputy Governor is appointed premier of the regional government.[35]

Until 1996–97, most governors were appointed by President Yeltsin, among them Yevgeniy Komarov in Murmansk and Pavel Balakshin and later Anatoliy Yefremov[36] in Arkhangelsk, all recruited from the old party nomenklatura. In the run-up to the gubernatorial elections of Murmansk Oblast in late 1996, Komarov enjoyed substantial economic and moral support from the Kremlin. Prime Minister Chernomyrdin even visited Murmansk on the eve of the elections with the apparent intention of supporting the incumbent. Nevertheless, Komarov did not succeed in bringing victory home. None of the candidates achieved the necessary 50 per cent of the votes in the first round of the elections. In the run-off, Komarov (40.7 per cent) lost to Yuriy Yevdokimov (43.5 per cent), former First Secretary of the Oblast Committee of the Communist Party and former Chairman of the Oblast Soviet (1990–93). Yevdokimov's political platform was the Congress of Russian Communities, the party for which General Aleksandr Lebed had ran in the duma elections in 1995, and his candidacy was supported by Lebed's new Honour and Motherland movement. Yevdokimov has later been associated with the Fatherland movement of Moscow's Mayor Yuriy Luzhkov and threw his support behind Putin after he had been installed as Acting President.[37] In the following elections in March 2000, Yevdokimov was re-elected with 59.8 per cent of the votes in the first round of elections. He stands forth as an active and entrepreneurial governor who succeeds relatively well in defending the interests of the region *vis-à-vis* federal authorities. Within the military, he is particularly popular for having launched an adoption campaign for the vessels of the Northern Fleet, whereby other federal subjects, cities and business enterprises contribute material supplies to the crisis-ridden fleet.[38]

In Arkhangelsk Oblast, the incumbent succeeded in securing a popular mandate in the 1996 election. Anatoliy Yefremov had been in office for less than nine months and was probably less associated with the negative impact of economic and social reform on the population. Running against the Communist Yuriy Guskov, he could also draw on the entire reform-oriented electorate in the run-off. He won a solid victory, 62.0 per cent as against Guskov's 28.8 per cent. In the 2000 election, Yefremov won 49 per cent in the first round to former oblast Prime Minister Nikolay Malakov's 32.3 per cent. In the run-off, Yefremov won 58.5 percent of the vote while Malakov got 31.6 per cent.

As follows from the first section of this chapter, bilateral power-sharing agreements between Moscow and the federal subjects have become an important instrument in filling the legal vacuum in Russian centre–region relations. Among the Northwest Russian federal subjects, only Murmansk Oblast has concluded a power-sharing agreement with federal authorities (Murmansk Oblast 1997a). The agreement was signed by President Yeltsin and Governor Yevdokimov on 30 November 1997. By this time, the process of developing Russian federalism through such agreements was on the wane, and the agreement was not as advantageous to the oblast as the early bilateral agreements of 1994–95. In addition to declarations on co-operation, it lists a range of areas as joint responsibilities, including the environment and management of natural resources. Arkhangelsk began drafting an agreement, but negotiations seem to have stalled.[39]

Federal authorities are heavily represented on the territory of Northwestern Russia. First, some 40–55 federal agencies have their representations in each federal subject of the region.[40] The Northwestern Federal Okrug, which has its main office in St Petersburg, is also represented. Second, the region is heavily militarised, and as a result large parts of its territory are under federal (military) control. In addition to military base areas, there are six so-called closed towns in Murmansk Oblast – rendering Murmansk the federal subject with most closed towns in the entire Russian Federation – and one in Arkhangelsk. These are the direct responsibility of federal, not regional authorities. In 1992, a new law, On the Closed Administrative-Territorial Formation (Russian Federation 1992), gave some forty-five formerly secret cities in Russia civilian names and established a division of responsibility between civilian and military authorities within them. A study by the authors of this book (Hønneland and Jørgensen 1998, 1999a) concludes that the closed towns on the Kola Peninsula have not been significantly more integrated into the surrounding civil society since the disintegration of the Soviet Union; politically, economically and socially, the inhabitants and authorities of the closed towns relate more to Moscow and other parts of the Russian Federation than to the regional centre of Murmansk.

Finally, it should be observed that the federal subjects of Northwestern Russia have tended to be less confrontational towards the federal centre than Russian regions in general. They have only to a very limited extent adopted legislation that contradicts federal law, and the elected governors in the area have generally been eager to be on a good footing with the Kremlin. There are several possible explanations for this deference. First, it can be assumed that federal authorities have more control over such a militarised region as Northwestern Russia than less strategically important regions. Second, the abundant natural resources of the region may have made federal authorities particularly eager to maintain control here. Third, it can be argued that the economic vulnerability of the region – Arkhangelsk is a net recipient of the federal budget; Murmansk is a donor, but its industrial future is insecure due to the large concentration of mono-industrial towns here – reduces its leaders' wish to challenge the authority of the federal government.[41]

Conclusions

The object of study of the present investigation – the implementation of international environmental agreements in Russia – renders the status and application of Article 72 in the Russian Constitution particularly interesting. The management of natural resources and the environment falls under this article and hence under the joint jurisdiction of federal and regional authorities. According to Article 76 of the Constitution, federal law has priority over regional law in areas of joint jurisdiction, but the regional authorities nevertheless enjoy considerable room for manoeuvre. First, federal legislation is still poorly developed, and it can become difficult for federal authorities to change a practice that for years has been followed in accordance with regional legislation. Second, there is an almost unlimited number of approaches to an area of law, and Article 76, Paragraph 5, refers only to instances of direct contradiction between legislation of the two levels. In addition to this is the fact that individual bilateral agreements have come to fill the legal vacuum between the federal centre and more than half of the subjects of the Russian Federation.

More interesting for our investigation than the legal peculiarities is the political 'tug-of-war' between various agencies at various levels. A main line of conflict clearly runs between the federal and regional level in general. The former is represented by ministries, state committees, supervisory agencies and others (see above), the latter by the regional administrations under the leadership of governors (in the republics: presidents). We have seen that the governors strengthened their position during the second half of the 1990s, but President Putin in 2000 introduced various measures that may curb their authority. A second line of potential conflict is in the interface between regional authorities and the representations of federal agencies located on their territories. There are indications that representatives of the latter tend to 'go native', becoming primarily spokespersons of their own geographical entity in relation to federal authorities. Third, one can imagine conflicts arising between various agencies at the same administrative level. At the federal level, different ministries or state committees may fight over formal powers since these are normally accompanied by allocations from the federal budget. This is particularly likely in the functional fields of our study since the responsibility to manage natural resources often implies control of revenues from extraction of these resources, and the management of the environment in recent years has come to involve considerable transfers of financial assistance from the West. At the regional level, the number of actors is more limited. A certain degree of conflict is often found between the regional administrations and the regional legislature. However, this has so far not been a major issue in Russian regional politics since the authority of the latter is so limited compared to the regional executive. Finally, the political clout of the former industry complexes – in Soviet times performing both economic activities at enterprise level and the implementation of state politics – and various political bodies at both federal and regional level continues to be of interest and will be reverted to in the case studies of the book.

The implementation of international environmental agreements in Northwestern Russia takes place in a political and administrative setting that is still in the making, and in an atmosphere of economic insecurity. Both Murmansk and Arkhangelsk Oblasts have been hard hit by the general economic crisis in Russia during the 1990s. Production has fallen markedly in most sectors of the economy; the result is increased unemployment and decreased population in the region. Prospects for the future are particularly insecure for the mono-industrial towns of Murmansk Oblast. Nevertheless, Murmansk is so far the only federal subject in Northwestern Russia that is a net donor to the federal budget.

The federal subjects of Northwestern Russia have generally sought a co-operative, rather than a confrontational stance in relation to federal authorities. This preliminary 'conclusion' will be further tested in the sector analyses of this book: first, have regional authorities given federal agencies the upper hand also in matters of fisheries management, nuclear safety and air pollution control? Second, how are power relations between regional authorities and representations of federal authorities in the regions? Little is known about the relations between these two categories of government in Northwestern Russia in general. The issue to be raised in the case studies of the book is whether they tend to side with each other or represent competing positions. For instance, do regional agencies of the federal system for fisheries management mainly defend the interests of the regional fisheries complex? Third, are there conflicts between different agencies at the same administrative level? The governors and their regional administrations are by far the most important political figures in Northwestern Russia, but do the regional legislatures nevertheless have a certain influence in environmental matters? Finally, how is the role of the former 'industry complexes' to be understood? This last question is highly relevant for all three case studies. Is the old concept of the 'northern fishery basin' – previously gathered under the Sevryba umbrella – still a relevant category in discussions about Northwest Russian fisheries management? What is the role of the 'nuclear complex' – mainly understood as the power plant at Polyarnye Zori, the nuclear icebreaker fleet of Murmansk Shipping Company and the military nuclear installations – in securing nuclear safety in the region? Is the mining and metallurgical complex a significant actor in issues of air pollution control? And how has the representation of 'industry-complex' directors in the regional duma of Murmansk Oblast affected regional legislation?

Notes

1 This and the next section are partly adapted from Hønneland and Jørgensen (1999a), which in turn was based on Blakkisrud (1997).

2 The Russian empire was organised in gubernii which were ruled by governors and directly subordinate o the cabinet in St Petersburg. With a few exceptions, their borders were not drawn in accordance with ethno-demographic realities.

3 The first federal unity within the RSFSR, the Volga–German Autonomous Workers' Commune, was established in October 1918, but it was only after the end of the Civil War that the federalisation process gathered momentum.

4 Since their unity was maintained through power at the centre, some observers have described them as pseudo-federations (Duchacek 1987).

5 There was arguably a fourth hierarchy, that of the central ministries whose enterprises (each with its own party cell) operated independently of the Soviets and the executive committees, see Whitefield (1993).

6 Among other things, they included a proposal to dissolve the ethnically defined entities and create fewer and larger territorially defined federal subjects. See Hanson (1994) and Sakwa (1993) for a discussion.

7 The Jewish Autonomous Oblast (Birobidzhan) was the only autonomous oblast not to gain the status of republic. It was, however, recognised as an independent federal subject separate from the kray of Khabarovsk, to which it had previously been subordinate.

8 The designations sobraniye (assembly) and soviet (council) could also be used.

9 This section is based on Risnes (2001).

10 A striking example is the regulation of ownership of land. The federal authorities were working on drafts of a land code for a number of years, but succeeded in passing a final code only in autumn 2001. The reason for this delay was disagreement between the President and the state duma. In the meantime, more than fifty federal subjects had adopted their own land codes.

11 There were twenty-four ministries until October 2001, when the Ministry of Federation Affairs, Nationalities and Migration Policies was disbanded. However, in December the same year a new minister without portfolio was appointed to co-ordinate government institutions on

nationalities issues (RFE/RL Russian Federation Report, 6 December 2001).

12 A system of presidential representatives in the oblasts and krays was first introduced immediately after the coup attempt in August 1991. Later, it was extended to the republics, and eventually institutionalised in the 1993 Constitution. Such representatives were not sent to all federal subjects. Generally, Yeltsin seemed more reluctant to station his representatives in ethnically defined than in territorially defined federal subjects.

13 This section is based partly on Blakkisrud (2001b).

14 A famous statement representing this development is Boris Yeltsin's, then newly elected Chairman of the Supreme Soviet of the RSFSR, invitation to the autonomous areas of the Union to 'take as much sovereignty as you can swallow'.

15 Several regional elections were actually held, where heads of administration were replaced by representatives of the local elite. See Hanson (1994) for details.

16 However, the picture is not unambiguous. In general, leaders of the ethnically defined federal subjects were elected, and they also tended to escape the interference of presidential representatives.

17 This section is based on Maurseth (2001).

18 During the first years of the existence of the Russian Federation, there were signs of regional authorities providing services that were obviously a federal responsibility, like issuing 'surrogate money'. This seems to have become less widespread in recent years.

19 The VAT rate was 20 per cent in 2000, tax on profit 30 per cent and tax on personal income 13 per cent.

20 The Federal Fund for Financial Support of the Regions was set up in 1994 to create a more coherent framework for channelling resources to the most needy regions. The fund, partly financed by VAT receipts, still constitutes the major source for federal transfers to the regions.

21 Referred in Maurseth (2001).

22 Keeping the rouble within the predetermined 'rouble corridor' was viewed as essential to deflate the economy. This had been achieved since 1995, and the economic growth since 1997 was regarded as a well-deserved result of this monetary stabilisation.

23 These terms are mainly used for statistical purposes.

24 All of Russia's 89 federal subjects except for Chechnya belong to one of eight inter-regional economic associations set up between 1992 and 1994, and based on Soviet-era economic-administrative divisions (i.e. planning regions). The ambitions and work practices differ somewhat among the associations, but their common goal is to co-ordinate internal co-operation as well as their relations with the political centre. The

Siberian Accord is often referred to as the most ambitious, extensive and successful of the inter-regional associations.

25 For the sake of language variation, the geographical terms are sometimes used without indication of federation subject category (oblast, republic or okrug). This might serve to confuse the two oblasts of the region with the cities of similar names. However, the cities are always referred to specifically, e.g. as Murmansk City or the city of Arkhangelsk.

26 The presentation is based on Hønneland and Jørgensen (1999a) and Blakkisrud and Hønneland (2001). Statistical material is from Makfol and Petrov (1998) and Goskomstat Rossii (1998).

27 The Terskiy Coast (the eastern part of the peninsula) came under the control of the Republic of Novgorod in the thirteenth century, but there are no records of permanent Novgorodian settlement on the peninsula until the first half of the fifteenth century. Following the collapse of the Novgorodian state in 1487, the area became a relatively neglected northern outpost of the Muscovite Principality. Almost a century later, permanent settlements were established along the northern coast at Kola and Pechenga, the first centred around a new fortification, the latter around a monastery. In 1708, Kola Uyezd (district) was included in the new Arkhangelsk Guberniya. In 1883, however, the uyezd was re-established within the guberniya and subsequently renamed Aleksandrovsk Uyezd in 1899 after the newly founded town of Aleksandrovsk (the present closed military town of Polyarnyy).

28 The new oblast consisted of the territory of the former Murmansk Okrug, as well as Kandalaksha Rayon, which was transferred from Karelia. In 1945, the former Finnish territory of Petsamo (now Pechenga) and the port of Liinakhamari were transferred to the oblast.

29 During most of the Soviet period known as the Kirov Railway.

30 See Blakkirud (2001a, 2001b) and Risnes (2001) for discussions of the relationship between Arkhangelsk Oblast and Nenets Autonomous Okrug.

31 This section is based on Hønneland and Jørgensen (1999a), Hønneland and Blakkisrud (2001) and Maurseth (2001).

32 At the turn of the millennium, the industrial production of the oblast had stabilised at 65 per cent of the 1991 level as compared to 50 per cent for Russia as a whole. The corresponding figure for Arkhangelsk Oblast was 61 per cent.

33 These cities make up two clusters of urban settlements: Severodvinsk, which is a centre for the military–industrial complex and the shipbuilding industry, and Novodvinsk with its wood-processing industry are satellites of Arkhangelsk, whereas Koryazhma is a satellite of Kotlas, the centre of the southern, agricultural region. On the other hand, Novaya Zemlya and Frantz Josef Land as well as the northern parts of the mainland are more or less uninhabited.

34 As seen in Figure 3.5, the production of oil and gas enjoyed a considerable increase in the period. Since energy prices were extremely low in the Soviet Union as compared to world market prices, the Russian integration into the world economy boosted the price of oil and gas dramatically, hence increasing profits and thereby also production of oil and gas.

35 The introduction of this new institution seems to have had very limited consequences.

36 Balakshin was removed from office in February 1996, allegedly due to economic mismanagement.

37 Hedenskog (2000) points out that Yevdokimov displays an astonishing proclivity to play on the wrong horse among the top politicians in Russia: as leader of the regional Soviet in 1993, he supported Vice President Aleksandr Rutskoy and Chairman of the Supreme Soviet Ruslan Khasbulatov in their struggle with President Yeltsin. Later, he supported Sergey Kiriyenko in August 1998 and Yevgeniy Primakov in April 1999, at times when both prime ministers were on the threshold of being removed from power.

38 When asked in a television interview in October 1999 what had been his most important achievement as a politician, Yevdokimov referred to this adoption campaign. For more detailed descriptions of the campaign, see Hønneland and Jørgensen (1999a) or Jørgensen (2001).

39 See Blakkisrud (2001b) and Risnes (2001) for differing views on the prospects of Arkhangelsk Oblast eventually concluding a power-sharing agreement with federal authorities.

40 The exact figure varies. In late 1999, the number for Murmansk was 40 and for Arkhangelsk 54 (Blakkisrud 2001; Risnes 2001). No investigation has been carried out of the degree to which these have 'gone native' (see first section of this chapter). This question will partly be addressed in the case studies of this book.

41 Relations between Moscow and the federal subjects of Northwestern Russia are discussed at length in Hønneland and Blakkisrud (2001).

4 Fisheries management

The Barents Sea fish resources have for centuries constituted a main foundation for life in the northern parts of Fennoscandia. As follows from Chapter 1, these resources have since the mid-1970s been managed by a bilateral Norwegian–Russian regime, which in turn partly serves to spur the implementation of these countries' obligations in accordance with global and regional fisheries agreements. The main objective of this chapter is to discuss how Russian authorities since the break-up of the Soviet Union have implemented their international obligations in the fisheries sector of the country's northwestern region. How have federal and regional authorities coordinated the management of marine resources within the territorial waters of the Russian Federation, which according to the Constitution is an area of 'joint jurisdiction' (Article 72)? Have regional authorities abstained from interfering with the management of resources in the Exclusive Economic Zone (EEZ), since the Constitution defines this as a federal responsibility (Article 71)? To what extent is fisheries management still performed by the corporate structure of the 'fisheries complex', as this was done in Soviet times? Implementation is discussed with reference to more overarching political developments in the Russian Federation in general and Northwestern Russia in particular, and also seen in relation to the nature of the problem at hand and of the obligations to be implemented. A brief overview of the resource basis, with an emphasis on the joint Russian–Norwegian fish stocks, and main target groups is given before we embark upon the discussion.

Background: resource basis and industry structure

The Barents Sea fish resources

The Barents Sea contains a rich abundance of fish stocks of a variety of species. The basis for the abundance of these fish resources is the high rate of plankton production in these waters, which provide food for large stocks of pelagic fish – i.e. fish living in the space between the sea floor and surface. The pelagic fish stocks, first and foremost capelin and herring, are in turn the prey of ground-fish, like cod, haddock and saithe. Both pelagic and groundfish serve as food for sea birds, marine mammals and people. Cod, capelin and herring are key species in the ecosystem. Cod feed on capelin, herring and smaller cod, while herring feed on capelin larvae. Periods with good recruitment to the cod and herring stocks and a reduced capelin stock tend to alternate with periods when herring is absent from the Barents Sea, while recruitment to the cod stock is moderate and capelin abundant.

The Barents Sea capelin (*Mallotus villosus*) stock used to be among the largest and most important fish stocks in the northeast Atlantic. One major trait of this stock is that large variations in individual growth from year to year lead to substantial fluctuations in stock size, which have considerable implications for the whole ecosystem. During the last quarter of the twentieth century, the total biomass fluctuated from close to 9 million tonnes (1975) to 0.2 million tonnes (1986). The capelin stock size was rather stable during the 1970s; in the 1980s, it decreased profoundly. Overfishing reinforced a natural downward fluctuation, bringing the stock close to total breakdown. Commercial fishing for capelin was halted in 1986, and the stock started to recover. Fishing was resumed again in 1991. A new collapse occurred in 1993. The stock recovered once again – at least partly. Fishing was resumed in 1999 for the first time since 1993. The quota that has been established is quite moderate.

The stock of Atlanto-Scandinavian herring (*Clupea harengus*) was the largest fish stock in European waters until its collapse in the late 1960s. The normal migration pattern from the North Sea to the spawning grounds off the Norwegian coast was broken in 1970. The stock had then been reduced to such an extent that the remaining fish found sufficient food off the Norwegian coast. The old migration pattern was only resumed in the mid-1990s. The stock has increased considerably in recent years, and herring catches in the

North Sea are approaching those of the 1950s. However, the stock is now thought to be in decline. The cohort groups from 1993 onward seem to be weak. Some herring fry drift with the Gulf Stream into the Barents Sea each year, although their numbers are highly variable. Each age group spends three years here, feeding on capelin as they drift northward. While contributing to the total herring stock, the young herring of the Barents Sea may be considered a threat to the capelin. However, the herring also relieves the pressure on capelin, since it is itself preyed upon by cod. Although herring is not commercially exploited in the Barents Sea, its presence does affect the fishing in the area.

Norwegian–Arctic cod (*Gadus morhua*) spawn along the coastline of Norway from the age of seven. After spawning, they return to the Barents Sea. Fry of this species also drift into the northern parts of the Barents Sea. From the age of four, cod prey upon capelin as the latter species moves southward to its breeding grounds. The cod stock reached a total of some four million tonnes at the end of the 1960s. The stock decreased steadily throughout the 1970s to reach less than one million tonnes in 1984. Strong age groups were recruited in the years from 1983 to 1985, but these cohorts were reduced in 1986–88 due to a lack of food and heavy fishing. Only at the beginning of the 1990s was the level of the late 1970s regained. This increase was mainly realised through quota regulation, which significantly moderated the fishing effort for cod. The stock of cod has shown a decline since 1993. Furthermore, stock estimates were regulated to lower levels in 1998, as scientists discovered that the method used previously had resulted in an overestimation of the stock. The quota for cod has been cut significantly in recent years.

The development of the Norwegian–Arctic haddock (*Melanogrammus aeglefinus*) stock in the Barents Sea tends to follow the same pattern as the cod. Having reached an all-time low in 1983–84, an increase was brought about by strong age groups from the years 1982–83. Another decline took place in the late 1980s. From 1990, recruitment improved markedly until 1995. In recent years, a modest overall decrease has been observed, but the spawning stock has increased. Fluctuations in the size of each age group are more significant for haddock than for cod, and the total stock is also considerably smaller. Thus, it is thought that it will be difficult to sustain a stable haddock fishery over time.

The Northwest Russian fishing industry

The fishing industry of Northwestern Russia developed rapidly after the Russian Revolution in 1917. The Murmansk Trawl Fleet was established in 1920, and a development programme for the fisheries sector was launched in 1926 by the central Soviet power. The building of the Murmansk Fishing Combinate, which was to become the largest industrial fish processing complex in the Soviet Union, was started via this government initiative. As in other areas of the industrial sector in the Soviet Union, the *sector principle* was the guide used to organise the fisheries sector. This implied that the economic sphere of the union was divided into a certain number of sectors each of which was subordinated to its respective ministry. Apart from Khrushchev's attempts during the period 1957–64 to implement a *territorial* organisation of Soviet industry, the sector principle prevailed until the post-Soviet privatisation project started in 1992.

The association of fishing companies in *the northern basin* of the Soviet Union, Sevryba (meaning *North Fish*), was founded in 1965. It was given the status of General Directorate of the Soviet Ministry of Fisheries in Northwestern Russia. Similar bodies were set up in the Far East (Dalryba), the Baltics (Zapryba), the Caspian Sea (Kaspryba) as well as the Azov Sea and the Black Sea (Azcherryba, later re-named Yugryba). After several less comprehensive reorganisation efforts, Sevryba was made into a private joint-stock company in the autumn of 1992. Twenty-three companies with various core activities (ranging from shipowners, on-shore processing factories, a shipyard, research institutions, sales and supply organisations and various other firms) constituted the founders of the company. In April 1993, the Union of Private Fishery Enterprises in the North (Sever) was included in the A/O Sevryba structure. This union, founded in 1992, comprises more than 130 small private firms directly involved in or connected to the fishing industry in Northwestern Russia. However, only 70 of these are involved in the catching of fish, and no more than 18 of them have a cod quota in the Barents Sea. The core activity of most is not fishery; they have recourse to the catching or selling of fish primarily to raise funds for other types of production or trade.

The main structure of the fishing companies was upheld within the new institutional framework, which means that the majority of the approximately 450 fishing vessels located in Northwestern Russia are still controlled by a handful of fishing companies. The rest are distributed between kolkhozes (the collective fleet) and other so-called new small private fishing companies. The total number of vessels has been relatively stable since the early 1990s as few old vessels have been decommissioned (despite exceeding their anticipated lifetime), and few new vessels have been purchased. The existing fishing companies in Northwestern Russia can be placed in five different categories as seen in Table 4.1.

Table 4.1 *The main user groups in the Northwest Russian fishing industry*

Inside Sevryba	*Outside Sevryba*
The old Soviet fleets (Murmansk Trawl Fleet, Murmanrybprom, Sevrybkholodflot, Sevrybpromrazvedka, Arkhangelsk Trawl Fleet Base, Arkhangelskrybprom and Karelrybflot)	Thirty-one kolkhozes (fishing collectives) organised in Roskolkhozsoyuz
The Union of Private Fishing Enterprises in the North (about 130 enterprises, of which approximately 55 are involved in fishing)	Eight kolkhozes organised in the Union of Fishing Collectives in the North
	The Union of Coastal Fishers (about 40 enterprises conducting fishery with passive gear from vessels of less than 36 metres)

Source: Hønneland and Nilssen (2001).

The old Soviet fleets consist mainly of medium-sized (50–70 metres) and large (over 70 metres) vessels, and each company owns between 30 and 95 vessels. All in all, there are 250–300 vessels. Before the dissolution of the Soviet Union, their main activity was the exploitation of pelagic species in distant waters and pelagic and demersal species in the Northern Atlantic Ocean and the Barents Sea. Now, they mainly fish for cod in the Barents Sea. The kolkhozes represent in some respects similar fleet structures as the traditional fishing companies, but have significantly fewer vessels, ranging from one to ten vessels each. They count around 80–100 vessels altogether. Nearly all are mid-sized (50–70 metres). An important characteristic of the fishing collectives is the wider diversification of their business activities than the other fishing companies and they are more engaged than the others in the catch of pelagic species. The new companies (including the coastal fishing fleet) have the smallest fishing fleet, both in terms of number and size, clearly limiting the cruising range of the vessels and, in practice, also the geographical sales markets of the fish. At present, the fleet consists mainly of fresh/salt fish combination vessels and some round freezer and fresh fish vessels. It counts some 100 vessels in all, including approximately 30 coastal fishing vessels of less than 50 metres. The rest are mid-sized (50–70 metres). It should be noted that the Russian perception of 'coastal fishing' is somewhat different from that found in its neighbouring Scandinavian countries. While a Norwegian 'coastal' fishing vessel normally has a crew of 1–3 persons and goes to port for delivery of catches each day, a Northwest Russian 'coastal' fishing vessel has a crew of more than a dozen men and stays at sea for a couple of weeks at a time before returning to deliver the catch.

The fisheries sector of the northern basin employed some 80,000 persons in the 1980s. The Murmansk Fish Combinate alone accounted for more than 6,000 employees in the land-based processing industry, while the largest fleet, the Murmansk Trawler Fleet, employed more than 17,000 persons at its peak. A sharp reduction in catches, and subsequently in employees, set in at the beginning of the 1990s. Throughout the 1990s, the total annual catch of the fishing fleet based in Murmansk Oblast (accounting for the bulk of the Northwest Russian fishing fleet) has dropped year by year, from 1.06 million tonnes in 1991 to 0.4 million tonnes in 1997. The main reason for this catch reduction is a major decline in distant fishing by the fleet of Northwestern Russia caused in turn by increased fuel costs. Adding to the problems of the land-based processing industry in Murmansk, Russian landings of fish abroad increased markedly during the same period. Russian landings of cod to Norway (fished in both Norwegian and Russian waters) reached 94,000 tonnes in 1992, while in 1988 they had only totalled 10,000 tonnes. Thereafter, the Russian landings in Norway increased further to nearly 150,000 tonnes around the mid-1990s. Since that time, there has been some reduction, and Russian deliveries of cod to Norway totalled 119,800 tonnes in 1998. The reason for this considerable increase in the export of fish is twofold. First, it became legally easier to export fish to Norway. Second, Northwest Russian fishers had to compensate both for the termination of state subsidies and an overall reduction in total catches. The main consequence of most Russian-caught fish being landed in Norway is a loss of job opportunities in Murmansk, both in the active fishing fleet and in processing industries ashore. The Murmansk Fish Combinate has been practically at a standstill since the mid-1990s. The total employment in the northern fishery basin is believed to have dropped to some 35–40,000 people.[1]

Premises for implementation

Before we turn to the implementation activities of public authorities and others, the premises for implementation in this concrete case will be briefly discussed. Environmental and resource management problems vary in their nature; so do the international agreements aimed at their solution. Problems are of varying malignity; clearly, it is more difficult to solve a 'malign' environmental problem than a relatively 'benign' one, just as it is easier to solve a 'simple' than a 'complex' problem. The importance of the problem-creating activity to target groups also influences the potential for problem-solving. The greater the importance of the activity to the target groups, the more difficult it becomes, presumably, to make them change their behaviour. Moreover, one can assume that the potential for successful implementation depends on possibilities for monitoring target behaviour. It is easier and less costly to detect violations if the activity is concentrated in one or a few locations than if it is widely scattered. Finally, the nature of the agreements to be implemented influences the potential for success. In particular, it is more difficult to achieve full implementation of agreements the more specific and ambitious they are.

Nature of the problem

As demonstrated above, the Barents Sea contains a variety of fish species at various levels of the food chain. The state of species at one level is dependent upon the state of species at levels below and above. For instance, the state of the ground-fish stocks at any particular time depends on the level of the pelagic stocks as well as of the marine mammals in the area. Hence, the size of the Norwegian–Arctic cod stock decreases in times with little herring and capelin in the Barents Sea and when the occurrence of seal and whale is high. Moreover, the different species are sensitive to changes in their natural environment, e.g. fluctuations in the water temperature. A picture emerges of a highly 'complex' problem area: first, the problem is not influenced by human activity alone. Second, it consists of numerous causal connections about which human knowledge is imperfect. Third, to the extent such knowledge is available, the potential for human manipulation is limited. Nevertheless, it should be emphasised that it is only human action that can seriously harm the fish stocks in question. With the development of ever more efficient catch methods in the post-World War II era, it has become technically possible to bring the Barents Sea fish stocks to extinction.

At the moment of writing, the state of several Barents Sea fish stocks – among them the important Norwegian–Arctic cod stock – is, if not catastrophic, then at least pretty serious. What is the potential for their recovery? Are target groups willing to sacrifice rewards from valuable catches? The most important aspect here is that the targets of public regulatory measures (emanating partly from international commitments) are the same people that are suffering from the problem. This makes the potential for effective implementation better than in many cases of classical environmental problems where the polluters are not the same as those suffering from the pollution. On the other hand, the 'penalty' makes itself felt only some time after the problem has been 'created', a circumstance that is supposed to reduce the willingness of targets to abstain from immediate benefits in order to contribute to implementation.

The problem-causing activity is also of great importance to the target groups in question. The fishery is a key industry in Northwestern Russia, which has concrete and symbolic implications at both individual and regional level. In Soviet times, Northwest Russian fisheries were significant in terms of food supplies not only at the regional, but also at the union level. Today, when much of the fish caught by Northwest Russian fishing vessels is delivered abroad, the fisheries are primarily of importance for regional authorities in terms of employment and revenue. Although both catches and employment have been significantly reduced since Soviet times, the fisheries sector is still a cornerstone of the regional economy. Symbolically, many inhabitants of Northwestern Russia still think of Murmansk as the 'fishery capital' of Russia. It might be assumed that the actual and symbolic importance of the fisheries to the region reduces the potential for successful implementation of international obligations that require a reduction in catches, in particular during the present economic crisis in the region.

At the individual level, the potential for personal economic gain from fishing activities has increased substantially since the early

1990s, when the fishery enterprises were privatised and it became possible to sell the catches abroad. Hence, it can be argued that the fishery has become more important to the individual fishers than was the case in Soviet times, when their wages were only very loosely dependent on the amount of fish caught.[2] The political and economic instability in Northwestern Russia since the early 1990s might have further reduced the propensity of fishers in the region to give priority to the long-term welfare of the fish stocks over short-term private gain. The combination of political and economic insecurity on the one hand and the possibility of rapid personal profit on the other significantly increases the 'malignity' of the problem at hand; fishers in such a situation are supposedly far more difficult to regulate with a view to increasing the long-term common good (which is most often the objective of regulatory measures at both national and international level) than fishers with prospects of a financially secure future.

The potential for monitoring target activities may in this case be characterised as relatively good.[3] The number of targets is limited, but they do operate over a rather large area. The chance of detecting violations also varies with the actual type of violation.[4] Effective monitoring is possible, but costly. In the current financial situation in Russia, it has proven difficult. We return to this topic later in the chapter.

In sum, the problem appears to be not particularly malign in itself, but present circumstances give grounds for concern. On the one hand, the problem is complex, but 'solvable' by manipulation of human activities (since natural phenomena alone can hardly bring the fish stocks to extinction). Moreover, the number of targets is limited and, most importantly, the targets are also the main 'losers' if implementation fails. On the other hand, the problem-creating activities are of great importance both to the individual targets and to the economy of the region, which, presumably, would make it more difficult to achieve behavioural change that supports the implementation of Russia's international obligations in fisheries management. Political instability and economic hardships may also increase the propensity of targets to think short-sightedly, reducing the clout of the authorities' argument that non-compliance will eventually lead to a reduction in stock sizes that will not be in the target groups' long-term interests.

Nature of the commitments

Chapter 1 describes the bilateral Norwegian–Russian regime for fisheries management in the Barents Sea and how it is partly nested in regional and global instruments. A striking feature in recent years has been the tendency to co-ordinate a growing number of regulatory measures of national responsibility in the bilateral regime. In particular, the establishment in 1993 of the Permanent Committee has furthered this end. During the latter half of the 1990s, regulatory matters such as the closing and opening of fishing grounds and satellite monitoring of fishing vessels have been codified by bilateral agreement in the Permanent Committee. New regulatory measures such as compulsory use of selection grid by fishing vessels, have also been introduced by this body. From the start in the mid-1970s, the bilateral regime has taken care of the most important regulatory mechanism of the Barents Sea fisheries, namely the establishment of total allowable catches (TACs) of the most important fish stocks in the area. All agreements between the two parties are binding.

Hence, Russia's international obligations related to fisheries management in the Barents Sea – or to be more precise, to the activities of the Northwest Russian fishing fleet[5] – are quite specific. To a large extent, the development of concrete regulatory measures takes place at the interface between obligations following from international agreements and federal standards to be applied also in the other fishery basins of the Russian Federation. Often, this makes it difficult to judge whether a particular measure emanates from the international regime or would have appeared through the national regulatory process independently of the state's international obligations. In this context, we perceive as Russia's international obligations all concrete measures codified through some sort of inter-state agreement, ranging from the general provisions of the global fisheries instrument (see Chapter 1) to concrete regulatory standards agreed upon by Russia and Norway in the Permanent Committee of the bilateral regime.

Public authorities' implementation activities

National implementation of international obligations starts with the incorporation in national legislation of requirements necessary to bring target behaviour into accordance with these obligations. Action must thereafter be taken by public authorities to enforce such requirements; it is this type of action we refer to as 'implementation activities'. In a Russian context, keeping in mind the 1993 Constitution's definition of resource management in the territorial waters of the Russian Federation as a 'joint responsibility' between the centre and federal subjects, these activities are expected to involve both federal and regional authorities. After a brief comment on the status of implementation in national legislation, changes in the role of federal authorities, regional authorities and federal agencies in the region in the 1990s are set out. Emphasis is on formal and actual role in the implementation process. The issue of implementation performance – whether implementation is achieved or not – is occasionally referred to here, but will be more thoroughly discussed in the last section of this chapter. We remind the reader that unless otherwise specified, all information is based on personal interviews with representatives of Russian fishing industry and fisheries management. In order to protect our interviewees from untoward repercussions, the concrete interviews are not indicated in the text (see pp. 17–18 on methodology in Chapter 1).

Implementation in national legislation

In Chapter 3, we observed that post-Soviet Russian politics have evolved in a virtual legal vacuum. Although a new constitution was in place as early as in 1993, the elaboration of a complementing legal framework has been slow and fumbling, partly as a consequence of the continuous conflict between the presidential administration and the Federal Parliament. The centre–region tension has also hampered the legislative process. The Parliament's upper house, the Federation Council – consisting of the leaders of the executive and legislative authorities of Russia's 89 federal subjects[6] – has often rejected bills after they have passed the necessary readings in the state duma.

Since the early 1990s, a law on Russian fisheries and the protection of maritime biological resources of the Russian Federation has been under preparation by the Federal Parliament. After having been rejected several times, the bill was finally approved by the state duma on 7 July 2000. However, the Federation Council a few weeks later refused to vote over it due to strong disagreement among the leaders of the different regions. A working group was established to review the most 'burning' issues of the draft. The Governor of Murmansk Oblast and the President of the Republic of Karelia, who had both emerged as strong opponents of this version of the bill, were represented on the working group. When the Federal Parliament finally passed the bill in the spring of 2001, the President refused to sign it due to alleged inconsistency with other federal legislation. The bill was returned to the Federal Parliament for further clarification.

The centre–region tension was allegedly a main hindrance to reaching agreement on the Fisheries Act in the Federal Parliament.[7] The present draft foresees the continuation of federal control over fisheries management, including the economically important quota allocation. It also evoked fear among regional actors of the introduction of payment for quota shares, increase in the amount of quotas sold to foreign shipowners and stricter control by more federal agencies than those already involved in the enforcement of fisheries regulations.

The fact that a federal fisheries act has not yet been adopted does not imply that Russian fisheries management takes place in a total legal vacuum. The Law on the Russian Exclusive Economic Zone was adopted in 1998 (Russian Federation 1998), laying the legal foundation for state enforcement in the EEZ. More importantly, a range of fisheries management issues are regulated by presidential decree, governmental resolution and management decisions at lower levels of the legal hierarchy.[8] The problem is by no means a lack of transformation of international commitments into national legislation; on the contrary. An extremely large amount of presidential decrees and governmental resolutions are issued – in the fisheries sector as well as other sectors of Russian politics and economy – but they are simply not enforced. There is abundant anecdotal evidence of decrees and resolutions concerning fisheries management for which not even the slightest enforcement attempt has been made; hence, they can at best be interpreted as symbolic expressions of political will.[9]

As observed in the discussion of the nature of the international commitments above, it is sometimes hard to decide whether a certain management decision reflects the implementation of international commitments or national policy objectives; the two clearly evolve to a large extent in tandem. We also noted above that the regulatory measures of the bilateral regime between Norway and Russia have become ever more specific during the 1990s, and that a growing number of such measures have been co-ordinated between the two countries. Many of the decisions in the bilateral regime are only codified in a form whereby information about the decision is distributed by management or enforcement bodies to the fishing fleet by fax or telex. Typically, Sevryba or the enforcement body Murmanrybvod will inform all fishing vessels that Norway and Russia have agreed on a particular regulatory measure, and that the fishing vessels are obliged to comply with this decision from a specific date. In sum, the transformation of Russia's international obligations into national legislation seems to be characterised by inertia at the higher levels of the legal hierarchy and a multiplicity of legal documents at its lower levels. The problem is not so much inability to produce legal documents as the opposite: the ease with which presidential decrees, governmental resolutions, orders and provisions at ministerial level are issued probably reduces the probability of their enforcement. Hence, sending a telex from Sevryba to the fishing fleet of the Barents Sea might prove a more effective 'legal' measure than having the decision elevated to the level of presidential decree. This is further discussed in the section on target compliance below.

The role of federal authorities

There are currently two major federal bodies responsible for fisheries management and enforcement in the Russian Federation: the State Committee for Fisheries and the Federal Border Service, respectively. The former is the direct successor of the Soviet Ministry of Fisheries. The status of the federal body responsible for fisheries was reduced from that of a ministry to a state committee in connection with the break-up of the Soviet Union and the establishment of the Russian Federation in December 1991. As mentioned in Chapter 3, ministries and state committees are different types of 'independent' administrative bodies at the federal level; the ministries are placed higher in the political hierarchy since their leaders are members of the federal Government, but the state committees are not subordinate to any ministry. Hence, the federal body for fisheries management was 'degraded' in connection with the dissolution of the Soviet Union, but kept its status as a separate administrative body.

The State Committee for Fisheries is the federal body responsible for all aspects of fisheries management in the Russian Federation other than enforcement at sea (see below). Research institutes under the Committee collect and analyse data on fish stocks in waters under Russian jurisdiction. The Committee is responsible for regulatory action with a view to preservation of these fish stocks. It represents the Russian Federation in international fisheries negotiations – the Russian delegation to the Russian–Norwegian Fisheries Commission is always headed by the Chairman or Deputy Chairman of the Committee – and has the main responsibility for implementation of Russia's international obligations in fisheries. Clearly, the Committee has taken the task of overseeing implementation of these obligations seriously, but it is itself only marginally involved in implementation activities directed towards target groups. Most importantly, it decides major regulatory principles and has an important role in advisory or decision-making bodies where several agencies from both the regional and the federal level are represented. Moreover, it has the last word in all management decisions where other agencies are responsible for the practical work leading up to these decisions. For example, the Russian shares of the Barents Sea quotas are distributed among the federal subjects of Northwestern Russia by the so-called Technical-Scientific Catch Council and further distributed among shipowners in fisheries councils within each federal subject. However, the decisions of both the Technical-Scientific Catch Council and the fisheries councils have to be approved by the State Committee for Fisheries.[10]

The most conspicuous issue related to the status, responsibilities and performance of the State Committee for Fisheries in recent years is its fight to defend itself against interference from other federal agencies, in particular the Ministry of Economy and various 'power agencies'. First, an attempt was made to 'dissolve' it by temporarily depriving it of its status as a state committee and incorporating it into the Ministry of Agriculture and Foodstuffs as a department for fisheries in April 1997. Its status as state committee was restored in September 1998. Second, responsibility for enforcement at sea was transferred from Rosrybvod, a department under the Committee until then in charge of all enforcement activities, to the Federal Border Service in accordance with a presidential decree from August 1997 (Government of the Russian Federation 1997a).[11] The decision to strip the Committee of responsibility for enforcement was followed by a media campaign, obviously arranged by the presidential administration, depicting it as corrupt and hence unfit for this type of task.[12] However, the decision met with fierce resistance throughout the fishing industry and was only implemented a year later, on 1 July 1998. Third, the old tradition of appointing leaders of the Committee from within the fishery complex has been broken. During the last years of the 1990s, leaders of the Committee were changed frequently and primarily selected among candidates with their professional background from 'power agencies'. Employees of the Committee complain about the lack of 'professionals' in its leadership of recent years.[13] Finally, the Ministry of Economy has recently 'forced' the State Committee for Fisheries to carry out a system for the sale of fishing quotas by auction, a procedure which the Committee is opposed to.[14]

In sum, the Russian Federation has a centralised system for fisheries management with the State Committee for Fisheries responsible for research and regulation and the Federal Border Service in charge of enforcement at sea. These federal bodies are responsible for the implementation of Russia's international fisheries obligations, but are only to a limited extent involved in implementation activities aimed at target groups; the practical work is for the most part delegated to representing agencies in the regions. The State Committee for Fisheries of the Russian Federation is the successor of the Soviet Ministry of Fisheries and reflects an attempt to continue the Soviet type 'industry-complex approach' to fisheries management, implying that one federal body is responsible for all aspects of fisheries. However, it has repeatedly had to defend itself from attacks aimed at reducing its traditional all-embracing influence on fisheries management. Its attempts to strike back have been partly successful. On the one hand, the Committee has succeeded in maintaining its own existence as a separate administrative body. On the other hand, it has been deprived of important tasks and had to accept interference from other federal agencies in areas that have traditionally been the responsibility of the Committee alone. One might rightly ask whether the problems of keeping one's 'head above water' in recent years has led to a displacement of goals: has survival in itself become the main objective of the Committee? At the very least, one could speculate whether its insecure existence has reduced the ability of the Committee to conduct effective fisheries management.

The role of regional authorities

Regional authorities, in Soviet times totally subordinate to federal authorities and in turn the CPSU, have traditionally had no role in the management of Northwest Russian fisheries. The 1993 Constitution also states that the management of natural resources in the

EEZ is an exclusive federal responsibility. As we saw in Chapter 3, however, the role of regional authorities, especially the governors and their regional administrations, has been strengthened quite markedly during the 1990s. Have the regional administrations of Northwestern Russia attempted to expand their sphere of influence to include fisheries management?

The answer to this question is that they have indeed tried to do so, but that the results are more uncertain. A major attempt by the Northwest Russian federal subject to gain influence in fisheries management was made in the early 1990s. Murmansk, Arkhangelsk and Karelia established fisheries departments under their regional administrations in 1993–94 and demanded a say in the quota distribution, then dominated by Sevryba, which, in reality, functioned as a regional representative of the State Committee for Fisheries. In late 1993, the Governor of Murmansk Oblast boasted about having reached an agreement with the Committee that the regional administration was to take over Sevryba's management responsibilities. This conclusion appeared to be premature, but the regional administrations were from now on represented on the bodies where fishing quotas were distributed.[15]

The quotas of Russia's northern fishery basin have in recent years been distributed in two stages. The Technical-Scientific Catch Council divides the catch between the federal subjects and decides how much of the catch is to be allocated for 'basin purposes', i.e. to finance necessary tasks such as research and monitoring. Roughly 60 per cent of the catch has over the past years been allotted to Murmansk Oblast, whereas Arkhangelsk Oblast and the Republic of Karelia have received some 20 and 10 per cent, respectively.[16] A certain share of the catch is usually designated for exchange purposes with the counties of Kaliningrad and Leningrad. Grigoriy Tishkov,[17] long-standing managing director of Sevryba, was head of the Technical-Scientific Catch Council throughout the 1990s. The regional fisheries councils are led by the head of the fisheries division of the regional administration (i.e. representing the governor/republican president), but Sevryba has also largely maintained its position here. All decisions made in both the Technical-Scientific Catch Council and in the regional fisheries councils must be approved by the State Committee for Fisheries.

A central discussion topic in Russia's northern fisheries community at the end of the 1990s was the question of establishing a new 'basin management body', i.e. an official body in charge of managing the entire northern fisheries basin. Scientists from the Kola Science Centre proposed creating such an organisation in a memorandum to the Murmansk Oblast administration in 1997. The 'basin body' would be based on the remains of Sevryba and be placed under both the State Committee for Fisheries and the executives of the four federal subjects in Northwestern Russia. In May 1999, the Murmansk Oblast administration made a formal proposal to the State Committee for Fisheries to establish a new 'basin body'. The proposal gained support at a meeting of the Northwestern Association in early autumn of that year, but it was suggested that the main office be located in St Petersburg. This led to more intensive lobbying from Murmansk. When Acting Chairman of the State Committee for Fisheries Yuriy Sinelnik visited Murmansk in October 1999, he announced to the press that a 'basin body' would be established in Murmansk as a trial project and that similar organisations would later be created in the other fisheries basins of the country. A possible outcome would be its creation, thus 'strengthening' the regional fisheries management with an organisation that is 'stronger' than Sevryba and the regional administrations are today, while keeping federal authorities' control and sanction possibilities for decisions made in the region. As of autumn 2001, the 'basin body' had not yet been established.

In conclusion, the regional authorities of Northwestern Russia have during the 1990s above all displayed great aspirations to get involved in fisheries management. They have established their own fisheries departments, although each employs only a handful of people, which have achieved at least a certain measure of influence over the most important practical management measures, namely the distribution of quotas. However, the regional fisheries departments are not involved in the elaboration of other regulatory measures or enforcement. Apart from their participation in the regional fisheries councils that distribute the quotas among shipowners in the region, they above all seem to perceive their role as an advocate of the fishing industry of the region articulating its cause in relation to federal authorities. The regional legislatures of Northwestern Russia have played a very minor role in fisheries management. The regional Duma of Murmansk Oblast has passed a law on coastal fisheries (Murmansk Oblast 1997b), but it was later annulled by the regional legal authorities. Former Director of Sevryba Grigoriy Tishkov was elected to the

Murmansk regional Duma in 1997, but this does not seem to have had any influence on fisheries management in the region.

The role of federal agencies in the region

Federal agencies located in the region have traditionally played a very important role in the management of Northwest Russian fisheries. As noted earlier in this chapter, Sevryba was originally created as the General Directorate of the Soviet Ministry of Fisheries in Northwestern Russia. Although its name was changed several times, it retained its role as both an association of all fishing industry actors and the main fisheries management body of the region throughout the Soviet period. Sevryba was the 'extended arm' of the Ministry of Fisheries in the region, in other words: a typical 'implementing' body. It 'governed' the entire fishing industry of the region down to the specifics of deciding where each particular vessels was to fish at any given time. It was in control of the distribution of quotas between the shipowners (or 'fishing organisations', as they were designated in the Soviet period) of the region and issued other regulatory measures on behalf of the Ministry of Fisheries.

The privatisation of Sevryba in 1992 initiated a process that in a few years rendered the status and competence of the association as both an industry and a management actor highly unclear. An immediate consequence of privatisation was loss of control over the enterprises that formed the association. The administration of Sevryba, having employed more than five hundred people in the 'good old Soviet times', saw its number reduced to a few dozen in the course of less than five years, since most financial and 'industrial' tasks were now taken care of at the company level. Hence, in the first years after privatisation it appeared important for Sevryba, i.e. the *administration* of the association, to maintain its role in the management process (since the other former tasks had been lost to its founding companies). When the regional administrations of Northwestern Russia in 1993–94 attempted to get involved in the management process, Sevryba retaliated vigorously, arguing that the fish stocks in the EEZ are indisputably a federal responsibility and that practical regulatory experience in the region lay within Sevryba, not the governors' apparatus. As the previous section showed, regional authorities were partly successful in their aspirations and acquired some influence in the process of quota distribution. However, Sevryba retained considerable power in this area along with continued responsibility for most other regulatory issues.

In the mid-1990s, the Sevryba administration acquired its first vessel purchased on a bare-boat charter basis, the Sevryba-1. The administration was then in a position to secure favourable quota conditions for its own vessel, registered it in Cyprus, and suddenly emerged as a small, but lucrative one-boat fishing company. At the same time, the management tasks were increasingly handed over to the regional administration (see previous section). The institutional identity of Sevryba was again changing; with the emerging possibilities for Sevryba-1 and several sister ships already under way, it seemed increasingly to be ready to let go of management responsibilities.

Another important federal agency located in the region is the enforcement body Murmanrybvod. It is subordinate to Rosrybvod, the department of the State Committee for Fisheries responsible for enforcement. Murmanrybvod has traditionally been in charge of the enforcement of fishery regulations in the rivers and lakes of Murmansk Oblast, in the Barents Sea and in international convention areas where the Northwest Russian fishing fleet conducts fishery, notably NEAFC and NAFO.[18] Most of the 300–400 employees of Murmanrybvod have been involved in the enforcement of fishery regulations in the rivers and lakes on the Kola Peninsula; only some twenty inspectors have been assigned to enforcement tasks in the Barents Sea and the international convention areas.

As follows from the section on the role of federal authorities above, responsibility for fisheries enforcement at sea in the Russian Federation was transferred from Rosrybvod to the Federal Border Service in August 1997, a decision made effective as of July 1998. In the northern fishery basin, the Murmansk State Inspection of the Arctic Regional Command of the Federal Border Service was established to take care of fisheries enforcement. The main argument put forward by supporters of the reorganisation in Northwestern Russia was that the Border Service had far more and far faster vessels than Murmanrybvod's two old rebuilt fishing vessels. As in the rest of Russia, the decision to strip the traditional enforcement body of responsibility for enforcement at sea met with fierce resistance also in the northwestern region. Both the fishing industry and the rest of the fishery management apparatus supported Murmanrybvod in its battle with the 'intruders' from the 'power agency' of the Border Service.[19] As in Sevryba's battle with the regional administrations, Murmanrybvod's main argument was that the necessary expertise and experience were to be found in the 'traditional' body. Murmanrybvod turned out to be less successful than Sevryba – the Federal Border Service was obviously a stronger opponent than the regional administrations – and was forced to relinquish responsibility for enforcement at sea. However, it is only responsibility for physical inspections at sea that has been transferred to the Border Guard. Murmanrybvod is still in charge of keeping track of how much of the quotas has been caught by the individual shipowner at any one time.[20] It has also retained its responsibility for the closing of fishing grounds in areas with excessive intermingling of under-sized fish, a very important regulatory measure in both the Russian and Norwegian part of the Barents Sea. Finally, Murmanrybvod is still responsible for enforcement in international convention areas. In practice, Murmanrybvod places its inspectors on board Northwest Russian fishing vessels that intend to fish in the NEAFC of NAFO areas.

A fisheries department has been established under the Northwestern Federal Okrug, the new administrative layer introduced by President Putin in May 2000 (see Chapter 3). This department, located in St Petersburg and mostly occupied with the co-ordination of fisheries research, has not been given a role in the regulatory process. It is not represented in the Joint Russian-Norwegian Fisheries Commission or the Technical-Scientific Catch Council.

In sum, federal agencies located in the region appear as the main participants in Russian public authorities' efforts to manage the Northwest Russian fishing fleet, including efforts to implement the country's international obligations. The federal bodies themselves interfere only to a limited extent in the management process, and regional authorities have not proven 'strong' enough to gain any significant influence. The old general directorate, Sevryba, retained much of its influence well into the 1990s notwithstanding its ever more dubious formal status in the regulatory process. Murmanrybvod has been stripped of its enforcement tasks at sea, but is still an important actor in the regulation and enforcement of Northwest Russian fisheries. A new federal agency has been established in the region in connection with the enforcement reorganisation, the Murmansk State Inspection of the Arctic Regional Command of the Federal Border Service. Hence, most practical 'implementation activities' directed towards the target groups of Northwest Russian fisheries take place in Murmansk – by Sevryba, Murmanrybvod and the Border Service's Murmansk State Inspection – although they have to be approved of by federal authorities.

The role of others

The distinction between public authorities and others might be somewhat blurred in the former Soviet Union since much of the administrative structure of the plan economy has been maintained, formally or informally, into the era of the Russian Federation. The experience with Sevryba is a good case in point. Formally, Sevryba was an association of all major fishing enterprises in Northwestern Russia; more or less informally, it has during the 1990s emerged at times as the 'extended arm' of the State Committee for Fisheries in Northwestern Russia and at times primarily as a small fishing company pursuing purely commercial interests. The 'traditional' actors of Northwest Russian fisheries – i.e. all parties involved except 'intruders' of recent years, notably the Federal Border Service and the regional administrations – are in Russia clearly perceived as above all belonging to the 'fishery complex'. The division between governmental agency and 'user group' hence becomes less relevant.[21] Nevertheless, we will in the following attempt to give an overview of how actors other than public authorities have influenced the management of Northwest Russian fisheries during the 1990s.

Target groups

It should be fairly obvious by now that target groups – i.e. the region's fishers and their representative bodies – have traditionally been highly involved in the management process of Northwest Russian fisheries. Sevryba has at one and the same time been the main fisheries management body in the region and the association of its fishers. The 1990s showed how organisational constructions like Sevryba have had to struggle in the post-Soviet period to defend their existence; partly they have clung on to their old functions, partly they have adapted to the new environment and created a 'commercial' basis for themselves. It seems fair to conclude that Sevryba's role in fisheries management in recent years has been significantly reduced. At the same time, Sevryba no longer emerges as a representative of the large shipowners in the region; although formally still constituting the association Sevryba, these enterprises now appear as independent industry actors. Hence, to the extent that Sevryba maintains its old management tasks, it represents the 'lucrative, small fishing company' that its administration has created for itself in recent years, rather than the larger shipowners of the region. On the other hand, these industry actors – Murmansk Trawl Fleet, Murmanrybprom, Arkhangelsk Trawl Fleet Base etc. (see above) – have increased their *direct* influence on fisheries management. Whereas they were earlier mainly represented through Sevryba, they now participate in their own right in the bodies responsible for quota distribution in Russia's northern fishery basin. Table 4.2 shows which governmental bodies and user groups are represented at various levels in the quota distribution process. A main observation is that all large shipowners, as well as the Union of Private Fishing Enterprises in the North – representing the smaller shipowners – are represented at international, inter-regional and regional level. However, these bodies are occupied mainly with quota distribution; the influence of user groups on other management issues is limited. It is also unclear how 'strong' user groups emerge *vis-à-vis* governmental agencies in these corporate bodies.

A conspicuous trend of late has been the increased influence of some of the small shipowners organised in the Union of Private Fishing Enterprises in the North. Probably the most famous example is shipowner Vladimir Gusenkov. He used his position as a *nouveau riche* to gain broad popular support though his *cheap fish* programme, an initiative aimed at providing fish products at reasonable prices to the population of Northwestern Russia. In 1997, he was elected to the regional duma. Two years later, he succeeded in becoming one of two deputies from Murmansk Oblast to the state duma. Before ending up in Moscow, Gusenkov had become an influential person in Northwest Russian fisheries. Allegedly, he paid for much of the costs of organising negotiations in the Russian–Norwegian Fisheries Commission in Murmansk in November 1999 and was in return given representation in the Russian delegation.[22] After very difficult negotiations – Norway wishing to follow the recommendation of the ICES scientists to reduce the cod quota drastically, and Russia to disregard the scientific advice – the cod TAC was set at nearly four times above the scientists' initial recommendation. Negotiations stalled for several days, and Norway eventually agreed on the high quota level only with reference to 'the importance of fisheries to the crisis-ridden population of Northwestern Russia' (Ministry of Fisheries 1999, Article 5.1). In the subsequent negotiations between Russia and Norway in November 2000, Gusenkov allegedly emerges as an informal leader of the Russian delegation, again insisting on a quota far above the scientific recommendations. This not only reflects the increased influence of Russian target groups and regional actors in

Table 4.2 *The main decision-making bodies of Northwest Russian fisheries and governmental bodies and user groups represented in them*

Decision-making body	*Represented governmental bodies*	*Represented user-groups*
The Joint Norwegian–Russian Fisheries Commission (responsible for establishing TACs for the joint stocks in the Barents Sea)	The State Committee for Fisheries (head of delegation) The Oblast/republican administrations of Murmansk, Arkhangelsk and Karelia VNIRO (federal fisheries research institute) Regional fisheries research institutes from Murmansk and Arkhangelsk (PINRO, SevPINRO) Regional control bodies in Murmansk and Arkhangelsk (Murmanrybvod and Sevrybvod) Sevryba	The administration of Sevryba Murmansk Trawl Fleet Murmanrybprom Arkhangelsk Trawl Fleet Karelrybflot Murmansk Collective Fishing Fleet The Union of Private Fishing Enterprises in the North
Technical-Scientific Catch Council (responsible for distributing quota shares between Murmansk, Arkhangelsk and Karelia)	Sevryba (leader) The Oblast/republican administrations of Murmansk, Arkhangelsk and Karelia Regional fisheries research institutes in Murmansk and Arkhangelsk (PINRO, SevPINRO) Regional control bodies in Murmansk and Arkhangelsk (Murmanrybvod and Sevrybvod)	The administration of Sevryba Murmansk Trawl Fleet Murmanrybprom Arkhangelsk Trawl Fleet Karelrybflot The collective fishing fleets of Murmansk, Arkhangelsk and Karelia The Union of Private Fishing Enterprises in the North
The regional fishery councils (responsible for distributing quota shares between individual companies in the respective regional entities)	The oblast/republican administration in the respective regional entities (leader) Sevryba Research and control bodies from the respective regional entities	The administration of Sevryba The largest fishing companies in the respective regional entities The collective fishing fleets of the respective regional entities The Union of Private Fishing Enterprises in the North

Source: Hønneland (2001).

the formulation of the Russian position in the bilateral negotiations with Norway;[23] more than anything, it reflects the growing 'malignity' of the problem at hand (see the section above on the nature of the problem). With increased political and economic insecurity on the one hand and the possibility of rapid personal profit on the other, target groups might end up less willing to think about their own and their community's long-term interests. We return to this question in the discussion on implementation performance below.

NGOs and research institutes

The number of external agents, i.e. those other than governmental bodies and user groups, involved in Russian fisheries management is very limited. NGOs are practically absent in Northwest Russian fisheries. The only exceptions are labour unions and various types of fishers' associations, but they have no role in fisheries management, nor in implementation of international obligations.[24]

The main 'external' agents in Northwest Russian fisheries management are fisheries research institutes at the federal and region level, notably the All-Russian Scientific Institute for Fisheries and Oceanography (VNIRO) in Moscow and the Knipovich Scientific Polar Institute for Marine Fisheries and Oceanography (PINRO) in Murmansk. It is indeed doubtful whether these institutions should be labelled 'external'; they are both directly subordinate to the State Committee for Fisheries.[25] While VNIRO is the main supplier of scientific input to the Committee at the federal level, PINRO is the major participant in the management process at the regional level in Northwestern Russia. The state of the fish stocks in the Northeastern Atlantic and the Barents Sea are constantly assessed by PINRO researchers, often in co-operation with Norwegian marine scientists. The results of their investigations are discussed by ICES' Advisory Committee for Fisheries Management (ACFM) and further channelled to national authorities as assessments of the fish stocks and recommendations for their exploitation. Hence, the advice that Russian and Norwegian authorities receive concerning the Barents Sea fish stocks is based on the work of both Russian (primarily from PINRO) and Norwegian scientists. In other words: the State Committee for Fisheries, as the main governmental agency responsible for Russia's fisheries management, receives scientific input from an international organisation (ICES) which is based on the work of scientists from an institution administratively subordinate to itself.

The most striking feature of PINRO's role in the management process in recent years is the disregard by Russian authorities of ICES' scientific advice. The Joint Russian–Norwegian Fisheries Commission has increasingly since the mid-1990s established TACs well above the scientific recommendations after pressure from the Russian party. This clearly demonstrates the impotency of Russian scientists in the face of government authorities and other pressure groups within the Russian delegation.

The role of PINRO scientists in the management process is not reduced to their co-operation with foreign colleagues in ICES. PINRO is highly integrated in the 'day-to-day' management of the Barents Sea fisheries. Most importantly, PINRO's research ships assist the exploration fleet Sevrybpromrazvedka in finding concentrations of fish for the fishing fleet. The unclear distinction between government and user groups discussed above is also reflected in the way fishers perceive the role of marine science and enforcement. In the West, it is generally considered legitimate (or even preferable) for the two to have somewhat divergent interests from the user groups (being obviously more concerned about protection of the resource base than exploiting it), at least to the extent that user groups are thought to be solely concerned with their own interests (see above). In Northwest Russian fisheries, marine science and enforcement bodies still largely seem to be perceived by fishers as belonging to the same unity – the *fishery complex* – as themselves. For instance, to the extent one sees discontentment among Russian Barents Sea fishers about marine science, it seems to be directed towards the alleged inability of scientists to predict the presence of fish in a short-term perspective.[26]

Joint implementation

Joint implementation in this context denotes implementation activities directed towards Russian targets and performed by Russian agents in co-operation with foreign nationals. A problematic aspect of discussing joint implementation in Northwest Russian fisheries is that decisions made at one level can be regarded as implementation of decisions made at higher levels. For instance, should research and regulatory activities between Russians and Norwegians under the framework of the bilateral regime be perceived as joint implementation? We are inclined to answer this question in the negative, but maintain that co-operation between representatives of the two countries in efforts to implement decisions made at the bilateral level should indeed be regarded as such.

Throughout the 1990s, joint implementation between the fisheries enforcement bodies of Norway and Russia in the Barents Sea has expanded consistently. The Permanent Committee under the Joint Commission was established in 1993 as a response to Russian overfishing in the Barents Sea.[27] When most Russian vessels started to deliver their catches in Norway, the old system for quota control in Russia – based mainly on catch control in port – proved inadequate. The Permanent Committee established a system for exchange of catch data between the enforcement bodies of the two states which reintroduced a mechanism for effective quota control in Northwest Russian fisheries. Co-operation with their Norwegian counterparts seems to have remained an important component of the work of Northwest Russian fisheries enforcement bodies throughout the 1990s. First, most Russian vessels still deliver their catches in Norway, so Russian enforcement bodies depend on data from Norwegian authorities to keep track of how much of their quotas the vessels have fished. Second, Norwegian enforcement bodies regularly assist their Russian counterparts in organising physical catch controls when Russian vessels land their fish in Norwegian ports.[28] Third, many enforcement tasks – such as routines for closing and opening of fishing grounds – have been co-ordinated between the authorities of the two states. Fourth, Norwegian enforcement bodies have partly assisted their Russian counterparts materially and financially. Interestingly, federal agencies in the region predominate in the Russian delegation to the Permanent Committee: the State Committee for fisheries was only represented in connection with the establishment of the Committee in 1993.[29] Enforcement co-operation between Norway and Russia can generally be characterised as successful. As far as problem-solving is concerned, the effects are uncertain, but the manner in which co-operation functions today clearly represents an improvement over the earlier situation (Hønneland 2000b).

Implementation performance and target compliance

The main question to be asked in this section concerns the degree to which Russian authorities have succeeded in implementing their international obligations related to the activities of the Northwest

Russian fishing fleet. First, have Russian authorities succeeded in setting up a system for fisheries management in accordance with their international obligations? Second, if so, has this system functioned as intended? Can any tendency be traced as to the type of management body (e.g. at what level of governance) that functions most satisfactorily? Third, have implementation activities affected the behaviour of target groups? Another major issue to be analysed is whether problems in implementation can be ascribed to the nature of the problem or the quality of implementation activities.

From global agreements Russia has concluded derive obligations, *inter alia*, to manage fisheries in the country's 200-mile EEZ in accordance with the principle of MSY, to establish TAC for each fish stock within the EEZ, to co-operate with other coastal states in the management of shared stocks, and to promote compliance with fishery regulations among all vessels under Russian flag. Already prior to the conclusion of the LOSC, the Soviet Union had a system in place for fisheries management and enforcement, which could now be adjusted to contribute to Soviet implementation of the new international obligations. Naturally, the Soviet Ministry of Fisheries was the central actor at the federal level. As far as the northern basin is concerned, a regulatory body existed in Sevryba, an enforcement body in Murmanrybvod and a fisheries research institute in PINRO. The tasks of these bodies were now adapted to the new surroundings, reflected mainly in the specific research, regulatory and enforcement obligations following from the newly established bilateral regime with Norway. PINRO's scientific results were already integrated in the work of ICES and were now used as a basis for recommendations to the regulatory authorities of the two countries. Sevryba was already the main regulatory body in the region and was now given the task of implementing regulations agreed upon in the Joint Fisheries Commission, notably to oversee the distribution of Russian quota shares. Murmanrybvod was already involved in monitoring of fishing activities, but was now given responsibility for enforcement in the entire ocean area up to 200 miles from shore. Hence, the Soviet Union took the necessary administrative steps to adjust the existing system for fisheries management to the new international obligations. Although data on the functioning of this system during the Soviet period are poor, it seems fair to assume that research, regulatory and enforcement bodies were well suited (in terms of competence and material resources) for their respective tasks, that they performed these tasks quite satisfactorily, and that target compliance was generally high.[30] The command system of the plan economy generally implied a high degree of control over the activities of target groups. Moreover, the latter had less incentive to cheat than they would have had in a market economy. Notably, all involved agencies belonged to the 'fishery complex', administratively subordinate to the Ministry of Fisheries.

In the post-Soviet period, three features stand out in the development of Northwest Russian fisheries management, one partly following from the other: the diffusion of management responsibility; the degeneration of implementation performance; and the reduction in target compliance. We have seen throughout this chapter how the established fisheries management system during the post-Soviet period has been challenged from different angles. Various 'power agencies', notably the Federal Border Service, have successfully challenged the task of the State Committee for Fisheries and its subordinate regional agencies to conduct enforcement at sea. The Ministry of Economy has interfered in the quota allocation process through its introduction of a system for auctions of fish quotas. The regional administrations of Russia's federal subjects have, somewhat less successfully, attempted to take over the management role of federal agencies located in the region.

A decline in implementation performance has followed partly from the fact that the 'newcomers' are less fit for their tasks than the traditional agencies, and partly from confusion following unclear division of responsibility between 'new' and 'old' management bodies. The former refers to poor standards in both competence and material resources. The regional administrations have had only a handful of persons of varying backgrounds employed in their fisheries departments; in comparison to Sevryba's large and well-experienced staff they have had little to show for their efforts. More apparent is the lack of experience and resources in the Border Service (whose tasks have also come to be more extensive than those of the regional administrations). For one thing, officers in the Murmansk State Inspection of the Federal Border Service generally lack experience in fisheries management and enforcement; this has partly been compensated for by transfer of some of Murmanrybvod's inspectors. More apparent is the lack of material resources to maintain presence at sea. Quite contrary to the intentions of the reorganisation of the enforcement system, the presence at sea by monitoring vessels declined since the Border Guard took over this duty in 1998. Precise data for presence at sea and inspection frequency are not available, but Jørgensen (1999, pp. 88–90) estimates that the Border Guard performed around 160 inspections at sea in 1998, which represents a significant reduction compared to an estimated 700–1,000 annual inspections at sea by Murmanrybvod prior to the reorganisation. For several months on end during 1998, not a single enforcement vessel was present on the fishing grounds in the Russian part of the Barents Sea. Officials of the Border Service explain this as lack of funds to purchase fuel. Critics question the genuineness of the Border Service's will to play a role in fisheries management. The result of the reorganisation has in any event so far been a tangible reduction in the effectiveness of Russian enforcement in the Barents Sea.[31]

Unclear task delineation might also have led to a reduction in implementation performance although it is more difficult to point to concrete effects here. Again the conflict between Rosrybvod/Murmanrybvod and the Federal Border Service is the most striking example. After the decree prescribing the reorganisation was issued in 1997, both agencies continued for a long period to perform enforcement duties, but at a low intensity and without co-ordination between them. A lack of co-ordination has remained a problem also after the decree was actually implemented – i.e. when a clear delineation of duties was established – in 1998. The same can partly be said about the relationship between Sevryba and the Murmansk regional administration, particularly in the early and mid-1990s, when a pretty fierce battle was going on between the two institutions. A kind of 'peace' was settled towards the end of the decade when Sevryba proved 'stronger' than its opponent but at the same time conceding to the latter a certain influence in quota allocation. The 'confusion' again mounted when Sevryba started to lose interest in management issues as its role as 'lucrative, small ship-owner' became more important. As mentioned, it is difficult to point to concrete management deficiencies as a result of the 'confusion'; we can only assume that a certain reduction in performance took place.

Data on target compliance in Russian fisheries are not publicly available. We assumed above that target compliance was generally high in the Soviet period, partly as a result of lacking incentives to cheat. It seems fair to conclude that the overall compliance level in the Russian part of the Barents Sea has decreased in the post-Soviet era. For one thing, Norwegian authorities in 1992 took extra steps to calculate the total Russian catch in the Barents Sea that year.[32] The figures indicated over-fishing by the Russians at a rate of more than 100,000 tonnes. Over-fishing hence constituted one quarter of the total cod quota in the Barents Sea in 1992. Russia had 170,000 tonnes at its disposal, of a TAC of 396,000 tonnes, after internal quota exchanges with Norway. This estimate was supported by export statistics, which indicated that close to the total Russian cod quota in the Barents Sea had been exported to Norway. At the same time, considerable quantities had been exported to other Western countries. Some cod had also been landed in Murmansk. The sudden rise in over-fishing coincided with Russian fishers starting to deliver the bulk of their catches abroad, primarily in Northern Norway. At the same time, the direct export of their product increased the incentives for fishers to underreport their catches (since they were paid better abroad), and reduced the chance for Russian authorities to keep track of the catches since control had traditionally been conducted in connection with landings of fish in Russian ports. The joint implementation (i.e. enforcement) practice described above halted as anticipated the opportunity for Russian fishers to conceal their real catches for Russian authorities when delivering in Norway. Nevertheless, the increased incentive to violate the regulations as compared to Soviet times has probably led to a reduction in target compliance. Combined with the significant reduction in performance of the Russian enforcement system – notably the absence of monitoring vessels at sea for considerable periods – there is reason to assume that the fall in target compliance is not insignificant. Interviews with Norwegian and Icelandic fishers who operated in the Russian part of the Barents Sea in 1997–99 indicate that a considerable illegal fishery of undersized fish took place in periods when enforcement vessels were absent (Jørgensen 1999, pp. 105–6).

In conclusion, a certain degeneration in implementation capabilities and performance among Russian authorities has taken place in the northern fishery basin throughout the 1990s. The traditional 'fishery complex' management bodies, which had taken care of implementation in a satisfactory way until the break-up of the Soviet Union, were now challenged by other governmental agencies wanting a piece of the budgetary cake and a growing 'malignity' of the problem. So far, the 'traditional' agencies – mainly the State Committee for Fisheries, Sevryba and Murmanrybvod – emerge as more successful in their implementation activities than the 'newcomers', notably the Federal Border Service and the regional administrations. The former are far better off in terms of competence and, to some extent, also material resources than the latter. To the extent that 'newcomers' have taken over, this seems to have led to a reduction in implementation performance and target compliance. On the other hand, with rumours of corruption in the State Committee for Fisheries and Sevryba having become more of a commercial actor than a management body, it seems rash to simply regard the various reorganisations as errors of judgement.

Notes

1 See Nilssen and Hønneland (2001) for a recent overview of the post-Soviet restructuring of the Northwest Russian fishing industry.

2 Admittedly, Soviet fishers were rewarded for over-fulfilling the production plans, but their personal economic gains were far smaller than is the case today. Moreover, since goods were considerably scarcer than purchasing power, the minor extras paid for this were probably of little significance.

3 Of course, this depends on what you compare with. Our point is that this case lies somewhere between cases where the target is either three pipelines or a million cars.

4 For instance, it is relatively easy with modern surveillance equipment to detect a vessel operating in an area closed for fishing. The under-reporting of a few tonnes of fish is, on the other hand, relatively difficult to discover due to the difficulty of conducting precise physical checks of the catch once it is stored in the ship's hold.

5 The Northwest Russian fishing fleet operates mainly, but not exclusively, in the Barents Sea.

6 As of 2002, the regional leaders will not themselves take place in the Federation Council; instead, they will appoint their representatives. This change was part of Putin's 'spring reorganisation' of 2000 (see Chapter 3), but has not been implemented at the time of writing.

7 The contents of the draft Fisheries Act has not been made public. However, some details are known from Russian media, and the authors have also received some information in conversations with involved actors.

8 For instance, quota allocation has in recent years been regulated by a preliminary provision issued by the State Committee for Fisheries (State Committee for Fisheries 1999a) while monitoring and enforcement activities are regulated by a so-called 'order' from the same committee (State Committee for Fisheries 1999b).

9 Famous is the story of Yeltsin's presidential decree that presidential decrees are henceforth to be complied with. In the fisheries sector, there are numerous decrees and orders aimed at redirecting the deliveries of fish to the home market, which have not been enforced.
10 In practice, the decisions of the Technical-Scientific Catch Council and the regional fisheries councils are almost always approved by the State Committee for Fisheries.
11 A 'service' (*sluzhba*) is also an independent federal agency immediately below ministry level. Although often referred to as a 'military' agency, the Federal Border Service is not answerable to the Ministry of Defence.
12 An example is the major headline on the front page of *Izvestiya* on 12 September 1997: 'The Mafia Has Beaten the Fishery Inspection. Can the Border Guard Beat the Mafia?'
13 It should be mentioned that this new strategy is more like the Western tradition of using political all-rounders for ministerial posts. For most Russians, used to ministers who are specialists in their field of responsibility, this is a new thing.
14 This is an example of how more general legislation appearing before the Fisheries Act reduces the scope of action for fishery management authorities. The provision on quota auctions is printed in *Rossiyskaya Gazeta*, 13 January 2001.
15 See Hønneland (1998) for a more detailed presentation of these events.
16 See Hønneland and Nilssen (2001) for a discussion of quota allocation in Russia's northern fishery basin.
17 Tishkov was ousted as director of Sevryba in late 2000.
18 Similar bodies are found also in Arkhangelsk Oblast and the Republic of Karelia, Sevrybvod and Karelrybvod, but these are responsible for enforcement of fishery regulations in rivers and lakes only (as well as the White Sea in the case of Sevrybvod). Responsibility for ocean fisheries by the Northwest Russian fishing fleet is wholly under Murmanrybvod.
19 A representative of the fishers in Murmansk made the following statement to *Polyarnaya Pravda* (19 September 1997, p. 1): 'The situation in our fishing industry is still difficult. The last six months' disintegration of the federal management bodies renders it extremely alarming, too.'
20 Fish quotas are in Russia given to shipowners, not to individual vessels.
21 See Hønneland and Nilssen (2000) for a further discussion of this dilemma.
22 In the protocol from the session, Gusenkov is identified as member of Murmansk regional duma (Ministry of Fisheries 1999). It seems rather odd to include deputies from the regional legislatures in the delegation since these have no role in fisheries management. Representatives from the legislatures of the other federal subjects of Northwestern Russia are

not included. This supports the argument that his role as shipowner and economic benefactor was more important for his inclusion in the Russian delegation than his status as representative of the regional duma.

23 Interview data indicate that representatives of federal authorities in the Russian delegation were more prepared to make a compromise with Norway than were representatives from Northwestern Russia.

24 Both labour unions and fishers' associations are mainly engaged in welfare work.

25 So-called 'departmental' (*vedomstvennye*) research institutes are very common in Russia. They are subordinate to various governmental agencies and intended to serve their needs. More basic scientific research is carried out at institutions under the Russian Academy of Science.

26 In an article in the newspaper *Polyarnaya Pravda*, fishers from Murmansk complain that they were not warned by the scientists that the big cod had already migrated into the Norwegian zone: 'If no fish is found in the ocean, then fishers are convinced that science is to blame' (*Polyarnaya Pravda*, 18 February 1998, p. 1). The message is: the main task of marine scientists is to help us fishers.

27 See Hønneland (1998, 2000b) for a more detailed account of these events.

28 These inspections are defined as Norwegian while the Russia inspectors participate as observers. However, Russian authorities may file charges against a vessel for violations discovered during such an inspection.

29 During the greater part of its existence, the Russian delegation to the Permanent Committee has been headed by the director of Murmanrybvod. Sevryba and PINRO are also represented. In 1999, a representative of the Murmansk State Inspection of the Arctic Regional Command of the Federal Border Service was given a place in the delegation.

30 One could discuss whether the decisions of the Joint Fisheries Commission are in accordance with international obligations of the two countries (e.g. whether they reflect international principles for fisheries management), but we limit our discussion here to decisions made at national level in Russia.

31 The reader might ask: 'Why did Russia choose this solution when the old system functioned well enough?' We see two possible answers to this question. One is that it indeed makes sense to transfer responsibility for enforcement to an agency independent of the rest of the fisheries management system as long as the latter is surrounded by allegations of corruption. Another answer is that there is probably no uniform strategy behind the decision to strip the State Committee for Fisheries/Rosrybvod of its enforcement capacity; rather, the reorganisation was the result of a fight over budget funds. With increased responsibility come increased funds, and the Border Guard was more interested in

the latter than the former, the argument – often employed by representatives of the 'fishery complex' – goes.

32 The Norwegian inspectors used the catch logs of the Russian vessels to calculate the individual vessel's total catch that year. Normally, they would only have been interested in catches taken in Norwegian zones, but on this occasion they included catches taken in the Russian EEZ.

5 Nuclear safety

As pointed out in Chapter 1, the threats posed by the nuclear complex of Northwestern Russia have attracted no little attention in recent years, not least from neighbouring Western countries. Thus, the issue of nuclear safety stands forth as the most highly profiled problem area among the three we have chosen to focus on in this study. It also differs from the other two by way of being far more heterogeneous in nature: some of the activities under scrutiny are of a civilian nature; others take place within the military sphere. Partly, the focus is on 'actual' polluting activities, such as the dumping of waste; partly it is on the risk of accidents in connection with activities that do not result in contamination under normal circumstances. Moreover, in the area of nuclear safety, environmental and security concerns tend to be closely intertwined. As will be shown in this chapter, the complexity of the problem area itself tends to be mirrored both in the multitude of international efforts undertaken to address it and in the related implementation processes.

Background: the 'nuclear complex' and radiological hazards

The build-up of the 'nuclear complex' in Northwestern Russia was linked partly with the nuclearisation of the Soviet Armed Forces, and also with civilian needs in transportation and energy production. Its history dates back to the late 1950s, when the Soviet Union's first nuclear-powered submarines and icebreakers were constructed and stationed on the Kola Peninsula. Well over a decade later, in 1972, the construction of the largest nuclear installation in the area, the Kola Nuclear Power Plant, was completed. Thus, the nuclear-powered vessels of the Northern Fleet, the icebreaker fleet of Murmansk Shipping Company and the Kola Nuclear Power Plant, together with their service and storage facilities, constitute the main elements of the Northwest Russian nuclear complex. A brief description of the development of each of these elements and their state today is given in the first sub-section below.

Perhaps contrary to popular belief, the extent of radioactive contamination in the region is relatively low and mainly due to external sources and practices that have been permanently or temporarily discontinued, e.g. atmospheric nuclear tests and the dumping at sea of radioactive waste (Bergman and Baklanov 1998; Lønne *et al.* 1997). The issue of contamination and its sources is elaborated in the second sub-section. While the release of radioactive substances is negligible in the normal operations of the nuclear installations in Northwestern Russia, an accident or other unforeseen incident at one of the installations, service or storage facilities could have very serious implications. The risks posed by the nuclear complex are addressed in the third sub-section below.

The 'nuclear complex' of Northwestern Russia

The Soviet Northern Fleet was officially established as late as in 1933, despite the fact that the strategic potential of the Kola Peninsula, with its year-round ice-free harbours, had been recognised in Russian naval circles as early as in the second half of the nineteenth century (Skogan 1986). The fleet headquarters were originally based in Polyarnyy on the western shore of the Kola Fjord, but subsequently moved to Severomorsk across the fjord. For more than two decades, the Northern Fleet remained the smallest of the Soviet Navy's four fleets. In the 1950s, however, a period of expansion set in, which coincided with the onset of the Soviet Union's struggle to achieve nuclear parity with the United States. The country's first nuclear-powered submarine was completed at a submarine construction facility in Severodvinsk in Arkhangelsk Oblast in 1957 and stationed at Zapadnaya Litsa on the Kola Peninsula in 1958. The Northern Fleet's expansion continued in the following decades, and the fleet acquired a large number of nuclear-powered submarines.

The fleet's prize possessions are its strategic submarines. They are armed with long-range ballistic missiles able to reach targets on the American continent from the Russian coast. The strategic submarines are protected by multi-purpose submarines, which are also nuclear-powered. The tactical missiles of these submarines may be equipped either with nuclear or with conventional warheads. Russia has declared that the multi-purpose submarines will not carry nuclear warheads in peacetime. In addition to the submarines, the Northern Fleet has a large number of surface vessels, many of which are armed with nuclear weapons and three of which are nuclear-powered.

The Northern Fleet reached the height of its power in the mid-1980s. Since 1988, the number of ships taken out of service has exceeded the number of new ships acquired, a tendency that has intensified since 1991 (see Table 5.1). This was due to the combined effect of a climate of economic downturn and the need to implement obligations laid down by the START I treaty. In addition, the nuclear submarines of the first generation started to reach the end of their service life from the late 1980s. A total of about seventy nuclear-powered submarines were removed from service in the Northern Fleet during the period 1991–98. This gave the Northern Fleet a new challenge: to dismantle a huge number of nuclear-powered submarines in a very short period of time. The process is very costly, and so far only a fraction of the submarines removed from service have actually been dismantled. The majority are stored afloat awaiting dismantlement, and many have not even been de-fuelled, i.e. the spent nuclear fuel has not been removed from the reactors. Some of these submarines are in a poor condition, and some observers claim there is a real danger of them sinking. Moreover, international co-operative programmes so far only cover the dismantlement of strategic submarines. Hence, there is no dismantlement capacity left for multi-purpose submarines, which are mostly at the end or have passed far beyond their service life.[1]

Table 5.1 *Number of ships in the Northern Fleet in 1991 and 1998*

Category	*1991*	*1998*
Strategic submarines	36	13
Other submarines	90	43
Large combatants	83	45
Smaller combatants	73	27
Landing- and amphibious vessels	20	12

Source: Hønneland and Jørgensen (1999a).

The full dismantlement of a nuclear-powered submarine involves several steps. The first step – and the most important from an environmental point of view – is the de-fuelling of spent nuclear fuel from the submarine's reactor. Afterwards, the reactor compartment is removed, and subsequently the rest of the hull can be cut up for scrap. The process generates a certain amount of spent nuclear fuel and other liquid and solid waste (including the reactor compartment itself) which has to be transported to special facilities for further treatment and/or intermediate storage. Spent nuclear fuel may either be stored as it is or reprocessed. The Russian policy with regard to spent nuclear fuel favours reprocessing, if possible. Reprocessing generates large amounts of high-level liquid waste. Liquid waste is usually solidified before storage, and some forms of solid waste can be compressed.

The Northern Fleet has limited capacity in all stages of the dismantlement process. First, the existing infrastructure has only allowed for the de-fuelling of a handful of submarines a year. Second, existing intermediate storage facilities for spent nuclear fuel and for liquid and solid waste are long since filled to capacity, which means that large amounts of spent nuclear fuel and radioactive waste are stored under unsatisfactory conditions. Third, the spent nuclear fuel that is supposed to be reprocessed is leaving the region very slowly, partly because Russia only has two special train carriers for spent nuclear fuel transportation, partly due to constraints at the reprocessing facility, Mayak in Siberia, and to the Northern Fleet's limited capability to pay for such shipment.

Up to 1992, although the situation was less critical then, the Northern Fleet disposed of large amounts of radioactive waste by dumping it at sea. Since 1993, Russia has observed a voluntary moratorium on such dumping, but the lack of capacity to deal with spent nuclear fuel and nuclear waste has, according to Russian authorities, rendered it impossible for Russia to ratify the parts of the London Convention that deal with the dumping of radioactive substances. The problems related to the decommissioning of nuclear-powered submarines is the most urgent nuclear safety issue in the military sector. However, as demonstrated by the Kursk and Komsomolets accidents, there are risks associated with nuclear-powered submarines in operation as well. Moreover, nuclear-powered submarines normally have to have their reactors refuelled twice in the course of their service life; thus, active submarines also contribute to the accumulation of spent nuclear fuel and to binding up de-fuelling infrastructure. These issues will be discussed further towards the end of the section.

In 1959, the Soviet Union's first nuclear-powered icebreaker – the *Lenin* – was stationed in Murmansk. Over the following years, a whole fleet of nuclear icebreakers was built.[2] The main task of the icebreakers was to escort vessels navigating the Northern Sea Route (i.e. the Northeast Passage), which stretches along the northern shores of the Eurasian continent from the Barents to the Bering Sea. Thus, the icebreaker fleet played an important role – and to some extent still does – in securing the *severnyy zavoz*, i.e. the transportation of foodstuffs and other important goods to outlying northern areas, as well as the transportation of various raw materials out of these areas, mainly from Siberia.

The icebreaker fleet is a subsidiary of Murmansk Shipping Company, one of the largest enterprises in Murmansk Oblast. This fleet, which in 1998 counted seven icebreakers and one nuclear-powered container ship, was needed less and less during the 1990s because transport volumes on the Northern Sea Route fell significantly. The remaining ships are approaching the end of their service life. Like the nuclear-powered submarines, the icebreakers have to have spent nuclear fuel removed and the reactors refuelled at regular intervals. Murmansk Shipping Company has three service ships of its own, *Imandra*, *Lotta* and *Lepse*. Spent nuclear fuel from the icebreakers used to be stored for an initial six months on board the *Imandra* and then moved to one of the other ships for further storage. However, by 1993 all three ships were filled to capacity. As for *Lepse*, the whole ship is now considered nuclear waste, since a large portion of the spent nuclear fuel on board is classified as 'damaged' and the ship itself is also contaminated. This damaged fuel stems mainly from the nuclear-powered icebreaker *Lenin*, which suffered a reactor accident in 1966.

The Kola Nuclear Power Plant, located in the town of Polyarnye Zori in the southern central part of the Kola Peninsula, was put into operation in 1972. The plant is by far the largest employer in Polyarnye Zori with approximately 6,000 employees (out of a population of some 18,000). As was customary in the Soviet Union, the company provided a large share of the local social and technical infrastructure, and many of these functions have been retained. The Kola Nuclear Power Plant and the eight other nuclear power plants currently in operation in Russia are joined together under the Rosenergoatom umbrella. Rosenergoatom is a subsidiary of Minatom, the Russian Ministry of Atomic Energy, which reportedly wants to see closer integration of the enterprises of the Russian nuclear energy sector. In June 1999, then Minister of Atomic Energy Yevgeniy Adamov decided to let Rosenergoatom have direct control of the revenue generated by all nuclear power plants. Plans to continue the reorganisation of the nuclear power sector towards full integration have met with considerable opposition at the regional and local levels. Workers at the Kola Nuclear Power Plant fear that both their pay cheques and general industrial rights will suffer, while local as well as regional authorities expect the merger process to result in significant cuts in revenue from the Kola Nuclear Power Plant to the local and regional coffers.

The Kola Nuclear Power Plant plays a significant role in the total supply of energy in Murmansk Oblast. Total yearly output is approximately 12 TWH. Altogether, the Kola Nuclear Power Plant provides some 60 per cent of the electric power consumed annually in the oblast (Hansen and Tønnessen 1998). Most of this is consumed by the industry, since electric power accounts for only a marginal share of the energy consumed by private households. In addition, the Kola Nuclear Power Plant exports energy to the Republic of Karelia. The plant has four nuclear reactors, each of which yields an effect of 440 MW. The two oldest ones, contained in one building, came on line in 1973 and 1974, respectively, while the two reactors contained in the other building have been in operation since 1981 and 1984. The two oldest reactors in particular are viewed with concern by the international community. The locations of some important nuclear safety sites in Northwestern Russia are displayed in Figure 5.1.

Radioactive contamination of the environment

The level of radioactive contamination of the terrestrial environment in Northwestern Russia is relatively low and comparable to that of neighbouring countries (AMAP 1997, 1998; Bergman and Baklanov 1998; Lønne *et al.* 1997). As in Norway, Sweden and Finland, the main sources of contamination are fallout from atmospheric nuclear tests and the Chernobyl accident. A total of 87 atmospheric tests were carried out on the Novaya Zemlya archipelago between 1955 and 1963 (Stortinget 1994, p. 31). Since 1963, subsequent to the conclusion of the partial test ban treaty prohibiting atmospheric

Figure 5.1 *Important Northwest Russian sites in a nuclear safety context*

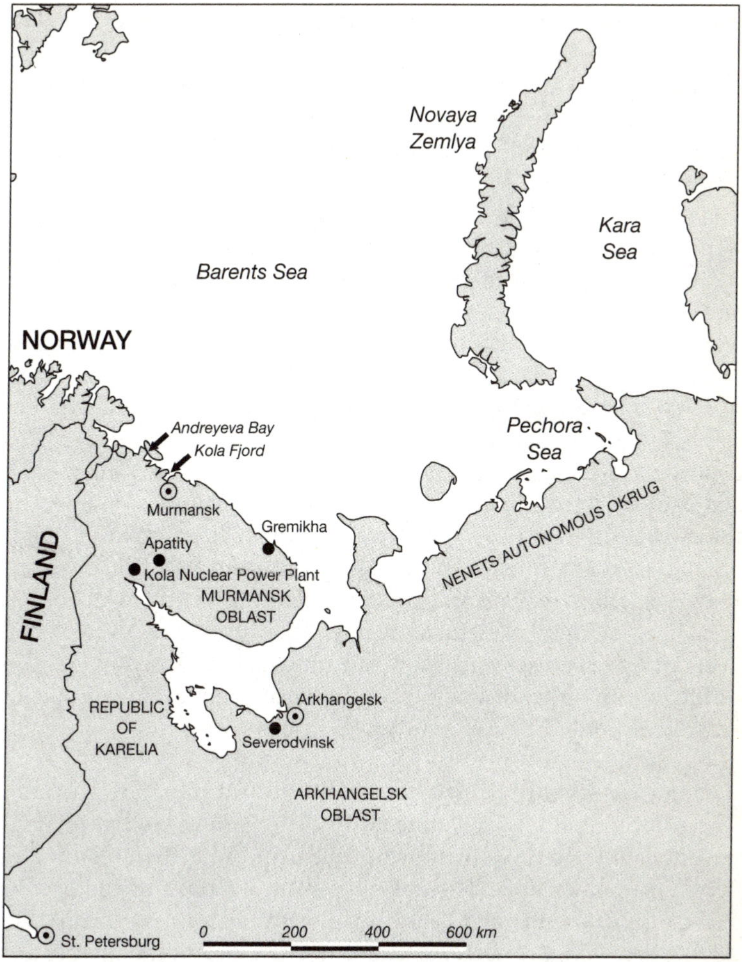

and underwater nuclear tests, all nuclear tests have been carried out underground.[3]

Despite the low contribution to the average level of contamination by regional sources, the localised character of such contamination must be taken into consideration. While fallout both from the nuclear tests and Chernobyl was dispersed over vast areas, more recent activities – particularly inadequate storage of waste – have resulted in a number of delimited areas where contamination levels are significant. On the Kola Peninsula as a whole, though, the main anthropogenic source of radiation affecting the population is radiotherapy, followed by radiation from construction materials. By contrast, production of nuclear energy and fallout from weapons testing and the Chernobyl accident make up less than 3 per cent of the average yearly individual doses to the population (State Committee for Environmental Protection 1998).

Compared to the Baltic Sea and the North Sea, the Barents and Kara Seas are very clean. This goes for radioactive contamination as well as for pollution in general. Besides fallout from atmospheric nuclear tests, the main sources of radioactive substances in these waters are routine releases from European reprocessing plants, first and foremost Sellafield in Great Britain. In recent years, contamination levels have been reduced, primarily due to a sharp reduction in releases from Sellafield. Releases from Russian facilities are also believed to have contributed to contamination increases via the Ob and Yenisey rivers. The total radioactivity of materials dumped by the Northern Fleet (until 1992) and Atomflot (until 1986) is comparable to the accumulated radioactivity of the Sellafield releases. However, all investigations carried out thus far have concluded that very little of this has actually leaked out. Moreover, even in the event of a worst-case scenario, with a simultaneous and rapid release of the remaining radioactivity to the environment, radiological consequences would be relatively low (Bergman 1997).

Radiological hazards associated with the nuclear complex

The principal radiological hazards to the region as well as to areas beyond it are posed not by previous activities but by potential future accidents or incidents. The risks posed by a release of radioactive substances to the life and health of humans fall into two main categories, depending on the distance to the site where the accident or incident takes place. Persons at or near the site will probably be in acute danger from intense radiation, as well as from other effects of the accident, such as fires and explosions. At greater distances from the site, the main dangers are usually related to long-range effects of more moderate exposure, for instance increased frequencies of certain forms of cancer in the exposed population.

It is problematic to distinguish between environmental risks and health risks where radioactive pollution is concerned. For a nuclear accident to constitute a real threat to the environment as such – that is, to the continued existence of various species of flora and fauna in a given area – the accident would have to have almost unimaginable dimensions. Usually, the main problem is that the presence of radioactive pollutants in the natural environment may pose a risk to people's life and health. The most seriously affected areas may be rendered uninhabitable. Moreover, as demonstrated by the Chernobyl accident, the problem of radioactive pollutants entering and accumulating in the food chain may affect vast areas, making certain foodstuffs – typically the meat of grazing animals – unfit for human consumption. Thus, in addition to the risks to life and health, radioactive contamination of the environment may have grave economic consequences, and it may even threaten the culture and way of life of certain people, notably those of indigenous peoples and fishers.

One study (Bergman and Baklanov 1998) substantiates the Kola Nuclear Power Plant's position as the most hazardous industry in the Kola–Barents region. Several operational incidents have taken place since the plant was put into operation, among them a loss-of-cooling incident in 1993, which might have resulted in a meltdown incident in the oldest reactor. The International Atomic Energy Agency (IAEA) has calculated the probability of a serious meltdown in the oldest reactors to be 25 per cent over a period of twenty-three years. Such an accident would not have Chernobyl dimensions, since the reactors are of a different and less dangerous design. Nevertheless, the local effects would be grave, and deposits of radioactive matter in parts of Russia and neighbouring countries would probably be high enough to influence both cancer statistics and patterns of food consumption.

Bergman and Baklanov (1998) identify submarines during refuelling as another high-risk possibility, although the consequences of an accident would be less far-reaching. In 1985, radionucleids were released to the atmosphere and ten people were killed following an explosion during refuelling of a submarine in Chazma Bay in the Far East. For submarines in operation, submarines under decommissioning or scrapping, and stored spent nuclear fuel and radioactive waste, the risks are less certain. These are all classified by Bergman and Baklanov (1998) as sources of potential high risk.[4] Where the submarines are concerned, the main dangers are linked to criticality accidents (i.e. uncontrolled chain reactions) in reactors with releases of radionucleids to air. De-fuelling of decommissioned submarines may involve the same risks as refuelling. Accidents involving inadequately stored spent nuclear fuel and radioactive waste may ensue as a result of fire breaking out at a storage facility and/or a criticality accident if spent nuclear fuel elements are stored in too close proximity to one another and without sufficient barriers between them.

Spent nuclear fuel and other waste dumped at sea, as well as the sunken submarine Komsomolets and leakage from underground test sites, are all categorised as low-risk sources by Bergman and Baklanov (1998). Finally, their study identifies some potential risks where the consequences are as yet undetermined due to insufficient research of the problem. They include transportation of spent nuclear fuel and waste, accidental nuclear explosions and releases from underwater test sites.

Premises for implementation

The nature of the problem

At first glance, the problem of nuclear safety in Northwestern Russia appears to be relatively complex, with respect to the prospects of solving it. The activities that give rise to radiological threats in the region are linked to crucial sectors of society: defence, energy production and transportation. The 'nuclear objects' themselves are controlled by two very powerful agencies, the Ministry of Defence and the Ministry of Atomic Energy (see discussion below). Moreover, the costs related to problem-solving are generally high. For instance, the economic cost of transporting a reactor with damaged spent nuclear fuel to Novaya Zemlya and dumping it there is next to nothing compared to the cost of safe removal, transportation and storage of the spent nuclear fuel. In some cases, intervention is hardly feasible at all if this is taken to mean a reduction of risk to an acceptable level. This would certainly seem to apply to the prospect of securing the safe functioning of the two oldest reactors at the Kola Nuclear Power Plant.

On the other hand, the consequences of a large nuclear accident would be devastating, both in terms of life and health and economically. The dramatic progress of a nuclear accident and the arbitrariness and sneaking nature of the long-term health effects make the public much more sensitive to radiological threats than to 'classic' environmental problems. The sensitivity of people to these issues may not be as high in Russia as in Western countries, but the 'Chernobyl effect' is nevertheless thought to have contributed significantly to postponing the finalisation of at least one Russian nuclear power plant (Darst 2001). One must assume, then, that even the most cynical Moscow-based decision-maker will be interested in reducing radiological threats in the region as much as possible. Still, we must keep in mind that while down-scaling costs are large and sure to occur, it is, after all, less probable that an accident will occur than not. The attitude towards risk-taking is decisive in this respect; one might assume that more people are more willing to take risks in the uncertain political situation of contemporary Russia than is the case in Western countries.

This general discussion does not capture the full complexity of the nuclear safety issue, which, as demonstrated in the preceding section, involves a number of more or less interrelated problems that may well differ among each other with respect to their 'malignity'. Consequently, a brief examination of each problem area seems to be warranted.

The military sphere As follows from the preceding section, the threats that emanate from the day-to-day operations of Russian nuclear submarines are difficult to evaluate. The responsibility for the safe functioning of the submarines rests with the military authorities,[5] and this issue is not addressed by the international arrangements discussed in this book. However, threats in this category are likely to fall off in the years to come, since Russia is committed to further cuts in the number of submarines. The flip-side of the coin is, of course, the accumulation of even larger stockpiles of spent nuclear fuel and other radioactive waste that will result from the continued decommissioning of vessels. No one is presumably interested in a further aggravation of this situation, but nevertheless the problem is a tough one to solve. As described in the preceding section, the dismantlement chain consists of a number of operations, from de-fuelling of submarines to final storage of the waste, and a bottleneck at one stage may frustrate the whole process. Moreover, the debates on where to locate temporary and permanent storage facilities have proven difficult and time consuming. Finally, large investments in infrastructure are necessary to solve the waste problem, and the operations involved are costly to run.

The nuclear icebreakers The categories of risks related to the nuclear icebreaker fleet are the same as for the nuclear submarines.

Accidents may occur during day-to-day operation of the vessels, during refuelling/de-fuelling or in connection with inadequately stored spent fuel or radioactive waste. The most serious accidents known to have happened with Russian civil nuclear vessels affected the icebreaker Lenin in 1966 and 1967.[6] The largest risk of radioactive contamination from the icebreaker fleet is probably that posed by the storage vessel *Lepse*, not least because of its location in the Murmansk harbour in the immediate vicinity of a city of some 380,000 inhabitants.

The icebreaker fleet has played an important role in the Russian North for decades since they make the Northern Sea Route navigable outside the short summer season. They also seem to have an important symbolical function: they are considered by many as the ultimate symbol of the conquering of the north as well as the pride of the city of Murmansk. Even in today's constrained economic conditions, it is likely that the Murmansk Shipping Company will try to keep as many of them in operation as long as possible.

The Kola Nuclear Power Plant As pointed out above, the Kola Nuclear Power Plant is considered the most dangerous component of the Northwest Russian nuclear complex. In the opinion of the neighbouring countries, it should be shut down as soon as possible. At the same time, the plant is of great importance to the region, both as an energy provider,[7] as an employer and as a contributor to the regional and local budgets. Those who stand to gain most by a closing of the enterprise – e.g. the inhabitants of Polyarnye Zori – are the same people whose daily existence is most directly dependent on its continued operation. Moreover, the most important energy customers are large industrial complexes with great influence – if not direct, then at least indirect – on regional politics, partly with company leadership in Moscow.

The nuclear complex in Northwestern Russia is viewed with great concern by a number of Western countries. This enhances the prospects of practical problem-solving since these countries are willing to contribute money and expertise in order to alleviate the situation. At the same time, the active involvement of other states implies that they would probably want to have a say in defining and grading the threats, and to influence priorities where implementation of international commitments is concerned. Thus, for the USA the military threat from the nuclear submarines and possible proliferation threats are the main issues. For the European countries, and for the Nordic countries in particular, the Kola Nuclear Power Plant is seen as the most pressing problem, although the focus on nuclear waste has been higher. For Norway, a large exporter of fish, it has been an important goal to ensure that the Barents Sea remains free of radioactive pollution. Even the slightest rumour of radioactivity in fish could have grave economic consequences for the country.

The nature of the commitments

The picture of international agreements and other co-operative measures that Russia participates in, pertaining in some way or other to nuclear safety, is highly fragmented (see Chapter 1). While fairly strict commitments exist in the adjacent areas of disarmament and non-proliferation, commitments aimed at enhancing nuclear safety and protection of the environment are generally 'softer'.

Under the IAEA regime, a comprehensive framework for international co-operation on nuclear safety has been set up. The agency has worked out a detailed set of internationally recognised safety norms and standards (Nuclear Safety Standards – NUSS), which are continuously reviewed and updated. The IAEA's International Nuclear Event Scale (INES) is used to classify nuclear events and accidents according to seriousness. Upon request, the IAEA sends advisory and review teams to member states to observe and help improve safety standards and activities. Within the IAEA regime, 'hard' mechanisms have largely been avoided. The agency has been oriented mainly towards recommendatory norms and standards, rather than binding ones. Inspections are carried out on a voluntary basis, and enforcement procedures are generally non-existent. The safety obligations under the Convention of Nuclear Safety, which are legally binding upon the parties, are mostly of a very basic and general nature. For instance, parties are required to maintain a legislative and regulatory framework, including specific national safety requirements, a licensing procedure and inspection, assessment and enforcement policies.

In the course of the last decade, Russia has concluded a number of bilateral and multilateral agreements with Western states in the area of nuclear safety and security. Many of these are framework agreements aimed at facilitating co-operation with and assistance to Russia, e.g. by removing obstacles linked to issues like liability, taxes and access to sites and installations. The agreement on Co-operative

Threat Reduction (CTR) between Russia and the USA was set up in order to help Russia fulfil its disarmament obligations under the START I treaty. However, CTR also has environmental implications: since the problems with removal and storage of spent nuclear fuel threaten the speedy dismantlement of strategic submarines, some projects specifically addressing these issues have been included under CTR. Article I of the CTR agreement (US Department of State 1992) specifies that the parties shall co-operate in order to assist Russia in destroying nuclear and other weapons, in ensuring their secure transportation and storage, and in establishing measures against proliferation. Under the agreement, the US is exempted from liability (Article VII) and taxes (Article XI). Immunity is granted to government personnel (Article X), and the US has a right to 'examine the use of any material, training, or other services provided [. . .], if possible at sites of their location or use' (Article XIII).

The AMEC declaration – as the word 'declaration' implies – does not specify any such obligations for any of the parties. The document itself is simply a confirmation of the parties' intentions to co-operate in solving a rather broad and non-specific set of environmental problems, i.e. those resulting from military activities. In practice, AMEC has been directed first and foremost towards the issue of military nuclear waste in Northwestern Russia. Like CTR, AMEC is supposed to provide a framework for co-operation on concrete projects. However, since the parties have not yet been able to negotiate a set of legal protections for the non-Russian participants similar to those provided for in the CTR agreement, AMEC has not functioned as intended (Sawhill 2000; Sawhill and Jørgensen 2001).

BEAR is a non-binding co-operative framework, directed, *inter alia*, towards assisting implementation of other international environmental accords in Russia. Concrete assistance is provided by Western countries under various bilateral arrangements, notably the Joint Russian–Norwegian Commission on Nuclear Safety.

As follows from the above, a meaningful analysis of Russia's implementation of its international commitments in the area of nuclear safety requires a broad approach to the concept of 'commitments', i.e. one that includes more than the formal obligations laid down by treaties and conventions. Only within the IAEA regime, and only in recent years, have formal obligations been included as a mechanism in international efforts to enhance nuclear safety. At the same time, international co-operative arrangements directed towards capacity-building and assistance play a very important part in Russia. Thus, in the subsequent sections on implementation activities and performance, we include in the discussion Russian actors' will and ability to facilitate co-operation and assistance under CTR, AMEC and the bilateral arrangements, as well as their part in implementing concrete projects initiated under these framework arrangements.

Public authorities' implementation activities

According to the Russian Constitution, protection of the environment as well as implementation of international agreements belong to the category of issue areas that are subject to the joint jurisdiction of federal and regional authorities (see Chapter 3). However, the Constitution also states that nuclear energy and fissile materials are subject to exclusive federal jurisdiction (Para. 72, Article 1, section i). Naturally, the same applies to the armed forces. In practice, this means that federal authorities and their representative bodies in the regions according to the Constitution should have a greater say relative to regional authorities in matters concerning nuclear safety than in more general environmental matters. This extends also to the implementation of international agreements. Moreover, the Ministry of Atomic Energy and the Ministry of Defence are both bureaucratic 'heavyweights', also compared to other federal bodies of governance.

Implementation in national legislation

Unlike in the case of fisheries management (see Chapter 4), Russian authorities have succeeded in putting in place a legislative framework for nuclear safety at the level of law. A law on the use of nuclear energy (Russian Federation 1995a) was adopted by the State Duma, 20 October 1995, and signed by President Boris Yeltsin on 21 November of the same year. The law is a large framework document, consisting of seventy articles. Its Preamble states that:

> The present Federal law defines the legal basis and principles for regulating issues arising in the use of nuclear energy. It is aimed at protection of the health and life of people, the environment and property in relation to use of nuclear energy. It shall contribute to the development of nuclear science and technology and to *the strengthening of the international regime for safe use of nuclear energy*. (Our emphasis.)

Article 3 defines the objects of nuclear energy use as, among other things, nuclear installations, radiation sources, storage points for nuclear materials and radioactive substances, storage facilities for radioactive waste, nuclear materials, radioactive substances and radioactive waste. Article 4 lists the range of activities covered by the law:

- siting, design, construction, operation and decommissioning of nuclear installations, radiation sources and storage points;
- development, production, testing, transportation, storage, disposition and use of nuclear charges for peaceful purposes and their handling;
- handling of nuclear materials and radioactive substances, including handling in exploration and mining of materials containing those materials and substances, in production, use, reprocessing and storage of nuclear materials and radioactive substances;
- safety assurance in the use of nuclear energy;
- oversight of assurance of nuclear and technical safety, radiation and fire protection of nuclear installations, radiation sources and storage points, of the sanitary-epidemiological well-being of citizens in the use of nuclear energy;
- physical protection of nuclear installations, radiation sources, storage points, nuclear materials and radioactive substances;
- control of and accounting for nuclear materials and radioactive substances;
- export and import of nuclear installations, equipment, technologies, nuclear materials, radioactive substances, special non-nuclear materials and services in the use of nuclear energy;
- state radiation monitoring within the territory of the Russian Federation;
- training of specialists for the use of nuclear installations, radiation sources, storage points, nuclear materials and radioactive substances;
- performance of other activities in the use of nuclear energy (Russian Federation 1995a, Article 4).

A law on radiation safety of the population (Russian Federation 1995b) was adopted by the State Duma on 5 December 1995 and signed by President Boris Yeltsin on 9 January 1996. Radiation safety is here defined as conditions under which present and future generations are protected against ionising radiation harmful to their health (Article 1). The law establishes principles for standardisation, grounding and optimisation in radiation protection assurance (Article 3) and basic hygienic standards for exposure caused by the use of ionising radiation sources on Russian territory (Article 9). Other important federal laws and normative acts in the sphere of nuclear safety include the laws on certification of production and services (Russian Federation 1993) and on the administrative liability of organisations for the violation of legislation in the use of nuclear energy (Russian Federation 2000) as well as the provision on licensing of activities in the use of nuclear energy (Government of the Russian Federation 1997b).

As the first among Russia's federal subjects, Murmansk Oblast acquired its own regional law on nuclear safety in 1997 (Murmansk Oblast 1997c). Referring to the federal laws on the use of nuclear energy and on radiation safety of the population, the regional law specifies, among other things, the authority of the regional duma (Article 8) and the regional administration (Article 9), and the rights and obligations of citizens and public organisations in matters of nuclear safety. The law states the major responsibility of various federal agencies to perform regulation and monitoring in the field, but lists a range of activities in which regional authorities can participate (Articles 8 and 9). Among these are the elaboration and implementation of federal nuclear safety programmes, monitoring of the radiological situation in the oblast, the location of nuclear objects (including storage of nuclear waste) and decision-making in the event of a nuclear accident.

It is difficult to judge precisely to what extent the legislative framework related to nuclear safety has evolved in response to the Russian Federation's international obligations in the field, and to what extent it is the result of internal political processes. However, one can assume that the international obligations of the state at least to some extent have influenced developments. The specific reference to the international nuclear safety regime in the preamble to the law on the use of nuclear energy speaks to this effect.

The role of federal authorities

The most important among the federal executive agencies participating in the implementation of nuclear safety measures and of international commitments in that area are the Ministry of Atomic Energy, Gosatomnadzor and the Department for Environmental

Protection under the Ministry of Natural Resources. In some co-operative arrangements, notably AMEC, the Ministry of Defence plays an important role.

The Ministry of Atomic Energy (Minatom) was established in 1986 as a Soviet ministry and merged in 1989 with the powerful Ministry of Medium Machine-Building, responsible for development and construction of nuclear weapons and reactors in the Soviet Union. Minatom was assigned responsibility for all aspects – civilian and military – of the nuclear energy industry and had about a million employees within its structure. This set-up continued when Minatom was reorganised into a Russian ministry in 1992. In 1998, responsibility for nuclear waste from military establishments was also transferred to Minatom. Minatom is a gigantic organisation and in many ways still epitomises a soviet-type industrial sector ministry. Far from being a mere regulatory body, it controls and co-ordinates the work of a large number of state enterprises, including nuclear power plants, weapons production facilities and research institutes. By participating in legislative processes and working out policy concepts and programmes, Minatom plays a key role in carving out the federal policy in the field of nuclear energy. At the same time, at least in principle, the ministry is in a position to implement this policy directly by issuing the necessary orders to its own subsidiary organisations.

Minatom participates actively in international processes related to nuclear energy management, nuclear safety, non-proliferation and disarmament, and in the implementation of international obligations in these areas. The ministry is a key Russian participant in the IAEA regime, and is responsible for fulfilling Russian obligations under the Non-Proliferation Treaty. In the Joint Russian–Norwegian Commission on Nuclear Safety, it is counterpart to the Norwegian Ministry of Foreign Affairs. Minatom is in charge of all fissile materials outside nuclear weapons, also of nuclear warheads once they are taken out of service, and of decommissioned nuclear submarines. This gives Minatom the central role in the implementation of projects under CTR, despite the programme's 'military' profile. It also means that the lack of a formal role for Minatom in AMEC may complicate the implementation of that agreement.

While Minatom represents the Russian Federation in bilateral and multilateral fora dealing with atomic installations and nuclear waste and also oversees the implementation of co-operative projects with other states, the concrete implementation of such projects is largely delegated to subsidiary or associated bodies, one of the most important being the Interbranch Co-ordination Centre Nuklid. This body was established in 1990 to co-ordinate attempts at commercialisation within the nuclear sector of the Soviet Union. It is not formally part of the structure of Minatom, but it is part of the 'Minatom system' and is organised as a so-called state unitary enterprise (*gosudarstvennoye unitarnoye predpriyatiye*). In practice, this means that it works on contracts with the Ministry and that ties between the two are tight. Nuklid's main office is in St Petersburg; branch offices are located in Moscow, Murmansk and Vladivostok. It has a staff of 55, but approximately 1,500 people work on a contractual basis for Nuklid. The major tasks of Nuklid are technology development (mainly of containers), certification in relation to IAEA and the US Agency for International Development (USAID) and innovation. In 1995, the director of Nuklid was assigned the task of elaborating a programme for nuclear waste treatment, and in 1998 the organisation was appointed main contractor for the AMEC projects and for the majority of the ten co-operative projects with Norway identified in the Framework Agreement between the two states.

In the Soviet Union, there existed no independent control agency in the field of nuclear safety. All functions pertaining to nuclear energy and weapons construction, including both regulation and control, were performed by various divisions within Minatom and its predecessors. In 1991, however, the Federal Inspectorate for Nuclear and Radiation Safety (Gosatomnadzor) was established in the Russian Soviet Federative Socialist Republic and endowed with the task of controlling and licensing activities related to the application of nuclear energy. From then on, Russia was in compliance with a central requirement of the IAEA Convention of Nuclear Safety, which states that the body which implements the regulatory function be separate from other bodies concerned with the promotion and utilisation of nuclear energy.

Gosatomnadzor was established as an executive body under the President. It is responsible for safety regulations in the use of atomic energy. Among its most important tasks are licensing of activities that involve the use of nuclear energy and radioactive materials, the development of standards for and monitoring of such use, non-proliferation of nuclear technology and materials, physical protection of nuclear installations and control of Russian implementation of relevant international agreements. The military sector has been excluded from its control since 1995. With the establishment of Gosatomnadzor, part of Minatom's control and licensing functions were removed from the ministry and placed with the new agency, making the latter, in effect, an outside 'watchdog' *vis-à-vis* Minatom's activities. As might be expected, this has created a lot of tension between the two agencies. Some of the conflicts have arisen around issues where the delimitation of competence between Minatom and Gosatomnadzor is unclear. In principle, as follows from the provision spelling out the functions of the agencies, Minatom is responsible for the implementation of rules and regulations in the field of nuclear safety, while Gosatomnadzor is responsible for implementation control (Ministry of Atomic Energy 1997). Thus, with regard to international obligations, one of Gosatomnadzor's main functions is to control the implementing activities of Minatom and other relevant agencies. Like Minatom, Gosatomnadzor participates in processes related to the IAEA regime, it controls implementation of requirements under the Non-Proliferation Treaty, and the agency is a participant in several projects under CTR as well as under the bilateral Russian–Norwegian regime.

The Russian environmental agency has experienced considerable ups and downs since it was first established in 1988. Until then, there had been no specialised agency responsible for environmental protection. However, as green issues came gradually to the forefront of public debate, the need arose for political responses, and a State Committee for Environmental Protection was created. In 1991, the Committee was elevated to the rank of a Ministry of Environmental and Natural Resources Protection. The agency retained this status until 1996, when it became, once more, a State Committee. Then, in 2000, came the final blow: as part of President Putin's bureaucratic spring-cleaning, which involved the reshuffling and merging of several ministries and was allegedly undertaken in order to streamline the bureaucracy, the State Committee for Environmental Protection was disbanded. The remains were incorporated into the Ministry of Natural Resources as a Department for Environmental Protection. Where nuclear safety is concerned, the main roles of the environmental agency are to carry out environmental impact assessments for facilities and installations prior to their construction, and to carry out inspections to ensure that environmental regulations pertaining to nuclear safety are observed.[8]

The most conspicuous trait in the Russian federal organisation of nuclear safety issues is the well-known Russian lack of horizontal integration between various agencies and the high level of conflict between them. A major line of conflict seems to run between Minatom and, in particular, Nuklid, on the one hand, and the 'softer' agencies of the State Committee/Department for Environmental Protection and Gosatomnadzor on the other. The two latter have seen their status reduced in recent years, both formally and informally. The federal agency for environmental protection lost its ministerial status in 1996. Gosatomnadzor has seen its major task to issue licences threatened by new regulations that provide Minatom (in practice: Nuklid) with the right to license activities related to the use of nuclear energy for military purposes (Government of the Russian Federation 1999). Hence, the loss of status of the environmental protection and nuclear safety supervisory agencies has taken place at the same time as Minatom and Nuklid have expanded their spheres of influence.

Working relations between the 'hard' and 'soft' agencies seem to be characterised partly by a *modus vivendi* between people who have been forced – for example, for the sake of international projects – to maintain a certain level of contact with each other. This seems to characterise relations between the representatives of Minatom and the State Committee/Department of Environmental Protection that are involved in co-operation with Norway (Hønneland and Moe 2000). Between others, i.e. Nuklid and Gosatomnadzor, the schism seems more volatile. There are also signs of internal conflict inside Minatom.[9]

The role of regional authorities

The formal role of regional authorities in relation to nuclear installations on their territory, as well as nuclear safety issues, is spelt out in the federal law on the use of atomic energy (Russian Federation 1995a). The law states that the regulation and exploitation of federal nuclear installations are a federal responsibility. The same applies to the implementation of international obligations and the co-ordination of international co-operation in this area (Article 9). However, a number of functions are defined as being the joint responsibility of federal and regional authorities, including decisions on the location of nuclear installations, environmental impact assessments and protection of people and the environment. Moreover, authorities at both levels are jointly responsible for working out and implementing 'complex programmes for the social and economic development and ecological safety of territories where nuclear energy installations are located' (Article 10). The joint responsibility of federal and regional authorities on these issues in the case of Murmansk Oblast is confirmed in the regional law on nuclear safety (Murmansk Oblast 1997b).

In practice, the vast dimensions of the nuclear-related problems as well as the bureaucratic strength of Minatom and the Ministry of Defence imply that the role of regional authorities remains essentially reactive rather than pro-active. The authorities of Murmansk Oblast have occasionally criticised the two ministries for the problems their activities have created in the region, but their main strategy has been to support federal attempts to deal with the situation and to lobby for stronger commitments in this field. The federal bodies, for their part, mostly recognise that regional support makes policy implementation an easier task. An agreement between Minatom and the regional administration of Murmansk on co-operation in the treatment of radioactive waste and spent nuclear fuel was concluded in 1998 (Murmansk Oblast 1998). A more general agreement on co-ordination of activities within the sphere of nuclear safety between Murmansk regional administration and a range of federal agencies present in the region, including Minatom, the State Committee for Environmental Protection, Gosatomnadzor and the Russian Navy (the Northern Fleet) was signed in early 2000 (Murmansk Oblast 2000). Being rather vague and non-specific, these agreements should perhaps be seen more as an expression of the parties' will to co-operate than as an operative framework for joint problem-solving. When concrete issues are to be tackled or conflicts of interest arise, representatives of the various interested parties are often invited to discuss the issue jointly. An example is the discussions of the suitability of Sayda Bay in the vicinity of the closed military town of Skalistyy as a storage site for submarine reactor compartments. The local authorities were sceptical about these plans and wanted to hold a referendum in Skalistyy on the day of the presidential election – 16 March 2000 – allowing the inhabitants to give their opinion.[10] When their right to do this was questioned, they turned to the regional administration, which agreed to invite all interested parties to discuss the issue, and to act as mediator between the local authorities on the one hand and the Northern Fleet and Minatom on the other.

Among the issues discussed at the meetings concerning Sayda Bay was that of material compensation to the inhabitants of Skalistyy. This is a question that could affect the policy of regional authorities as well. Increasing nuclear safety in the region is seen as very important, but in the current conditions economic considerations tend to take precedence over most other matters. So to the extent that regional authorities have to accept risks in the future too – for instance in the form of storage sites on their territory – they are likely to try to get as much economic mileage out of it as possible. Pushing for direct compensations is one way of achieving this. Efforts to improve nuclear safety could also spawn positive spin-off effects in the region through investments in infrastructure and increased demand for labour. In 1999, a Committee for Conversion and Nuclear Safety was set up under the regional administration to co-ordinate activities in the field of nuclear safety. The name of the committee reflects the dual objective of the administration, enhancing nuclear safety and simultaneously reviving the struggling naval shipyards.

A large share of the funds currently available for nuclear safety projects in Northwestern Russia comes in the form of assistance from abroad. As pointed out above, co-ordination of such co-operative measures are the prerogative of federal authorities. However, regional authorities are taking quite an active part in attracting and negotiating agreements of this kind. For instance, the Murmansk regional administration is represented in the Joint Russian–Norwegian Commission on Nuclear Safety.

The role of federal agencies in the region

As mentioned in Chapter 3, some forty federal agencies are represented in Murmansk Oblast and even more in Arkhangelsk Oblast. Some of them are relatively independent with regard to policy choices, including choices related to the implementation of Russia's international obligations. As noted in Chapter 4, federal agencies located in the region act as the main representatives of Russian public authorities in the efforts to manage the Northwest Russian fishing fleet, including implementing the country's international obligations. On the other hand, the autonomy of most federal agencies located in the region is probably rather limited *vis-à-vis* head offices in Moscow. This seems to be the case with the federal bodies involved in nuclear safety. Minatom and Gosatomnadzor have their representations in the region, but the 'balance of power' between federal and regional offices differs from what we found in fisheries management. While important decisions in fisheries management are made by federal agencies located in the region and normally sanctioned by the federal offices, the latter seem to have a greater thrust in the nuclear safety area or, put differently, the agencies located in the region are less autonomous in nuclear safety issues than in fisheries management. In addition to the presence of Minatom and Gosatomnadzor, the State Committee/Department for Environmental Protection has regional branches in each federal subject, including Murmansk and Arkhangelsk Oblasts (see Chapter 6). The Murmansk branch of the committee consists of several departments, including the State Control and Radiation Security Department, which is charged with addressing nuclear safety issues. In the military sphere, the Directorate of Ecological Security of the Armed Forces of the Russian Federation has 'regional' units, including one in the Northern Fleet. However, the responsibility for nuclear safety in the Northern Fleet rests with another body, the Radiological, Chemical and Biological Protection Service.

A recent addition to the measures already in place to organise the scrapping of submarines, treatment of nuclear waste and rehabilitation of submarine bases in the northern areas is the planned establishment under Minatom of a state enterprise, Sevrao, to handle these tasks (Northern Enterprise for the Treatment of Nuclear Waste) (Government of the Russian Federation 2000). Altogether nine such regional enterprises are planned in the Russian Federation. The first will be Sevrao and Dalrao (Far Eastern Enterprise for the Treatment of Nuclear Waste) in the Far East. An overarching federal structure, Rosrao, might also be set up under Minatom. Sevrao will have its head office in Murmansk and branch offices in Andreyeva Bay and Gremikha. It was supposed to be on track by March 2000, but was hampered by changes in Russian property regulations (Hønneland and Moe 2000).

Implementation performance and target compliance

To what extent have Russia's international nuclear safety commitments been implemented in Northwestern Russia? Due to the complexity of the problem, implementation of global, regional and bilateral commitments are discussed separately. We look in particular at the London Convention, the CTR and AMEC agreements and the bilateral agreements with Norway, respectively.[11] This section also covers aspects of the discussion found in Chapters 4 and 6 under the headings 'the role of others' and 'joint implementation'. The former refers mainly to the participation of target groups in the implementation process.[12] The latter involves construction projects financed by the US and Norway under the CTR and AMEC agreements and the Norwegian Plan of Action for Nuclear Safety in Northwestern Russia.[13]

The global level

Soviet/Russian implementation of the London Convention, here related to the dumping of radioactive waste that had taken place in the Barents and Kara Seas since the 1960s, is studied by Stokke (2000b). He distinguishes four stages in terms of access and participation patterns in the Soviet/Russian 'implementation game': (1) a period of military self-regulation until the late 1970s; (2) a time of gradually expanding participation during the 1980s; (3) a stage of acute politicisation at the beginning of the 1990s; and, lastly, (4) the mildly ambiguous situation in recent years in which domestic involvement in nuclear affairs is contracting while foreign participation is on the rise.

Since the 1960s, the Northern Fleet and the Murmansk Shipping Company experienced a widening gap between their needs and actual capacity to store radioactive waste and spent nuclear fuel. As a result, they resorted to dumping waste matter into the adjacent Arctic waters. During the 1960s and 1970s, dumping was secret, closed to public scrutiny and under the sole regulation of the military authorities. An interim storage facility for spent nuclear fuel had been built for the Northern Fleet as early as in 1962, but it was plagued by constant operation problems. In 1973, the Northern Fleet and the Murmansk Shipping Company started to transport spent nuclear fuel to the reprocessing plant at Mayak in the Urals.

The Soviet Union ratified the London Convention in 1976, and in 1979 the Soviet Council of Ministers passed Resolution 222 on Measures to Ensure Performance of the Soviet Side's Obligations Following from the 1972 [London] Convention (Stokke 2000b, p. 490). The resolution prohibited the dumping of high-level waste and made the State Committee for Hydrometeorology and Environmental Monitoring (Goskomgidromet)[14] responsible for issuing permits to dump low- and medium-level waste and for reporting permit allocation to the International Maritime Organisation (IMO). According to Stokke (pp. 491–492), the resolution – intentionally designed to spur

Soviet implementation of the London Convention – transformed the Soviet implementation game by shifting executive involvement to other levels of government, by prohibiting the dumping of high-level waste and by introducing a regulatory newcomer regarding low- and medium-level waste. All these measures were in line with the regulatory provisions of the London Convention and would be difficult to account for in the absence of the convention.

During the 1980s, Goskomgidromet confirmed its role as an independent agency with its own ambitions in the dumping issue. It participated in the elaboration of new standards for the dumping of radioactive waste; it permitted the Northern Fleet to continue dumping low- and medium-level waste on the condition that it built a waste-processing plant; and, when this did not happen, it withdrew its dumping permit. Murmansk Shipping Company, which had less waste to handle than the Northern Fleet, had already built a processing plant and stopped dumping liquid waste in 1984 and solid waste in 1986. The Northern Fleet, for its part, disregarded the instructions of Goskomgidromet and even increased the amounts of dumped waste towards the end of the 1980s. The newly established State Committee for Environmental Protection replaced Goskomgidromet at the head of the Soviet delegations to the London Convention in 1989.

Largely as a result of the Chernobyl accident, nuclear safety became a major issue in Soviet/Russian politics at the end of the 1980s and early 1990s. The barriers to involvement in nuclear safety issues were dramatically lowered as institutional rivalry during the transition from the Soviet Union to the Russian Federation enhanced participation in the decision-making process. Implementation of international nuclear safety obligations went from being a process involving a handful of regulatory bodies to a key issue at the highest political level with broad societal scrutiny and activity. However, during the 1990s interest in environmental affairs levelled off as the economic crisis claimed most ordinary citizens' attention. At the same time, foreign assistance directed towards nuclear safety in Russia increased. This foreign involvement, mainly at the regional and bilateral level, generally took the form of financial assistance to Russia to help the country comply with its obligations at the global level. Hence, implementation of obligations at the global level became linked to implementation at the regional and bilateral level (discussed below). The Kola Nuclear Power Plant's ability to comply with the IAEA standards and the Northern Fleet and Murmansk Shipping Company's ability to process radioactive waste and spent nuclear fuel in accordance with Russia's international obligations are in a major sense dependent upon the success of various bilateral projects under the Joint Russian–Norwegian Commission on Nuclear Safety.

The regional level

A thorough study of the implementation of the CTR and AMEC programmes is found in Sawhill and Jørgensen (2001).[15] The main objective of the CTR programme is to eliminate strategic weapons and their launching systems in Russia in order to enable the country to comply with its arms reduction obligations under START I. By 2007, 41 ballistic missile-firing submarines (SSBNs) and their associated missiles and missile launchers are to be eliminated through the CTR programme. While Russia would comply with the START II treaty by removing the missile compartment from submarine hulls and cutting the missile tubes in half, this is only one step in a comprehensive process of dismantling the entire submarine quota. In particular, the rate of the scrapping depends on how quickly the reactor fuel can be removed. In 1995, the rate was four submarine reactor cores (or two submarines) annually. The main obstacle was lack of capacity to handle spent nuclear fuel and radioactive waste.

In its initial years, the CTR programme provided mainly heavy industrial equipment to Russia, such as cutting tools, cranes and other things necessary for removing the missile tubes and scrapping submarine hulls. As the Russian shipyards from the mid-1990s became increasingly unable to pay their workers and maintain basic operational procedures, the CTR programme shifted from providing equipment and technology to signing direct contracts with Russian shipyards to dismantle submarines. The first contract was signed with the Zvyozdochka shipyard in Arkhangelsk Oblast in 1997. In addition to this shipyard, the Nerpa shipyard in Murmansk Oblast was later included in the scheme. After infrastructure improvements provided by the CTR programme, Nerpa can now dismantle two to three submarines and Zvyozdochka six per year. Spent fuel from six SSBNs will be reprocessed at the Mayak Chemical Combine. For spent fuel from the remaining SSBNs, the CTR programme is purchasing some 100 40-tonne storage casks, developed under the AMEC programme (see below), that can safely store the fuel for up to fifty years. Due to continued difficulties in getting the casks licensed, the problem of spent nuclear fuel remains a serious obstacle to submarine dismantlement. Nevertheless, 18 of the projected 41 SSBNs were dismantled by February 2001, see Table 5.2.

Table 5.2 *CTR accomplishments and projections (as of February 2001)*

	Original inventory baseline	*Eliminated February 2001*	*Eliminated 2004 (projection)*	*Eliminated 2007 (projection)*
Submarine-launched ballistic missiles (SLBM)	936	184	503	661
SLBM launchers	728	308	480	612
Ballistic missile-firing submarines (SSBNs)	48	18	32	41

Source: Sawhill and Jørgensen (2001).

The AMEC programme comprises seven project groups, five of which deal with spent nuclear fuel and radioactive waste management, see Table 5.3. Most importantly, a 40-tonne prototype container suitable for interim storage and transportation of spent nuclear fuel has been developed under the programme (project 1.1). The prototype was completed in late 1999, but the cask's certification has been complicated by disagreement between Minatom and Gosatomnadzor concerning which of these organisations should be the certifying agency. Concrete storage pads, of which up to fifty casks may be temporarily stored, should have been ready by mid-2001 (project 1.1-1). However, the construction of the pads has been delayed due to difficulties in obtaining land-use permits from regional authorities.

Project 1.2 aims at reducing the growing volume of low-level liquid radioactive waste through the development of a mobile waste-processing facility. The facility is intended to serve submarines at remote sites on the Kola Peninsula. The first mobile unit is under construction at the time of writing. Projects 1.3 and 1.4 are related to solid radioactive waste stemming from the dismantlement of submarines. Several facilities are scheduled to be completed during the years 2001–2.

In summary, the CTR and AMEC projects – mainly aimed at the scrapping of submarines and the development of infrastructure

Table 5.3 *Nuclear safety projects in the AMEC programme*

Project number	*Project description*
Naval spent nuclear fuel management	
1.1	Design and construct interim storage and transportation container
1.1-1	Design and construct temporary storage pad for spent nuclear fuel cask
Naval liquid radioactive waste treatment	
1.2	Design and construct mobile liquid radioactive waste processing facility
Solid radioactive waste volume reduction	
1.3-1	Assess technology for waste volume reduction
1.3-2	Manufacture a mobile pre-treatment facility
1.3-3	Manufacture a decontamination unit for metal wastes
Solid radioactive waste storage	
1.4-1	Assess surface coating technologies
1.4-2	Manufacture steel radioactive waste containers
1.4-3	Manufacture concrete radioactive waste containers
Radiation monitoring and personnel and environmental safety	
1.5	Equipment transfer, training and exchange of monitoring strategies
1.5-1	Radiation control at facilities

Source: Sawhill and Jørgensen (2001).

necessary for the unloading, transportation and storage of spent nuclear fuel and radioactive waste – are in the process of being implemented, but largely behind schedule. Delays are caused by a mixture of internal Russian factors and factors found in the interface between donor states and Russia. The major problem among the latter is slowness in the elaboration of an international legal framework, in particular related to indemnity against liability, access to nuclear sites, personnel immunity and tax exemptions. The internal Russian factors are mainly related to institutional controversies: cf. the disagreement between Minatom and Gosatomnadzor as to which agency has the right to license the 40-tonne cask developed under the AMEC programme. Apart from open conflict, the lack of co-ordination between various Russian agencies has reportedly created serious problems for the implementation of both CTR and AMEC. Moreover, there seems to be a positive correlation between the potential for financial gain for the institutions involved and implementation success. For instance, the enthusiasm of Minatom and the Ministry of Defence is related to the financial support channelled through these agencies by the programmes. Likewise, the defence industry gained substantially from the agreements, which enhanced their supportive attitude. Furthermore, Minatom's interest cooled off markedly when the ministry in the mid-1990s acquired control of the lucrative nuclear export market (and was thus no longer so 'dependent' on financial support from abroad). The Ministry of Foreign affairs, for its part, has often put on a tougher stance towards the US in CTR negotiations than other Russian agencies, which can probably be explained, at least partly, by the fact that this ministry has only had a co-ordinating role in the CTR process. Finally, the overarching political controversies of the Russian Federation – between the executive and the legislative and between the federal centre and the regions – have also hampered co-operation under the CTR and AMEC agreements. The key to the solution of the most pressing unresolved issues affecting AMEC co-operation – tax exemptions, liability and immunity – rests largely with the Federal Parliament. As far as centre–region relations are concerned, there are examples of projects having been exempted from taxes by federal authorities, yet having to face demands for taxes at the regional level.

The bilateral level

The Norwegian Plan of Action for Nuclear Safety in Northwestern Russia provides further infrastructure to facilitate implementation of the agreements at global and regional level. The Plan of Action was evaluated in 2000 by one of the authors of this book (Hønneland and Moe 2000).[16] Project participants were interviewed at various levels of government in both countries.

The evaluation comprised five of the projects covered by the Framework Agreement on Nuclear Safety between Russia and Norway, see Table 5.4. Project 202 involved the upgrading and expansion from 1200 m^2 to 5000 m^2 of the effluent treatment facility for liquid radioactive waste at the facility serving nuclear-powered icebreakers in Murmansk. The project was conceived in 1994

Table 5.4 *Projects financed by the Norwegian Plan of Action for Nuclear Safety in Northwestern Russia and included in the Framework Agreement on Nuclear Safety between Norway and Russia*

Project number and description	*Funding in USD*
Defence-related spent nuclear fuel projects	
211: Build ship for transport of spent naval nuclear fuel	376,000
212: Build four railway cars for transport of spent naval nuclear fuel	2,963,000
216: Empty/decommission spent naval nuclear fuel at Andreyava Bay	733,000
217: Establish interim storage facility for spent naval nuclear fuel at Mayak	186,000
230: Develop transportable storage cask for spent naval nuclear fuel	610,000
232: Build pad for temporary storage of spent naval nuclear fuel casks	595,000
Defence-related radioactive waste projects	
213: Modernise liquid radioactive waste storage facility in Severodvinsk	4,185,000
214: Deliver mobile equipment for processing liquid radioactive waste	0
215: Build temporary storage facility for solid radioactive waste at Andreyava Bay	8,578,000
226: Build system for processing solid radioactive waste from submarines	75,000
Civilian nuclear safety projects	
101: Enhance operational safety at the Kola Nuclear Power Plant	9,668,000
202: Modernise liquid radioactive waste treatment facility in Murmansk	1,996,000
203: Dismantle the floating technical base Lepse	2,852,000
229: Develop transportable storage cask for spent nuclear fuel	472,000

Source: Sawhill and Jørgensen (2001).

as a bilateral Norwegian–Russian initiative; the USA joined the project in 1995. The facility will serve both the nuclear-powered icebreaker fleet and the Russian Northern Fleet. The opening of the facility was postponed several times, but finally took place in June 2001. Main project participants in Russia were Nuklid and RTP

Atomflot, on whose premises the facility was built. A major goal for the Norwegian side was to sway Russia to accede to the London Convention's prohibition on the dumping of nuclear waste (including low-level waste) at sea. In the interviews, this was mentioned by all Norwegians who had something to say about this project, but by none of the Russians. They, instead, stressed the need to solve the increasing problem of liquid radioactive waste, and to expand activities and secure revenues at RTP Atomflot (by selling services to the Northern Fleet). The Russians and Norwegians agreed that the goals of the project had been 'nearly achieved'. The Norwegians here probably referred to the finalisation of the facility, not to Russian accession to the dumping ban in the London Convention. To explain the delays in finalising the facility, the Russian project participants referred to changes in the Russian security norms twice during the project period (in 1996 and 1998). On the Norwegian side, 'Russian bad [management] culture' and 'the culture clash between Americans and Russians' were given as reasons for the delays. Both parties mentioned the Russian need for pre-payment as a major obstacle. Nevertheless, bilateral co-operation between Norwegian and Russian project participants was generally perceived as unproblematic. The project has had a relatively high profile and was also mentioned frequently in evaluation interviews we had with people other than those directly involved in it. Most seemed to perceive it as 'partly successful'. For some time, it was clearly viewed as something close to an exemplary project since the parties did manage to get something done here. With the repeated delays in finalising it, however, enthusiasm dwindled. Several of the Russian interviewees peripheral to the project referred to it as 'too golden', indicating that the abundant financing dampened Russian enthusiasm to finalise it. Some said outright that the Norwegian side should have stood more firmly on its position and demanded the finalisation of the project with the funds initially allotted.

A Norwegian initiative resulted in the establishment of an international advisory committee to work for the solution of the environmental threat posed by *Lepse*, the nuclear-powered icebreaker fleet's old storage vessel for radioactive waste (project 203). The committee is led by Norway; the other participants are Russia, France, the USA, the European Commission and the Nordic Environmental Finance Corporation (NEFCO). Major participants on the Russian side include Minatom, Nuklid, Murmansk Shipping

Company (the owner of *Lepse*), the State Committee/Department for Environmental Protection, Gosatomnadzor and various research institutes and enterprises. The vessel was docked in the summer of 1999 and is assumed by Russian experts to be safe for another ten years. Documentation is being elaborated on the whole process of removing the damaged fuel and liquidating the vessel; the present project only embraces the former aspect. There has been very little progress in the project so far, except for a fruitful sub-project on licensing. From the point of view of the Norwegian leadership of the project, practical work cannot start until all Western parties involved have been secured tax freedom and indemnity against liability through framework agreements with Russia. Such agreements are still lacking for NEFCO and the USA. An agreement between Russia and France was signed in June 2000. During the interviews, Russian actors at both the project level in Murmansk and the co-ordinating level in Moscow showed little understanding for the Norwegian stance and complained about the lack of progress in the project.

It has long been acknowledged that Russia will need a specialised vessel for safe transport of spent nuclear fuel and possibly also other radioactive waste from decommissioned nuclear submarines from remote locations in Northwestern Russia to transfer terminals in Murmansk and the Sevmash shipyard in Severodvinsk. Spent fuel is transported in containers too heavy to be transported by road. The ship will be required to have independent propulsion machinery, a double hull and other safety features. The firm Moss Maritime was responsible for an elucidation (project 211); the main actors on the Russian side were Minatom and a co-ordinating body for Russian shipyards Morskoye Korablestroyeniye (Maritime Ship-Building). The original plan was to build a new ship. However, in 1998 the Russian party announced that it would instead reconstruct an old vessel, the *Amur*, arguing that it would be a less expensive solution. The Norwegian position was that the cost of reconstructing *Amur* would hardly be lower than that of building a new vessel. It also argued that *Amur* would not be fit to fulfil the tasks of the required specialised vessel. Separate expert groups were established in Norway and Russia in 1999, and in the autumn of that year they came to a joint conclusion: building a new vessel would be the better alternative. At the beginning of 2000, Minatom formally informed the Norwegian party that it would go in for a new vessel. Since then, planning has progressed rapidly. The Norwegian project participants assumed that external concerns were delaying the project. Minatom was out of ideas about how to rid itself of the old and polluted vessel, the *Amur*, and the planned specialised vessel for transport of spent nuclear fuel was perceived as a possible way of solving this problem. The Russian project participant viewed the Norwegian approach to the project as constructive and acknowledged that the delay was indeed due to problems on the Russian side.

In order to transport spent nuclear fuel from terminals in Murmansk and Severodvinsk to interim storage or reprocessing in Mayak, Russia will need specialised railway rolling stock able to provide safety-approved transport for the 40-tonne casks developed under the AMEC programme. Project 212 in the Norwegian Plan of Action involved procurement of four such specialised wagons, of which Russia already had four. The Norwegian firm Moss Maritime was responsible on the Norwegian side while Nuklid was main Russian contractor of the project. The wagons – finalised in March 2000 – were built at Tver Railway Factory in Central Russia. All subcontractors were also Russian. Negotiations on the realisation of the project started in September 1998. The Norwegian project manager claimed that they were 'forced' by the Norwegian Ministry of Foreign Affairs to accept Nuklid as main contractor on the Russian side. They would have preferred to control all activities in Russia itself, selecting subcontractors by means of tenders. Nuklid does not use tenders; it selects subcontractors on the basis of fixed prices. According to the agreement between the Norwegian project leader and Nuklid, the former has no right even to be informed of financial dispositions by the Russians. The only reason Moss Maritime accepted the idea was because it was a concrete project, with easily monitorable progress. The wagons were built without any particular problems. However, a major problem arose when they were being completed in spring 2000. The Norwegian project manager was informed that the Russian main contractor had changed ownership of the wagons. Moss Maritime's agreement with Nuklid states that the wagons shall be owned by the Mayak facility. However, it turned out that they had been transferred to a newly established firm, Atomspetstrans. Moss Maritime requested further information on this matter and immediately stopped remaining payments to Nuklid. Moss Maritime was concerned for the lack of respect shown to concluded agreements by the Russian party. They claimed not to have been informed about the change of ownership, nor about the status of Atomspetstrans. During the interviews, representatives of other agencies in Russia claimed that Atomspetstrans did not exist and that if it had in fact been established, it would be a 'paper firm' only performing an unnecessary middle-man role, leasing the wagons to the Mayak facility. The following interview extracts illustrate the antagonism between the Norwegian project management and Russian main contractor of this project:

> As far as our relationship with Moss Maritime is concerned, our functions are quite similar, but we're interested in the end result, and we know Russian management culture; Moss Maritime exaggerates its function; they're only interested in making money, which is quite understandable, but they shouldn't have been given so much money for doing it; they have only been a financial agent for the [Norwegian] Ministry of Foreign Affairs; I don't know how much Moss Maritime took from the Ministry of Foreign Affairs, and it really doesn't interest me, but I proposed to manage the project on my own and inform Moss Maritime of its progress; [. . .] it would have been financially beneficial also for Nuklid only to be a financial agent and receive money from Moss Maritime for our intellectual services, but it wouldn't have been beneficial for Russia. (Russian project participant and co-ordinator)

> [The Russians] view themselves as responsible for the project and us as donors; Nuklid thinks of itself as contractor, but they're not able to manage projects; the [Norwegian] Ministry of Foreign Affairs should support us here . . . , they should at least insist on professional project management; the Ministry of Foreign Affairs could avoid using Nuklid by arguing that experience from other projects is not too good, for instance in [Project 202]; [. . .] Norway displays naivety in relation to Nuklid, if the authorities suspect that not all money goes to the agreed measures, it's wrong to continue. (Norwegian project participant)

In contrast to project 212, Moss Maritime was given the opportunity to carry out the upgrading of storage tanks for liquefied radioactive waste at the Zvyozdochka shipyard in Severodvinsk (project 213) without the involvement of Nuklid. The project involved the upgrading of two existing tanks and the modernisation of piping systems and control equipment at the premises. The tank facility is located next to a planned effluent treatment facility for liquid radioactive waste and will primarily function in connection with the dismantling of nuclear submarines at the shipyard. The project was started in May

1998 and completed in August 1999. It is generally perceived of as one of the most successful under the Plan of Action. It involved intensive work for fourteen months and ended in the completion of the modernised tank facility. Moss Maritime used a Russian employee as project manager. He remained for most of the project period in Severodvinsk. In contrast to several other projects under the Plan of Action, this one was completed without delay. The total costs amounted to NOK 5.7 million less than budgeted. In explaining the success of the project, Moss Maritime stressed its freedom to select Russian subcontractors itself, i.e. non-interference by Nuklid. At an early stage in the project, it discovered that payments from the Norwegian side had been used by the shipyard for other purposes than agreed upon. The project leader warned the Zvyozdockha leadership that he would have to report this to the Norwegian Ministry of Foreign Affairs. The shipyard then decided to take up loans to pay for the agreed equipment. Another problem was to make workers at the shipyard actually work. A rather unconventional measure by the project management was to physically show up at the yard and promise to pay the workers a reward if they performed the work they were supposed to do anyway. The project manager circumvented the requirement (in line with the provisions of the Framework Agreement) that inputs to the project be tax and customs exempted, by simply buying materials in the Russian market at whatever price was offered. The director of Nuklid – who was initially appointed by the Russian side as 'leader of the project's working group' – took exception to the project's objective. She recognises that the project was successfully implemented, but disputes its rationale, arguing that it was 'basically unimportant, [. . .] far too expensive, and directed towards a completely irrelevant goal'. However, her position seems to be in direct contradiction to her own government's nuclear safety priorities as presented to the international community: that Russia requires additional capacity to collect and process liquid radioactive waste from the Northern Fleet, the Murmansk Shipping Company and the shipyards that are dismantling decommissioned submarines (Gubanov and Akhunov 1995; Semenov and Bonne 1999).

The bilateral co-operation at state level between Norway and Russia in areas covered by the Plan of Action has found its form, although some problems and difficulties remain. Co-operation between environmental and nuclear safety authorities functions to the satisfaction of both parties. The signing of the Framework

Agreement and establishment of the Joint Commission for its implementation in 1998 represent major achievements at the highest political level in the two countries. Current problems, such as the inclusion of new projects under the provisions of the Framework Agreement, are mainly to be found on the Russian side. However, where the Norwegians feel that their Russian counterparts are moving too slowly, some Russians miss a more profound understanding by the Norwegians of the difficulties on the Russian side. Regional actors in Northwestern Russia also complain that the Norwegian party relies too heavily on contacts with federal agencies in Moscow. Collaboration at project level between the two nations can generally be characterised as very good. In our interviews, no major differences in the perception of goals, processes and results were revealed – except in some of the projects where Nuklid was involved. The role of this co-ordinating body in nuclear safety projects is highly disputed in both Norway and Russia, which is even more explicitly reflected in the analysis of concrete projects. First, Norwegian project managers object to the lack of financial transparency seen when Nuklid stands for project management on the Russian side. Second, working relations between Norwegian and Russian project participants are reported to be far more problematic when Nuklid is involved than when it is not.

Conclusions

If we compare the above with fisheries management, the nuclear safety sector is far more complex both with regard to issues and actors involved. We noted in Chapter 4 that Northwest Russian fisheries during the 1990s were characterised by a fragmentation of management responsibility, degeneration in implementation performance and a reduction in target compliance. For both the fisheries and nuclear safety sectors, we assumed implementation capacity to be quite good during the Soviet period. Implementation performance and target compliance in the fisheries decreased during the 1990s mainly as a result of bureaucratic controversies as well as changes in the targets' incentive structure brought about by the end of the command economy. In the area of nuclear safety, most of the Russian obligations we have reviewed in this chapter came into being in the post-Soviet period, and several of the problems met in the fisheries sector were encountered here too. In particular, bureaucratic controversies – notably between the 'hard' and 'soft' regulatory agencies at the federal level – have clearly hampered implementation. Moreover, foreign assistance has come to dominate the implementation of Russia's international nuclear safety commitments during the post-Soviet period. Some of the most serious problems encountered in implementation efforts can be ascribed to unresolved issues between Russia and the Western donor states, relating, i.e., to indemnity against liability, access to nuclear sites, personnel immunity and tax exemptions. So while there is some progress in the implementation of Russia's international nuclear safety commitments at the present moment, it is slow and it is fumbling.

Notes

1 On the other hand, strategic submarines sometimes go to dismantlement well before the expiration of their service life.
2 The icebreaker fleet also includes conventionally powered ships.
3 However, even underground tests, both US and Soviet, have been known to cause radioactive fallout on the territory of other states (Stortinget 1994).
4 The Kola Nuclear Power Plant and submarines at refuelling are both classified as sources of known or probable risks – i.e. 'release is known to have occurred or [. . .] significant probability for release has been confidently estimated' (Bergman and Baklanov 1998, p. 55). Sources of *potential* risk are 'those expected to constitute a risk for considerable release provided the outcome of further analysis for certain steps in the event chain' (*ibid.*).
5 Nevertheless, the regional branch of the State Committee/Department for Environmental Protection (see section on implementation by federal authorities below) allegedly has the right to inspect some military objects; see the section below on the role of federal agencies in the region.
6 In 1966, there was a major discharge of radioactivity from the reactor section, and as the fuel assemblies in the reactors were to be replaced the same year, it was discovered that several of them had expanded due to overheating. Forty per cent of them were removed and transferred to the *Lepse*. In 1967, there was a major leakage in the cooling system of one of the vessel's reactors (Bergman and Baklanov 1998, p. 32).
7 The possibility of substituting electricity from Norway for the nuclear energy has been discussed, but it soon became clear that Norway could not provide the necessary amounts. Substituting various forms of alternative energy for nuclear power, or solving the problem by way of

energy-saving measures will take a long time, if at all feasible. In a long-term perspective, gas from the Shtokmanovskoye field in the Barents Sea may prove the most realistic option.

8 Other federal agencies engaged in the implementation of international nuclear safety agreements are the State Committee/Federal Service for Hydrometeorology and Environmental Control (see Chapter 6 for further information about this agency), the Russian Ship-Building Agency, the Ministry of Economy and the continuously changing agencies for defence industry. However, their role is of a more peripheral character compared to those federal agencies discussed in this section.

9 For example, it turned out at the second session of the joint Russian–Norwegian Commission for Nuclear Safety that the Russian delegation leader did not know that a joint Russian–Norwegian secretariat for the joint commission had been set up at the premises of Minatom. An employee of Nuklid was paid through a bilateral Russian–Norwegian project to run the secretariat. The director of Nuklid claimed that not having been informed of the secretariat was a case of 'simple fraud' (Hønneland and Moe 2000). She fired the employee, and the Russian part halted the project. The secretariat could not have been established without Minatom's knowledge and acceptance. By other Russian interviewees in the Norwegian evaluation of the bilateral nuclear safety co-operation, these events were referred to as 'another attempt at centralisation by [the director of Nuklid]' (2000, p. 26).

10 Later, the regional electoral commission declared the referendum plans illegal, and it was not carried out.

11 The BEAR co-operation has mainly served to relate environmental concern to broader foreign policy issues (Stokke 2000a). This regime has not contributed funds and engaged in practical nuclear safety projects to the same extent as CTR, AMEC and the Norwegian Plan of Action.

12 Environmental NGOs are generally few and weak in Murmansk Oblast. The most important NGO in nuclear safety issues in Northwestern Russia is the Norwegian organisation Bellona, which has an office in Murmansk. However, Bellona's role has been more important in agenda-setting than in implementation of Russia's international agreements.

13 The title of the Plan of Action does not specifically refer to Northwestern Russia, but to 'areas adjacent to our northern borders' (Ministry of Foreign Affairs 1995).

14 See Chapter 6 for details on this agency.

15 This section is based mainly on Sawhill and Jørgensen (2001). Underlying documentation is found in Shields and Potter (1997) and Safranchuk (2000a). See, in particular, Orlov (1997), Pikayev (1997) and Safranchuk (2000b).

16 This section provides a summary of the report's evaluation of project implementation; see the report for a detailed account (Hønneland and Moe 2000).

6
Air pollution control

Norilsk Nickel is one of Russia's leading producers of non-ferrous and platinum-group metals and the country's largest air polluter. Three of the company's six subsidiaries are located on the Kola Peninsula: the Pechenganickel Combine at Zapolyarnyy and Nikel,[1] the Severonickel Combine at Monchegorsk and the Olenegorsk Mechanical Plant at Olenegorsk. Pechenganickel and Severonickel emit large quantities of sulphur dioxide (SO_2) which causes considerable acid precipitation both on the Kola Peninsula and in the neighbouring Fenno-Scandinavian countries. This chapter reviews the problem of air pollution on the Kola Peninsula, the status of the area's mining and metallurgical complex – with an emphasis on the Norilsk Nickel combines – and the role of various actors in the implementation of Russia's international obligations related to air pollution control.[2] Implementation performance and target compliance are reviewed mainly with reference to the LRTAP regime (see Chapter 1). Given the peculiarities of this case compared to fisheries management and nuclear safety, the section on implementation performance and target compliance is presented before the discussion of various actors' implementation activities.[3]

Background: polluters and pollution on the Kola Peninsula

The mining and metallurgical complex

RAO[4] Norilsk Nikel was founded in 1994 by joining six companies under a corporate umbrella. It has four main operation facilities: a mining and metal-processing facility at Norilsk in northeastern Siberia (see Figure 6.1); a metal-processing facility at Monchegorsk;

mining and metal-processing facilities at Zapolyarnyy and Nikel; and a precious-metals processing plant at Krasnoyarsk in central Siberia. In addition, the company has a research institute (Gipronikel Planning and Design Institute) in St Petersburg and a mechanical plant at Olenegorsk on the Kola Peninsula. Norilsk Nikel is the world's leading producer of nickel and palladium, and the company's sales constitute approximately USD 3 billion annually (Bond and Levine 2001).

The Pechenganickel Combine operates four small mines and a smelter in the northern parts of the Kola Peninsula, close to the Norwegian border. Mineral production in the region dates back to the early 1940s, when it was a part of Finland. At the end of World War II, the Petsamo (Pechenga) district was annexed by the Soviet Union, and mining and smelting operations were resumed at Nikel in 1946. In the mid-1960s, the focus of mining activities was shifted to the Zhdanov deposit near Zapolyarnyy. Eighty-five per cent of the company's mine output comes from two open pits of this deposit, scheduled to be worked out by 2005–6. The remaining output comes from three underground mines, which are projected for depletion at various times during the period 2005–15 (Bond and Levine 2001).

The metallurgical operations of Pechenganickel take place at the company's plant at Nikel. The plant processes ore concentrates from the mines near Zapolyarnyy and raw materials shipped over the Northern Sea Route (see Figure 6.1) from Norilsk. These shipments started in the late 1968s when local ores began to decline. During the Soviet era, Norilsk Nickel shipped approximately one million tonnes of ore from Siberia to its Kola facilities every year (Kotov and Nikitina 1998b). The shift to a market economy has forced the company to reduce these shipments and rely more heavily on its deposits on the Kola Peninsula. Consequently, annual shipments have been more than halved since Soviet times (1998b).

Pechenganickel sends its smelter output to the Severonickel Combine at Monchegorsk in the central parts of the Kola Peninsula. The combine has both smelting and refining facilities for processing nickel and copper. Production started in 1939, and since the late 1960s the combine has relied on non-local feedstocks, e.g. ore from Pechenganickel and Norilsk. Today, Severonickel operates Russia's largest capacity nickel refinery (Bond and Levine 2001).

Norilsk Nickel was privatised in 1993, although 51 per cent of the voting shares were to remain in government hands for another three

Figure 6.1 *Location of the RAO Norilsk Nickel companies and shipment route from Norilsk to the Kola Peninsula*

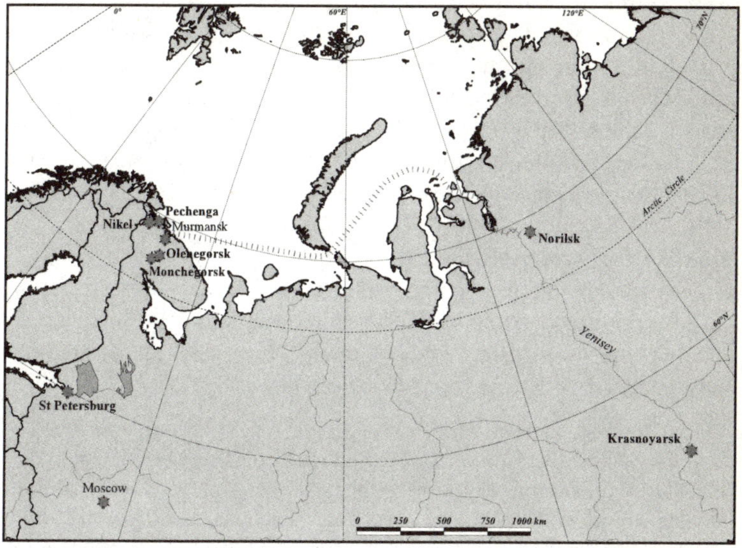

years. However, Kotov and Nikitina (1998b) argue that the government soon lost actual control over the company as a result of the general chaos of the period, and that the company's directors, largely free from shareholder control, consolidated their hold on the enterprise and restructured it to further their own interests:

> In the chaotic period following the company's privatization, neither the Russian government nor the other nominal owners of Norilsk Nickel were able to exercise effective control over the enterprise. Largely unaccountable to anyone, Norilsk's management (the so-called red directors) ran the company for personal profit rather than long-term viability. Naturally, they were not interested in making capital-intensive investments to benefit the environment. This situation highlights the crucial distinction between Norilsk's leadership and its owners. In the West, ownership implies that a company's managers are ultimately accountable to the company's owners, and thus will pay attention to promoting that company's long-term interests. Managers whose primary goal is to increase the value of their company will make the investments (including environmental investments) necessary to enhance its prospects. In Norilsk's situation, however, exactly the opposite occurred. (1998b, p. 565)

In recent years, Norilsk Nickel has increasingly oriented its productions towards exports, which now account for more than 50 per cent of the company's sales and nearly 85 per cent of all Russian exports of nickel (1998b). The company consolidated its economic position considerably during the 1990s. Like many other natural resource-producing companies in Russia, it got through the general economic crisis in the country fairly well. Since export taxes have become an important source of revenue for the Russian government, the authorities also have a vested economic interest in the company.

Pollution from the smelters

The Norilsk Nickel company towns have routinely ranked among the most polluted cities in Russia. Since the late 1980s, they have also become increasingly famous in the West as areas of environmental catastrophes. As Bond (1996) says:

> Anecdotal accounts are sufficient as an indication of the general magnitude of the problem [. . .]. On the Kola Peninsula, forests within a 20-km radius of the city of Monchegorsk were reported to be completely dead, with vegetation stress detectable as far as 60 km away in Apatity and across international borders in Finland [. . .]; at Nikel', nearly half the workforce was reported to be suffering from respiratory ailments [. . .], life expectancy is estimated at 42 years, and a 'black desert' spreading outward from the Pechenganickel smelter was wreaking sufficient havoc across international borders to compel Norwegian officials to undertake initiatives to reduce emissions at the Combine. (Bond 1996, p. 307)[5]

During the period from 1980 to 1987, the annual SO_2 emissions from Pechenganickel fell from 384,000 tonnes to 337,000 tonnes while emissions from Severonickel rose from 200,000 tonnes to 224,000 tonnes (Darst 2001). In 1994, Pechenganickel emitted 132,900 tonnes and Severonickel 111,000 tonnes of air pollutants (Kotov and Nikitina 1998b). In 2000, the corresponding figures were 160,860 tonnes and 57,397 tonnes (State Committee for Environmental Protection 2001).

The location of the Kola Peninsula smelters north of the Arctic Circle compounds the environmental problems as the Arctic ecosystems are more fragile and lack the assimilative capacity of those at lower latitudes. Hence, the activities of the Norilsk Nickel plants have led to wide-ranging environmental degradation and acidification. Close to the smelters, the forest is completely dead. According

Figure 6.2 *Approximate forest damage zones in the vicinity of Monchegorsk and Nikel and the visible-damage zones on the Kola Peninsula and in Finnish Lapland*

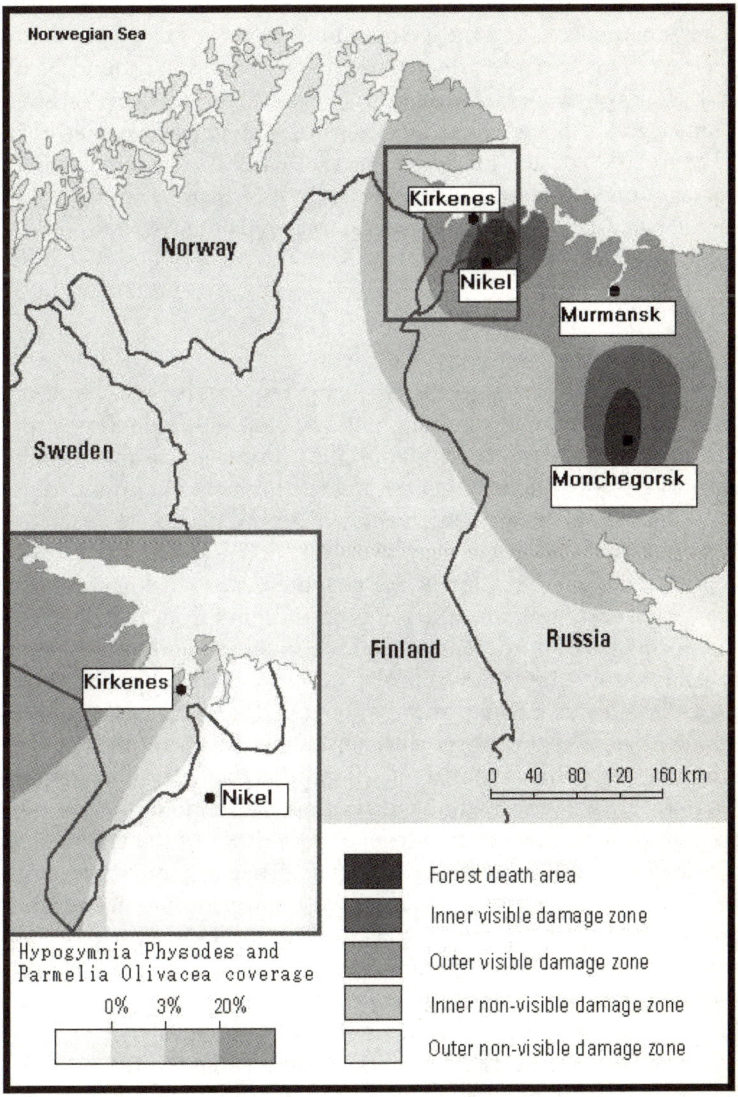

Source: AMAP (1998).

to the Arctic Monitoring and Assessment Programme's report on the state of the Arctic environment (AMAP 1997), the forest-death area around Monchegorsk covers 400–500 square kilometres and extends ten kilometres south and fifteen kilometres north of the smelter complex. The zone is expanding at a rate of half a kilometre per year. The area severely affected by air pollution around Nikel and Zapolyarnyy is considerably larger than the one around Monchegorsk. It increased in size from 400 square kilometres in 1973 to 5,000 square kilometres in 1988 (1997). The outer visible-damage zone extends into the eastern parts of Inari in Finland. Also on the Norwegian side of the border, trees and other vegetation have been damaged (see Figure 6.2).

Premises for implementation

Nature of the problem

The problem at hand seems in many respects to be a typically 'malign' one. First, the mining and metallurgical complex of the Kola Peninsula is of crucial importance financially to the regional authorities of Murmansk Oblast and is extremely important to the local authorities in the settlements where the plants are located – both as taxpayers and as employers. As noted above, the Norilsk Nickel companies weathered the economic crisis in Russia during the 1990s fairly well and extract good revenues from the export of their products. In turn, federal, regional and local authorities have a reliable source of income from the various taxes paid by the enterprises. Mainly as a result of the mining and metallurgical activities taking place on its territory, Murmansk Oblast is one of the few federal subjects in Russia that are net donors to the federal budget (see Chapter 3). Moreover, the main victims of the pollution are also those who have most to lose from a close-down of the enterprises. These factors will probably reduce their propensity to comply with international commitments that infringe on operations at the combines. Second, to the extent that the authorities are interested in manipulating enterprise operations to align them with the country's international obligations, public control over company operations has decreased drastically during the 1990s. As noted above, not only were the Norilsk Nickel companies privatised in the early 1990s, the influence of their nominal owners over their management was also far less than is normally the case in more developed market economies. Moreover, the Kola Peninsula combines are not only 'big' in a regional context; even more important is the fact that they form part of a company that is large and powerful enough to have influence at the highest political levels in the country. Norilsk Nickel is owned by one of the most powerful Russian oligarchs, Vladimir Potanin, who through his bank, Oneksimbank, acquired control over Norilsk Nickel in the mid-1990s.[6]

On the other hand, there are factors that reduce the impression of air pollution control on the Kola Peninsula as particularly malign compared to other environmental problems in the region. The polluters are concentrated within a few locations, and their activities are fairly easy to monitor. This seems particularly clear when we compare, for instance, the case of fisheries management, where the target group is made up of hundreds of individual fishing vessels constantly moving around a vast fishing area. Further, the results of bad implementation are in this case highly visible (in the form of lifeless forest),[7] and the problem at hand may also benefit from the fact that wealthy Western neighbours are affected by the polluting activity.

Nature of the commitments

The commitments of the LRTAP Convention and its protocols are both binding and relatively precise. Concrete reductions in annual emissions are set, and the contracting parties have obliged themselves to comply with these requirements. It can be argued that this makes implementation more difficult than is the case when agreements are vague and non-binding. The first concrete obligation, following from the first Sulphur Protocol (see Chapter 1), was to reduce the annual sulphur emissions or the transboundary fluxes by at least 30 per cent by 1993, using 1980 levels as the baseline. Since only a very small part of all sulphur emitted in the European part of the Soviet Union crossed the Union's western border, the Soviets chose – after having pressed for this to be an option – to reduce transboundary fluxes, not emissions.[8] Also, the signing of the LRTAP Convention and adoption of the first Sulphur Protocol coincided with several developments at the national level in the Soviet Union, which facilitated Soviet implementation of these international accords. Notably, Soviet energy policy was restructured towards the end of the 1970, implying a transition to natural gas, an increase in nuclear power production, the development of an energy complex in Siberia and a shift towards low-sulphur coals (Darst 2001; Kotov and Nikitina 1998a).

The second Sulphur Protocol incorporated a more integrated approach allowing wide variations in the reduction requirements made of different countries. For the first time, the concept of critical loads was used as a reference point to establish such requirements; critical loads are the pollution threshold above which sensitive ecosystems experience significant damage. The ceilings for emissions from the European part of Russia were set at 4.44 million tonnes in 2000 and 4.297 million tonnes in 2005. At the time the second Sulphur Protocol was signed, Russia was already in compliance with it; SO_2 emissions from European Russia constituted 2.98 million tonnes (Darst 2001). Hence, to the extent that implementation activities would be necessary, it would be in the form of measures to ensure that emissions did not increase beyond the targets set.

Other instruments at the regional or bilateral level – the AEPS/Arctic Council, BEAR and bilateral agreements with Finland and Norway – are of a programmatic and non-binding character, partly designed to facilitate implementation of the LRTAP commitments.

Implementation performance and target compliance

As indicated in the section on the nature of the problem above, there are factors both facilitating and hampering implementation of Russia's LRTAP commitments. However, in reviewing implementation performance and target compliance, all factors contributing to the malignity of the problem are offset by one simple fact: during the 1990s, the productivity of Russian industry decreased to such an extent that the country's LRTAP commitments were achieved without any particular effort. In addition comes the fact, already mentioned in the section on the nature of the problem above, that the signing of the LRTAP Convention and the first Sulphur Protocol coincided with several structural changes in the Soviet energy sector, which in sum reduced the emissions of SO_2. In accordance with the 30 per cent reduction target of the first Sulphur Protocol, SO_2 emissions from European Russia had by 1993 decreased by 51.7 per cent from their 1980 level (Kotov and Nikitina 1998a). Also as noted above, Russia was already in compliance with the second Sulphur Protocol when it was signed in 1994. Since then, SO_2 emissions from the Kola Peninsula smelters have been further reduced.

Public authorities' implementation activities

In Soviet times, implementation of the country's international environmental obligations was generally secured by including the commitments in the sector ministries' five-year production plans. There was no overarching governmental body responsible for the country's environmental policy. Moreover, regional authorities, in general politically impotent, had no influence on this sector of politics. All important decisions were made within the axis running from the sector ministries at the federal level to the enterprise leadership in the regions (which, in turn of course, were subordinate to decisions made by the CPSU). The main question to be asked in this section is how various federal and regional agencies have been involved in the LRTAP implementation of post-Soviet Russia, in particular related to the activities of the Kola Peninsula smelters.

Implementation in national legislation

Soviet participation in the LRTAP regime transferred the acid rain issue from general air-protection management to an independent element within Soviet environmental politics (Kotov and Nikitina 1998a). The first openly published Soviet national middle-term environmental programme, published in 1990, contained concrete requirements reflecting Soviet obligations under the first Sulphur Protocol and the NO_X Protocol (1998a). These have been repeated in several subsequent federal plans and programmes.

A new Soviet law on air pollution, prescribing a significant reduction in emissions and transboundary flows of the pollutants covered by the LRTAP regime, was adopted in 1982 (OECD 1999).[9] This law is still in effect, but after 1991 a gradual revision of Soviet environmental legislation has taken place. The single most important legal act is the 1991 law on environmental protection (Russian Soviet Federative Socialist Republic 1991). The law calls for a shift to economic instruments in environmental politics, such as charges for polluting emissions and the establishment of environmental funds independent of the federal budget. A separate federal provision on the system for environmental funds was adopted in 1992 (Government of the Russian Federation 1992). The federal environmental fund of the Russian Federation is an independent institution responsible to the government. The regional duma of Murmansk Oblast adopted a law on the regional environmental fund (already in existence) in 1997 (Murmansk Oblast 1997d), and according to regional environmental authorities this fund is the most important economic mechanism of environmental protection in the oblast (State Committee for Environmental Protection 2001). The income of the fund mainly comes from payments for emissions from the polluting enterprises and fines for violations of environmental regulations. Ten per cent of payments from the enterprises goes to the federal environmental fund, 30 per cent to the regional and 60 per cent to the local environmental fund of the municipality where the enterprise is located.

The role of federal authorities

Soviet implementation of the LRTAP regime commitments was co-ordinated by a governmental interdepartmental commission, headed by the State Committee for Hydrometeorology and Environmental Monitoring (Goskomgidromet) (Kotov and Nikitina 1998a).[10] The Commission had both a territorial form of representation – including representatives of the Soviet republics that contributed to westward transboundary pollution – and sector representation from various federal agencies. It issued orders to the industrial ministries responsible for polluting enterprises. The ministries in turn set standards for emission reductions for the enterprises, incorporating them into the national plans for economic and social development. Hence, the LRTAP standards were part of a more general mechanism of political and economic governance. For the most severe sources of transboundary pollution, among them the Kola Peninsula smelters, the Commission itself participated in setting the standards at the enterprise level (1998a).

As reviewed in Chapter 5, a State Committee for Environmental Protection was created in 1988, elevated three years later to the rank of Ministry of Environmental and Natural Resources Protection. The responsibility for co-ordinating LRTAP implementation was transferred from Goskomgidromet to the new State Committee once it was established.[11] Kotov and Nikitina (1998a) claim that the institutional framework for Soviet/Russian implementation of the LRTAP regime disintegrated as a result of this reform, arguing that the new environmental agency lacked the political authority and financial clout enjoyed by the interdepartmental Commission. This problem was compounded as the federal environmental agency gradually lost its formal status during the latter half of the 1990s, being deprived of its ministerial status in 1996 and disbanded altogether in 2000. The agency continues its activities as a Department for Environmental Protection under the Ministry of Natural Resources (see Chapter 5). The division of responsibility between the federal and regional level is further discussed in the next sub-section.

The role of regional authorities and federal agencies in the region

A general trait of the evolving Russian environmental legislation is that it foresees an increase in the role of regional authorities in environmental management. As we saw in Chapter 3, according to the 1993 Constitution this area of politics is the joint responsibility of the federal and regional level. The 1997 bilateral agreement on the sharing of responsibility between the Government of the Russian Federation and Murmansk Oblast (Murmansk Oblast 1997a, Article 2) states that the federal level is responsible for conducting a uniform state policy in the area of environmental protection (including the elaboration and implementation of national environmental plans), while the regional level is responsible for the actual regulatory measures, for instance issuing of permits to emit polluting substances (Article 4).

We saw in Chapters 4 and 5 that the Murmansk regional administration established departments for fisheries and nuclear safety within its own structure during the 1990s (in 1993 and 1999, respectively). Interestingly, the regional administration does not have its own department for environmental regulation. Rather, it seems as if the regional representation of the State Committee/Department for Environmental Protection (in the following referred to as the 'regional environmental committee') functions as an implementing agency not only for its superior federal office in Moscow, but also for the regional administration, in itself an interesting observation.[12] The regional administration determines environmental politics for the oblast by elaborating programmes, action plans and concrete regulations. The annual report of the Murmansk regional environmental committee (State Committee for Environmental Protection 2001) states that the regional environmental legislation is largely produced by the regional administration and only partly by the regional duma. Hence, although the Murmansk regional administration has established departments for fisheries management and nuclear safety, though not for environmental affairs, it seems more active in regulative measures in the latter case than in the two former (where such measures are almost exclusively designed by federal authorities). Moreover, the relations with the federal agencies in the region also seem to differ in the three cases. In the fisheries management, relations have at times been quite confrontational while the most important decisions have continued to be made at the federal level. In the field of nuclear safety, the regional authorities have aimed only at a co-ordinating role and not fundamentally contested the authority of federal agencies. In the case of air pollution control and environmental management more generally, there has indeed been a certain transfer of responsibility to the regional level. However, the regional administration has not found it necessary to establish a department for environmental protection within its own structure, but has continued the traditional close collaboration with the regional environmental committee, which formally speaking is a representation of federal authorities located in the region.

In addition to the elaboration of environmental programmes and regulatory standards, as well as the monitoring and enforcement activities performed by the regional environmental committee, the regional authorities are responsible for the regional environmental fund.[13] Table 6.1 demonstrates the income sources of the fund during the period 1995–2000. The major part of the fund's income comes from charges paid by enterprises for being allowed to continue pollution-creating operations. There was a dramatic increase in these payments in 1997, 1999 and 2000.

Table 6.1 *Income of the environmental fund of Murmansk Oblast during the period 1995–2000 (in 1,000 roubles)*

	1995	*1996*	*1997*	*1998*	*1999*	*2000*
Payments for pollution	4,868.0	3,641.7	16,068.6	10,504.0	23,005.7	44,567.4
Fines and confiscation	1,788.0	936.0	1,114.2	989.3	1,787.1	1,685.4
Interests from the fund	381.3	113.7	38.4	282.5	146.2	241.4
Other sources	1,892.9	1,074.9	974.3	432.5	2,294.2	1,530.3
Total	8,186.9[a]	5,766.3	18,195.5	12,208.3	27,233.2	48,024.5

[a] This is the total as given in the original source.
Source: State Committee for Environmental Protection (2001).

The money coming from enterprises as contributions for being allowed to conduct polluting operations or in the form of fines is first deposited into a special account controlled by the regional environmental committee. From there, 10 per cent is distributed to the federal environmental fund, 30 per cent to the regional environmental fund and 60 per cent to the local environmental funds of the oblast (Murmansk Oblast 1997d). The municipalities where the Kola Peninsula smelters are located, Monchegorsk and Pechenga Rayons, received 30.1 and 34.7 per cent, respectively, of this money in 2000 (State Committee for Environmental Protection 2001). Further, the regional fund in 2000 contributed financially to five environmental programmes at the regional level. One of them was aimed at the restoration of the environment around the Pechenganickel and Severonickel smelters. The programme was given 329,000 roubles from the fund in the period 1997–2000 (State Committee for Environmental Protection 2001).

Monitoring of air quality in the oblast is performed by another federal agency in the region, the regional branch of Rosgidromet (see note 10). The monitoring agency has seventeen control posts in nine of the municipalities of Murmansk Oblast. A significant problem in recent years has been the recurring destruction and looting of the control posts, reducing the ability to perform reliable measurements of the air quality.

The role of others

As the Soviet system for implementation of the country's international environmental obligations (led by the interdepartmental commission) dissolved, as the federal environmental agency gradually lost its authority, and as public authorities increasingly lost control of industrial enterprises, it can be argued that the enterprises themselves became the most important players in the Russian implementation game. There is little evidence that the managements of the Kola Peninsula smelters have been overly concerned with implementation activities related to the LRTAP regime. One obvious explanation, as already mentioned, is that the Russian commitments to this regime soon fulfilled themselves (see the section on implementation performance and target compliance above). Hence, there was no real need to engage in such activities. Moreover, the primary concern of the leadership of the smelters – apart from enriching themselves as quickly as possible, as noted by Kotov and Nikitina (1998b)[14] – has been to keep the enterprises profitable and sustain jobs in the mono-industrial towns of Monchegorsk, Zapolyarnyy and Nikel.

As noted by Darst (2001), Russian environmental NGOs had their heyday in the early 1990s. Along with the rising economic crisis of the country, the environmental concern of the Russian population has more or less vanished – at least in its organised form. Despite the grave environmental problems of Murmansk Oblast, environmental NGOs – apart from 'official' public organisations like children's 'green clubs' – are practically absent. To the extent that environmental NGOs have had any influence on air pollution control in Northwestern Russia, it has been in the form of Nordic NGOs (cf. the slogan 'stop the death clouds!' referred to in Chapter 1) pressing their own governments to contribute to the financing of purification equipment at the Kola Peninsula smelters.

Joint implementation

Foreign participation in the modernisation of the Kola Peninsula smelters first became an issue in the mid-1980s.[15] The immediate background was the economic co-operation between the Soviet Union and Finland that had taken place on a clearing–trade basis since the late 1940s. Metallurgy was one of the focused areas of Soviet–Finnish economic co-operation, and the Soviet delegation to the Soviet–Finnish Economic Commission in 1985 proposed that Finland take part in a modernisation project at the Kola Peninsula smelters. A Finnish engineering firm proposed completely refitting the Pechenganickel, permitting the recovery of over 95 per cent of the sulphur contained in the ore. In the end, nothing came of the project since the participants were unable to attract the estimated USD 600 million necessary for its completion. In 1993, a Norwegian-led consortium won an international competition for tenders to modernise the Pechanganickel plant organised by the Russian government. The costs were this time estimated at substantially less, approximately USD 257 million. Norway had already offered to contribute NOK 300 million (at the time some USD 50 million); Sweden and Finland also promised to contribute, although much less than Norway. When President Yeltsin visited Oslo in 1996, he finally declared that the Russian party was ready to contribute the remaining sum necessary to get the project off the ground. However, the project was temporarily halted by the final takeover of Norilsk

Nickel by Oneksimbank in 1997. The new leadership was more sensitive to the costs and benefits of various investment projects and less interested in subsidising the Pechanganickel smelter. The latter performed poorly compared to the combines at Monchegorsk and Norilsk, and there was insecurity as to its further viability due to the exhaustion of the local ore and the increasing costs of shipping ore from Norilsk. Hence, the new owners chose to concentrate on exploring the further resource basis of the plant rather than on modernising its nickel smelting facilities. Contrary to expectations, the project was suddenly revived in early 2001, and on 19 June that year the Norwegian Minister of the Environment and the Russian Minister of Economy signed an agreement on a modernisation project that would involve a 90 per cent reduction in emissions of SO_2 and heavy metals (Ministry of the Environment 2001). Norway promised to contribute NOK 270 million (approximately USD 30 million). The project, including a testing period of two years, is scheduled to be finalised in 2006–7.

Conclusions

The case of Russia and the LRTAP regime is clearly one of 'compliance without implementation'. The Russian commitments 'implemented themselves', rendering 'implementation activities' on the part of public authorities, target groups and others superfluous. Kotov and Nikitina (1998a) argue that the LRTAP regime contributed to certain behavioural changes domestically in the Soviet Union, mainly in the areas of planning, research and monitoring, but had little effect on actual emissions. It is also an open question whether Russian authorities during the 1990s would have been capable and willing to actively contribute to the implementation of the country's commitments under the LRTAP regime had emissions not been reduced to acceptable (according to the commitments) levels due to exogenous factors. First, the federal environmental agency was seriously weakened during the 1990s, culminating in its total dissolution and the subordination of its remnants under the Ministry of Natural Resources – a typical 'user agency' – in 2000. Second, the regional administration of Murmansk Oblast – although having significantly increased its political authority since Soviet times – would be expected to prioritise further industrial activity in the mono-industrial towns of the oblast (contributing both employment and considerable revenues for the regional budget) over environmental issues. Third, the capacity of public authorities to influence decisions in private enterprises was significantly reduced during the 1990s. Finally – and partly related to the latter circumstance – it is doubtful whether the authorities' compliance mechanisms (here: fines) are compelling enough to induce compliance among the nickel plants on the Kola Peninsula. In sum, Russia can show a high degree of formal compliance with its LRTAP commitments in the 1990s, but a correspondingly poor implementation record in the same period.

Notes

1 The *urban-type settlements* of Nikel and Zapolyarnyy are the largest settlements of Pechenga Rayon (district); see Chapter 3. There is also an *urban-type settlement* named Pechenga belonging to the rayon with the same name; this is considerably smaller than Nikel and Zapolyarnyy. For the sake of simplicity, the two latter are in this chapter referred to as towns.

2 This chapter is to a lesser extent than the two preceding chapters built on primary research by the authors. The material on the Norilsk Nickel combines derives mainly from Bond (1996) and Bond and Levine (2001); the presentation of air pollution on the Kola Peninsula builds on AMAP (1997, 1998); while data on implementation performance and target compliance are mainly from Darst (2001) and Kotov and Nikitina (1998a, 1998b).

3 As follows from this chapter, Russia's LRTAP commitments have 'implemented themselves', i.e. there has been no need for conscious efforts to achieve compliance in this case. In fisheries management and nuclear safety, compliance has been more imperfect, which warrants first a description of the various actors' efforts to reach compliance, then an assessment of actual implementation performance and target compliance.

4 *Rossiyskoye aktsionernoye obshchestvo* (Russian stock holding company).

5 We were recently reminded of how shocking it often is for people from the West to arrive in these areas: Passing Monchegorsk in a car on our way from Apatity to Murmansk, our Norwegian co-passenger noted: 'When I first came to this area in the late 1980s, I was simply unable to absorb the extent of environmental degradation. The only thing I could think of was that this was probably what it would look like after a nuclear war.'

6 See Freeland (2000) for an account of Potanin's takeover of Norilsk Nickel.

7 Compare again with the fisheries sector: poor fisheries management may lead to the depletion of stocks, but it is far more difficult to state beyond reasonable doubt that this has taken place than it is to demonstrate that forests are dead. If catches are not good, it could be argued that fishing gear or techniques are unsatisfactory, or that the migration patterns of the particular stocks have changed.

8 Since only the European part of the Soviet Union was covered by the LRTAP regime, some heavily polluting industries were moved eastwards, thus increasing air pollution in Siberia.

9 According to Kotov and Nikitina (1998a), this law came into force in 1980.

10 The Soviet State Hydrometeorological Service (Gidromet) was given the status of state committee and renamed the State Committee for Hydrometeorology and Environmental Monitoring (Goskomgidromet) in 1978, being elevated from a lowly meteorological service to the most prominent environmental protection agency of the Soviet Union (Darst 2001). Today, the institution has the status of a 'federal service' and is usually referred to by the acronym Rosgidromet. As follows from the discussion in both this chapter and Chapter 5, this agency is no longer among the most important bodies of governance in Russian environmental and nuclear safety management.

11 Goskomgidromet remained responsible for the monitoring of air pollution, but all other main functions related to air-quality control were transferred to the State Committee for Environmental Protection.

12 In an interview with a representative of one of the leading environmental NGOs in Murmansk Oblast, it turned out that our interviewee did not know that the regional environmental committee was formally subordinate to the State Committee/Department for Environmental Protection and not to the regional administration. This reflects how well integrated the regional environmental committee is in the overarching structure of regional politics despite its federal subordination.

13 Members of the fund's board are nominated by the Governor and confirmed by the regional duma. A Deputy Governor, the leader of the regional environmental committee and the Deputy Chairman of the regional duma have permanent seats on the board of the regional environmental fund (Murmansk Oblast 1997d, Article 8, sections 4–5).

14 Admittedly, the authors apply this formulation in speaking of enterprise leaderships in the post-Soviet 'market economy' in general. However, they also refer to how the managements of the Kola Peninsula smelters – at least up to the takeover of Oneksimbank in 1995–97 – were not responsive to the company's owners and mainly concerned with short-term profit. Towards the end of the 1990s, the situation changed somewhat and the managements of the Kola smelters tried to undertake

some measures towards air pollution control, partly to improve their environmental image as the smelters were turning into international companies (Elena Nikitina, pers. comm., December 2001).

15 This section builds mainly on Darst (2001). It is an open question whether Nordic attempts to modernise the Pechanganickel smelter should be labelled 'joint implementation' since the efforts are not directly aimed at the implementation of specific international commitments but rather geared at environmental protection in general; cf. comments on the use of the concept 'joint implementation' in Chapter 2.

7
Conclusions

We started this book by asking how Russian authorities have gone about implementing their international environmental commitments, noting that we were more interested in the political processes initiated with a view to achieving such implementation than in meticulously mapping the exact level of actual compliance in the various cases. This chapter sums up the major findings of our three case studies. Our primary focus is on the 'implementation activities' carried out in each case: what has been done to implement the various commitments, and how can the success or failure in each individual case best be explained? As a point of departure for this discussion, we set out some of our main conclusions from the case studies on implementation performance and target compliance. Rounding up the chapter, we attempt to extract some lessons of a more general nature from our study.

Implementation performance and target compliance

In Chapter 4, we observed that Northwest Russian fisheries during the 1990s could be described in terms of three main features, the one partly issuing from the other: the diffusion of management responsibility, the degeneration of implementation performance and the reduction in target compliance. However, the indication of reduced performance implies, of course, that Russian authorities had previously scored better on implementation performance and target compliance. Indeed, the Soviet Union had a system for fisheries research, regulation and enforcement – not to mention the production plans of the command economy – which enabled the country to manage fisheries in its exclusive economic zone in accordance with the principle of maximum sustainable yields, to establish total allowable catches for each fish stock within the exclusive economic zone, to co-operate with other coastal states in the management of shared stocks, and to promote compliance with fishery regulations among all vessels under Soviet flag.[1] The extent to which the existence of this regulatory system reflects the determined implementation of international obligations is disputable; probably, the national system for fisheries management developed in parallel with Soviet adjustment to the country's international fisheries obligations. Target compliance decreased during the 1990s, mainly as a result of changes in the targets' incentive structure brought about by the end of the command economy; suddenly, it became profitable for Russian fishers to cheat. At the same time, bureaucratic controversies (see next section) seriously reduced the management system's ability to monitor and enforce regulations.

In comparison with fisheries management, the nuclear safety sector is more complex both with regard to issues to be covered and actors involved. Most of the Russian nuclear safety obligations reviewed in Chapter 5 date from the post-Soviet period and several of the same problems have been encountered in their implementation as with the fisheries obligations. In particular, bureaucratic controversies – notably between the 'hard' and 'soft' regulatory agencies at the federal level – have clearly hampered implementation. Moreover, foreign assistance has come to dominate the implementation game of Russia's international nuclear safety commitments during the post-Soviet period. Some of the most serious problems encountered in the implementation can be ascribed to the interface between Russia and the Western donor states, i.e. problems related to indemnity against liability, access to nuclear sites, personnel immunity and tax exemptions. We can conclude therefore that while there is at the moment some progress in the implementation of Russia's international nuclear safety commitments, it is slow and fumbling.

As follows from Chapter 6, the productivity of Russian industry decreased to such an extent during the 1990s that the country's LRTAP commitments were achieved without any evident effort. In accordance with the 30 per cent reduction target of the first Sulphur Protocol, SO_2 emissions from European Russia had by 1993 decreased by more than 50 per cent from their 1980 level. Moreover, Russia was already in compliance with the second Sulphur Protocol when it was signed in 1994 and SO_2 emissions from the Kola Peninsula smelters have continued to fall since then.

Implementation activities

More interesting than the extent to which Russian environmental obligations have been complied with or not concerns the steps Russian authorities have taken in order to induce such compliance by target groups. A brief summary is given in the following of implementation activities taking place in fisheries management, nuclear safety and air pollution control.

Fisheries management

The implementation of the international fisheries obligations of the Soviet Union was the responsibility of the Soviet Ministry of Fisheries. In connection with the dissolution of the Soviet Union and establishment of the Russian Federation, the federal fisheries agency had its status reduced to that of a state committee. During the 1990s, the State Committee for Fisheries repeatedly had to fight off 'intrusions' from other federal bodies of governance. These attempts were only partly successful. On the one hand, the Committee succeeded in sustaining its status as an independent administrative body (except for the period 1997–98, when it was placed under the Ministry of Agriculture and Foodstuffs). On the other hand, it was compelled to relinquish responsibility for enforcement at sea to the Federal Border Service and to accept the introduction of a system of quota sales proposed by the Ministry of Economy. The federal agencies are only partly involved in implementation activities aimed directly at target groups; these are predominantly carried out by federal agencies in the region in co-operation with regional authorities. The most important federal agencies in the region are the enforcement body Murmanrybvod, the remnants of the former 'industry complex' of Sevryba and the newly established (1998) Murmansk State Inspection of the Arctic Regional Command of the Federal Border Service. While Sevryba has lost most of the powers it enjoyed in Soviet times as the 'extended arm' of the Ministry of Fisheries, it has not lost its role in the regulatory process altogether. Until recently, its general director led the Technical-Scientific Catch Council, which distributes quota shares among the federal subjects of the northern fishery basin. Also, Sevryba has retained some management tasks related to the practical regulation of fishing activities.

More than anything, important decisions related to the management of Northwest Russian fisheries seem to be made by a somewhat diffuse corporate leadership of the area's 'fishery complex', consisting of representatives of regional authorities, the various federal authorities located in the region, research institutes and target groups.[2] Such a constellation is visible in the bodies responsible for quota allocation at the intra-regional and regional levels, for instance the Technical-Scientific Catch Council and the regional fishery councils. The main reason for the drop in target compliance in Northwest Russian fisheries in recent years – apart from the change in the fishers' incentive structure – seems to be the negative consequences of the transfer of responsibility for enforcement at sea from Murmanrybvod to the Border Service. The latter so far has a poor record of presence at sea; for several months on end, not a single enforcement vessel was present in the Russian zone of the Barents Sea. This, it is believed, allowed a massive subsequent catch of undersized fish to take place. However, despite this flaw in enforcement – admittedly a necessary link in the implementation chain – there is nevertheless a system in place that takes care of the new and specific obligations continuously emanating from various international agreements and co-operative regimes, mainly the bilateral Russian–Norwegian regime and NEAFC. In other words, there is a 'capacity to govern' in the Russian system for fisheries management although reorganisations forced upon the existing system from the outside have reduced this capacity.

Nuclear safety

In the nuclear safety sector, the Ministry of Atomic Energy (Minatom) is the organisational heavyweight, responsible for the implementation of most of Russia's international agreements in the field. To some extent, Minatom delegates the implementation of concrete projects to the so-called Interbranch Co-ordination Centre Nuklid, which forms part of the 'Minatom system'. In the military environmental collaboration under AMEC, the Ministry of Defence is the responsible partner on the Russian side. The Federal Inspectorate for Nuclear and Radiation Safety (Gosatomnadzor) was established in 1991 to control and license activities related to the application of nuclear energy. This agency has also had an important role in the implementation of Russia's international nuclear safety obligations. There is a limited measure of horizontal integration between the various federal agencies involved in the implementation process. There is also a rather high degree of tension between the 'hard' agencies of Minatom and Nuklid on the one hand and Gosatomnadzor on the other. The two former have gradually expanded their sphere of influence at the expense of the latter.

Murmansk regional authorities have created a department for nuclear safety within their structure, but have seen its role as mainly to co-ordinate the various regional, national and, above all, international attempts at ensuring nuclear safety in the oblast. It has also had a certain 'negative' sway, halting projects planned by the federal authorities. The federal agencies located in the region are of less importance in the nuclear safety area than in fisheries management. Implementation failure or delay has mainly been caused by bureaucratic controversies at the federal level – primarily between Minatom/Nuklid and Gosatomnadzor – or by inadequacies in inter-state agreements with foreign donors. As was the case in the fisheries management, Russia does have the 'capacity to govern' also in the sphere of nuclear safety, but new patterns of joint implementation with other states have created new challenges that have yet to be overcome.

Air pollution control

Soviet implementation of the country's international obligations related to air pollution control was ensured by an interdepartmental commission charged with overseeing such implementation as well as the incorporation of the requirements of the obligations in national industrial production plans. The interdepartmental commission was led by the State Committee for Hydrometeorology and Environmental Monitoring (Goskomgidromet) (presently the Federal Service of Hydrometeorology and Environmental Monitoring, or Rosgidromet). A State Committee for Environmental Protection was created in 1988 and elevated to ministerial status three years later. The responsibility for co-ordinating Soviet implementation of international air pollution control requirements was transferred from Goskomgidromet to the new State Committee once it was established. The old implementation system disintegrated through this reform because the new governmental structure was not given the political authority and financial muscle that the interdepartmental commission had previously enjoyed. The Ministry of

Environmental Protection came under increasing pressure from other federal authorities in the mid-1990s. In 1996, its status was again reduced to that of a state committee and in 2000 it was disbanded altogether and its remnants incorporated into the Ministry of Natural Resources.

Unlike the cases of fisheries management and nuclear safety, the Murmansk regional administration has not established a department for environmental protection within its structure. Rather, the regional representation of the Department for Environmental Protection (under the Ministry of Natural Resources) functions as an implementing agency not only for its federal head office in Moscow, but also for the regional administration. The regional administration determines environmental policies for the oblast by elaborating programmes, action plans and concrete regulations. Hence, although the Murmansk regional administration has established departments for fisheries management and nuclear safety, though not for environmental affairs, it is more active in regulative measures in the latter area than in the two former (where such measures are almost exclusively set out by federal authorities). Relations with the federal agencies in the region also differ in the three cases. In the fisheries management, relations have at times been quite confrontational while the most important decisions have continued to be made at the federal level. In the field of nuclear safety, the regional authorities have aimed only at a co-ordinative role, preferring not to contest seriously the authority of federal agencies. In the area of air pollution control and environmental management more generally, there has indeed been a certain devolution of powers to the regional level. However, the regional administration has not found it necessary to establish a department for environmental protection, but has continued its traditionally close co-operation with the regional environmental committee, which represents the federal authorities in the region.

As the Soviet system for implementation of the country's international environmental obligations (led by the interdepartmental commission) disintegrated, as the federal environmental agency gradually lost its authority, and as public authorities increasingly lost control of industry enterprises, the enterprises themselves became more important actors in the Russian implementation game. There is little evidence that the managements of the Kola Peninsula smelters have been overly concerned with implementation of air pollution regimes. Hence, the case of Russia and the LRTAP regime is clearly one of 'compliance without implementation'. The Russian commitments 'implemented themselves', rendering 'implementation activities' on the part of public authorities, target groups and others superfluous. The LRTAP regime contributed to certain behavioural changes domestically in the Soviet Union, mainly in planning, research and monitoring activities, but had little effect on actual emissions. It is also an open question to what extent Russian authorities during the 1990s would have been either capable or willing to actively contribute to the implementation of the country's commitments under the LRTAP regime had emissions not been reduced to acceptable (according to the commitments) levels by exogenous factors. First, the federal environmental agency was seriously weakened during the 1990s, culminating in its total dissolution and the incorporation of its remnants under the Ministry of Natural Resources – a typical 'user agency' – in 2000. Second, the regional administration of Murmansk Oblast – although having significantly increased its political authority since Soviet times – would be expected to prioritise further industrial activity in the mono-industrial towns of the oblast (contributing both employment and considerable revenues for the regional budget) over environmental issues. Third, public authorities' chance to influence the workings of private enterprises declined significantly during the 1990s. Finally – and partly related to the latter circumstance – it is doubtful whether the authorities' compliance mechanisms (here: fines) are compelling enough to induce compliance among the nickel plants on the Kola Peninsula. In sum, while Russia can show a high degree of formal compliance with its LRTAP commitments in the 1990s, its record of implementation efforts during the same period is correspondingly poor.

Table 7.1 gives an overview of the most important actors in the Russian implementation of international commitments in fisheries management, nuclear safety and air pollution control. The relative strength of the agencies at the various levels is discussed in the next section.

Lessons

In Chapter 1, we set out the book's dual aim: to contribute to the literature on Russian politics, in particular by providing specifics on centre–region relations, and to make our findings relevant to the literature on the implementation of international environmental

Table 7.1 *Most important actors in the Russian implementation of international commitments in fisheries management, nuclear safety and air pollution control*[a]

	Fisheries management	*Nuclear safety*	*Air pollution control*
Federal authorities	State Committee for Fisheries Federal Border Service	Minatom Nuklid Ministry of Defence Gosatomnadzor Rosgidromet	Department for Environmental Protection (Ministry of Natural Resources) Rosgidromet
Regional authorities	Fisheries departments at the regional administrations	Nuclear safety department at the Murmansk regional administration	Regional administrations (no specific departments for environmental protection)
Federal agencies in the region	Murmanrybvod Murmansk State Inspection of the Arctic Regional Command of the Federal Border Service (Sevryba)	Minatom Gosatomnadzor Rosgidromet	Department for Environmental Protection (Ministry of Natural Resources) ('regional environmental committees') Rosgidromet
Target groups	Individual fishing companies	Northern Fleet Murmansk Shipping Company Kola Nuclear Power Plant	Pechenganickel Severonickel

[a] The table is not meant to be exhaustive. It includes those agencies and enterprises that are given most attention in the book's case studies.

agreements in general, and of implementation in the Russian Federation in particular. What lessons of a more general nature can be drawn from our case studies? In the following, we discuss this question first with reference to the overarching political cleavages in Russian politics outlined in Chapter 3, and then to other studies of the implementation of international environmental agreements, as summarised in Chapter 2.

Political cleavages in Russian politics

We concluded Chapter 3 with a set of questions related to the general direction of Russian regional politics: has there been any devolution of power from federal to regional authorities in fisheries management, nuclear safety and air pollution control? Are regional authorities and federal agencies in the region more concerned with rivalries or with working with each other? What is the level of conflict between the regional administration and the regional duma? Are the old 'industry complexes' still significant actors in Russian politics? And the key question related to federal politics in Russia: what is the level of conflict between the various federal agencies?

To address the latter question first, the level of conflict between various federal agencies proved very high in all three case studies. The 'sector' or protection-minded agencies of the State Committee for Fisheries, Gosatomnadzor and the former State Committee for Environmental Protection have all been involved in fierce battles with other federal agencies – 'power agencies', such as the Federal Border Service, and 'user agencies', such as Minatom and the Ministry of Natural Resources – and have seen their sphere of influence reduced. Second, while federal authorities are formally in charge of fisheries management, nuclear safety and air pollution control, there are signs of varying degrees of power delegation in the three cases, ranging from a very limited degree of delegation in nuclear safety issues to quite a considerable delegation of authority in questions of air pollution control. The case of fisheries management lies somewhere in between. Formal powers are limited, but the bulk of implementation activities are performed by regional authorities or federal agencies in the region. Third, the two latter authority levels tend to side with each other rather than engaging in rivalries. In the fisheries management, there were evident signs of rivalry in the early and mid-1990s, but the tendency in recent years has been towards coordination of efforts. In nuclear safety issues, regional authorities have more or less explicitly taken upon themselves a co-ordinating role, avoiding confrontations with federal authorities and federal agencies in the region. In air pollution control, the 'regional environmental committee' in practice functions as an implementing agency both for its head office in Moscow and for the regional administration. Fourth, there is little conflict between the regional administration and the regional duma in questions of fisheries management, nuclear safety and air pollution control. The latter has adopted regional laws on coastal fisheries, the radiation safety of the population and a regional environmental fund, legal measures that support rather than contest the positions taken by the regional administration. Notably, they also avoid contesting the authority of federal agencies, supporting the argument that Northwest Russian federal subjects have generally sought an accommodating, rather than a confrontational stance in relation to federal authorities. Finally, the old notion of 'industry complexes' as important actors in Russian politics is still relevant, but the form and role of these complexes have changed since the Soviet era. The 'fishery complex' of Northwestern Russia is still a highly relevant category, but it is no longer represented by the Sevryba association. Rather, the individual shipowners have increased their political influence at the expense of Sevryba. Likewise, the Kola Peninsula nickel smelters still enjoy considerable political influence, not as parts of the old administrative chain, but of a large industrial conglomerate owned by one of Russia's most powerful oligarchs. Hence, in both fisheries and pollution affairs the target groups still enjoy considerable political influence, but public agencies have lost most of their previous authority to govern them. In the nuclear field, the situation is more reminiscent of Soviet days, with the Northern Fleet and the Kola Nuclear Power Plant still state-owned. The political cleavages related to fisheries management, nuclear safety, and air pollution control are summed up in Table 7.2.

If we compare these findings with other studies of Russian politics, our first conclusion supports the general impression of a lack of horizontal integration and a high level of conflict within the Russian bureaucracy. Also as expected, the delegation of power from the federal to the regional level is greater in air pollution control than in the more sensitive area of nuclear safety. The extent of delegation is perhaps a bit more unexpected in the case of fisheries management – at least to the extent that we include federal agencies in the region in

Table 7.2 *Political cleavages related to fisheries management, nuclear safety and air pollution control*[a]

	Fisheries management	*Nuclear safety*	*Air pollution control*
Level of conflict between various federal agencies	High level of conflict	High level of conflict	High level of conflict
Delegation of power from the federal to the regional level	Federal authorities in charge, but considerable delegation to regional level and federal agencies in the region	Federal authorities in charge, limited delegation	Federal authorities in charge, but considerable delegation to regional level and federal agencies in the region
Regional authorities and federal agencies in the region siding or rivalling	Tendencies at rivalling, but mainly siding	Mainly siding	Siding
Level of conflict between the regional administration and the regional duma	Little conflict	Little conflict	Little conflict
Old 'industry complexes' still significant political actors	Not in its previous form, but increasing influence of individual shipowners	Old 'industry complexes' still important	Significant political actors

[a] The table is not intended to reflect measurement in any form. It is merely an attempt at visualisation of some of the main conclusions of the study.

the catchall phrase of a regional 'fisheries complex' (which there is good reason to do regarding the fisheries). Bearing in mind that federal authorities have exclusive jurisdiction over natural resources in the 200-mile economic zone (i.e. outside Russia's territorial waters), the influence of regional authorities in, for example, quota allocation in the economic zone is indeed greater than one would anticipate. Somewhat unexpected is also the apparent harmony between regional authorities and federal agencies located in the region, although this could be said to confirm the generally observed tendency of the latter to 'go native', i.e. side with regional authorities rather than their own leadership at the federal level. Furthermore, the level of conflict between the regional administration and the regional duma is also very low, which probably adds to the picture of the latter as relatively impotent political bodies in post-Soviet Russia.

Implementing international environmental agreements

How have these political processes affected implementation? We observed in Chapter 2 that an important lesson drawn from previous studies is that implementation failure is often unintentional, the result of difficulties encountered during the implementation process rather than a conscious choice by the state not to implement the commitment in question. We also noted that this is expected to be particularly true for post-Communist states, which, since the early 1990s, have seen a devolution of power, weakened fiscal strength and control over target groups, a slow legislative process, a tendency for sanctions to be ineffective and have only a short history of independent enforcement agencies. In the following, we systematically review our conclusions in relation to our initial hypotheses about how the nature of the problem, the nature of the international commitments, implementation in national legislation, implementation activities performed by public authorities and others have affected implementation in our cases.

Nature of the problem The problem areas within our three case studies can, on the one hand, all be characterised as relatively 'malign' in an implementation perspective: the fishery, nuclear and mining and metallurgical complexes are cornerstone activities in the Northwest Russian economy. In the hard economic climate of post-Soviet Russia, one would expect authorities to prioritise employment and tax revenues on the basis of continued resource extraction (as in the case of fisheries), risk behaviour (as in the nuclear complex) and polluting activities (from the mining and metallurgical combines) over environmental and natural resource protection. This would clearly be assumed to reduce the potential for successful implementation of international commitments that restrict industrial activities or resource extraction. Further, public control over target groups has declined since the major enterprises in at least the fisheries and air polluting sectors have been privatised. On the other hand, the chances for monitoring target activity range from 'relatively good' in fisheries management to 'very good' in nuclear safety and air pollution control. The targets of the two latter are mostly stationary; and while fishing vessels, nuclear icebreakers and submarines and surface vessels of the Northern Fleet admittedly move over a considerable ocean area, they are at least easier to control than a million cars. Moreover, the targets are themselves largely the main 'losers' if implementation fails – at least in the long-term perspective. Adding to the relative 'benignity' of the problem is the keen Western interest in solving the problems under scrutiny here.

Clearly, the role of fisheries, nuclear power and industry production companies as cornerstone enterprises in the region has influenced the propensity of public authorities to give priority to environmental and natural resource protection concerns. In the fisheries sector, this has been most obvious in the Russian positions *vis-à-vis* various international negotiations. For instance, the Joint Russian–Norwegian Fisheries Commission from the late 1990s established cod quotas far above the scientific recommendations of ICES, mainly as a result of Russian pressure within the Commission. However, there has been a determined effort to implement international obligations once they are established.[3] Likewise, while authorities would probably have been reluctant to accept or implement international obligations that seriously impeded further industrial activity in the mono-industrial towns of the Kola Peninsula, it is hard to argue that this factor accounts for the problems found in the implementation of Russia's international nuclear safety and air pollution control commitments in the northwestern region of the country. However, the loss of control over fishing and air polluting companies as a result of the privatisation of these enterprises seems to have hampered implementation, at least in the cases of fisheries management and air pollution control. Finally, the relatively good opportunities to monitor target group behaviour have improved the prospects of successful implementation, but cannot by themselves serve as a main explanation for the achieved implementation. In sum, factors related to the nature of the problems at hand can partly account for implementation performance, but hardly constitute any decisive element in this context.

Nature of the commitments The hypothesis on the varying influence of commitments on implementation performance is that agreements that are binding upon the signatories, contain precise obligations for the parties, and require a large degree of adjustment in the behaviour of target groups are more difficult to implement than accords that are non-binding, vague and demand only minor or no efforts on the part of target groups. Of our case studies, air pollution control is the one in which the nature of the commitments can obviously explain much of the actual implementation efforts taking place, or more correctly, not taking place. As a result of reduced industrial activity, the commitments more or less fulfilled themselves. In nuclear safety, the situation is the opposite: the international accords are so demanding upon the Russian party – requiring restructuring of certain elements of the Northwest Russian nuclear power complex to a so far unforeseen extent – that it can largely explain much of the trouble encountered in the implementation process. In both cases, the nature of the commitments proves an important explanatory factor in accounting for implementation success or failure. This is not the case in fisheries management. The commitments following from the bilateral Russian–Norwegian regime, reflecting the parties' commitments in accordance with regional and global agreements, are binding, precise and generally require not insignificant changes on the part of target groups . But even this does not account for implementation failure observable in the Barents Sea fisheries.

Implementation in national legislation Is the implementation of international commitments in national legislation (implementation at the national normative level; see Chapter 2) a prerequisite for their further successful *de facto* implementation (implementation at the national level in actual practice)? The elaboration of a national, and, to some extent, also regional legislation at the level of law has been quite successful in the areas of nuclear safety and air pollution control. Russia does not yet have a law on fisheries although the

Federal Parliament has been working on such a law since the early 1990s. Hence, the incorporation of international commitments in national legislation at the level of law does not seem to be a prerequisite for successful implementation of Russia's international fisheries agreements.[4] There is little reason to assume that the situation related to air pollution control would be much different had a law on environmental protection not been adopted in the early 1990s, i.e. that Russian authorities would have been able to pursue more or less the same air pollution policy as today in the absence of this law. It should also be observed that the existing law on air pollution is from the Soviet era. In nuclear safety, the situation might be a bit different, although this is mere speculation. One might at least imagine that public management of Russia's vast nuclear complex – with the conflicting public agencies involved – would have proven more difficult had not a legal framework at the level of law been in place.

Implementation by public authorities The lengthening of the previous chain of implementation has clearly been an obstacle to effective implementation in our case studies. Not only was Soviet implementation of the country's international commitments ensured by the incorporation of these commitments into national production plans; the Soviet Union also possessed administrative systems in areas such as fisheries management, nuclear safety and air pollution control that were indeed 'capable of governing'. When we claim the decreased implementation performance and target compliance in Northwest Russian fisheries in recent years to be the result of the disintegration of the previous enforcement system, this is clearly an example of 'unintentional' implementation failure. Rather than 'Russia' as a rational unitary actor deciding that 'from this moment on we will no longer adhere to our international fisheries commitments and therefore dissolve the existing enforcement system', the reorganisation was partly the result of genuine suspicion on the part of the presidential administration that the existing fishery inspection was incapable of performing its tasks,[5] and partly of more common bureaucratic battles over budget shares (which depend on areas of formal responsibility). The delays in the implementation of some of the international nuclear safety projects reflect intra-agency conflict between Minatom and Gosatomnadzor rather than an overarching Russian unwillingness to implement the projects. Likewise, some implementation processes in nuclear safety have reportedly been delayed by the Ministry of Foreign Affairs 'displaying political strength' to compensate for its lack of financial gain from international co-operation. We should also avoid the Western tendency to perceive the Russian 'hard' agencies as necessarily 'the bad guys' and the 'soft' ones as always 'the good guys'. While there is ample evidence of Minatom attempting to curb the independent nuclear safety protection agency, it is possible at least to imagine that Gosatomnadzor may 'be more meticulous than necessary' in its licensing activities, thus hampering the implementation of Russia's international agreements, in order to legitimise its own existence as an independent agency. Some would say that this is what happened when the 40-tonne cask developed under AMEC was denied a licence.[6] The point is that the devolution of power to new agencies – while being desirable either to ensure independent environmental control or to increase the influence of regional authorities or stakeholders – often involves the cost of lengthening the chain of implementation and hence reducing implementation effectiveness, at least in the short run. It should be observed in this context that delegation of power to the regional level has not hampered implementation. Quite the contrary, the co-ordinating role generally assumed by regional authorities in our case studies has sooner furthered rather than obstructed successful implementation.

In sum, implementation efforts by public authorities at both the federal and regional level can generally explain the failure or success of the individual cases of implementation. On the negative side, most of the problems found in all our three case studies can be accounted for by the high level of conflict between federal agencies. On the positive side, much of the successful implementation activity that is taking place can be ascribed to the existence of pretty well-functioning systems for environmental and natural resource management (i.e. well-functioning as long as they are protected from interference from other bodies of governance). Moreover, the inclusion of regional authorities and federal agencies located in the regions in some of the implementation processes seems to have had a positive effect on implementation performance.

Implementation by others Participation by other actors than public authorities in the implementation process is sometimes believed to enhance chances of success. In particular, the participation of target groups, research communities and NGOs is assumed to bestow legitimacy on the process and increase the knowledge base for implementation. We saw in the case studies that participation by such other actors was generally limited to target groups here. In addition, scientific institutes were also to some extent included in implementation activities, mainly in fisheries management. Where participation by target groups and researchers is observed, primarily in fisheries management, but partly also in nuclear safety, it has contributed positively to those aspects of the implementation process that have proven effective. But, again, this has not been a decisive element in explaining implementation performance.

An assessment of the explanatory power of the various factors we have reviewed in relation to implementation performance is given in Table 7.3. The nature of the problem seems to have had a moderate effect in explaining implementation performance in all three case studies. Most importantly, the fact that major target groups have been privatised during the 1990s has quite seriously hampered implementation. The nature of the commitments proved an important

Table 7.3 *Assessed explanatory power of various factors related to implementation*[a]

	Fisheries management	*Nuclear safety*	*Air pollution control*
Nature of the problem	(2)	(2)	(2)
Nature of the commitments	(1)	(3)	(3)
Implementation in national legislation	(1)	(2)[b]	(1)[b]
Implementation activities by public authorities	(3)	(3)	(3)[b]
Implementation activities by others	(2)	(2)	(1)

[a] 3: high importance; 2: some importance; 1: little importance.

[b] These assessments are made on the basis of contrafactual exercises: based on the experiences of the fisheries management, it is assumed that the incorporation of international commitments in air pollution control, and, to a degree, also nuclear safety, is not a prerequisite for their successful *de facto* implementation. Furthermore, it is assumed that the high level of conflict among federal agencies would have hampered implementation of Russia's international air pollution requirements had they not implemented themselves through the reduction in industry productivity.

explanatory element in the areas of nuclear safety and air pollution control, but not in fisheries management. The air pollution control commitments constituted no real challenge for the Soviet Union/ Russian Federation, while the nuclear safety accords require behavioural changes so far-reaching that, it may be argued, complete compliance should not be expected for some time yet. Based on the results in the fisheries sector, implementation of international commitments in national legislation at the level of law is no prerequisite for further implementation activities. The performance of public authorities is a major explanation to implementation success or failure, while implementation activities of others, mainly target groups and partly also scientific communities, play a certain role. In sum, the implementation performance in the case of fisheries management can be explained mainly by both positive and negative elements in public authorities' implementation efforts, but partly also together with research communities. In air pollution control, the nature of the commitments, i.e. the lack or very limited need of behavioural changes is the main explanation of implementation performance. Finally, the picture is a bit more complex in the case of nuclear safety where all the factors reviewed have had a moderate or considerable effect on implementation performance.

Conclusions

The break-up of the Soviet Union and establishment of a new Russian state in the early 1990s was accompanied by a green wave of environmental concern in the population and the reorganisation of the state structure to incorporate independent agencies for environmental protection and monitoring. The State Committee for Environmental Protection, created in 1988, was elevated to the status of a ministry in 1991. An independent control agency for nuclear safety, Gosatomnadzor, was established the same year. A contrary trend followed in the second half of the decade: the federal agency for environmental protection lost its ministerial status in 1996 and its status as an independent agency four years later. Gosatomnadzor has so far maintained its independence, but has seen its powers and areas of responsibility constrained by Minatom. Similarly, the State Committee for Fisheries lost its independent status temporarily in 1997 and has since been under constant attack from other federal agencies, notably the Federal Border Service and the Ministry of

Economy. Ironically, some of the present tensions at the federal level in Russia concerning the management of the environment and natural resources are the outcome of reorganisations encouraged by the West, partly even spurred by binding agreements with Western countries. Had Russia not established an independent agency for nuclear safety control, these tasks may very well have been performed successfully by Minatom and the difficulties encountered in the implementation of CTR and AMEC would not have occurred. If responsibility for fisheries enforcement at sea had not been transferred to the Federal Border Service – a reorganisation completely in line with the 'Western' view that such control should be performed by agencies with limited affiliation with their target groups (in many countries performed by the Border Guard or the Navy), our Barents Sea fisheries case study might very well have had excellent implementation performance and target compliance. While we do not intend to imply that Gosatomnadzor should not have been established – or that the transfer of enforcement powers to the Federal Border Service was necessarily a mistake in a long-term perspective – we would like to repeat that Russia in some areas of the management of the environment and natural resources has a considerable 'capacity to govern' as part of its Soviet heritage. This is particularly obvious in the management of fisheries.

Hence, while the general climate surrounding the protection of the environment and natural resources is not very promising in Russia at the turn of the millennium, our case studies have also revealed patterns of governance at the regional, federal and international level that do not bode too badly for the future. First, there is the established 'capacity to govern', often overlooked by well-meaning Westerners loaded with good intentions to 'teach the Russians'. Lack of knowledge of existing structures of governance in Russia might well lead to the destruction of systems that already work quite well. Second, the recent history of Northwestern Russia gives a certain hope for the future as far as the role of regional authorities in the implementation process is concerned. Apart from some initial confrontations in the fisheries management, regional authorities have in all three cases taken upon themselves a co-ordinating role that has clearly had a positive effect on implementation performance. Third, most joint implementation initiatives have had a similarly positive effect, not only on implementation problem-solving, but also in overcoming structural difficulties created by the lack of integration and high level of conflict between various Russian agencies of governance. In both fisheries management and nuclear safety, bilateral cooperation with Norway has 'forced' representatives of conflicting Russian agencies – e.g., the Federal Border Service and the 'traditional' fisheries complex, and Minatom and Gosatomnadzor and the State Committee/Department for Environmental Protection – to join forces, which, in turn, has had positive effects on Russian implementation efforts. Based on these conclusions, our main recommendation for the establishment of future environmental agreements with Russia would be to take into consideration the specifics of Russian political culture in drawing up implementation plans for the agreements. Moreover, the potential that lies in joint implementation at the micro level and in involving regional authorities in implementation processes should not be overlooked.

Notes

1 As we noted in Chapter 4, data on the functioning of the Soviet system for fisheries managemet are poor, but it seems fair to assume that management agencies were relatively well endowed in terms of competence and material resources to perform their tasks satisfactorily. Moreover, target compliance was probably quite high since the command economy implied a high degree of control over the activities of the target groups and the latter had low incentives to cheat.

2 Admittedly, important decisions have to be sanctioned by federal authorities, but as mentioned in Chapter 4, the State Committee for Fisheries does not interfere to any large extent in the day-to-day management of Northwest Russian fisheries.

3 Another question is whether the decisions of the Joint Russian–Norwegian Fisheries Commission reflect the parties' obligations as set out in the global fisheries agreements.

4 This is not meant to imply that the implementation of Russia's international fisheries agreements has been completely successful. However, to the extent that it has not been successful, it has not been a result of lacking incorporation of international commitments in national legislation. It could also be argued, as we do in Chapter 4, that the absence of a law on fisheries does not mean that the management of Russian fisheries takes place in a legal vacuum. Legal documents at lower judicial levels are constantly being issued. Further, the definition of 'incorporation in national legislation' is not obvious (e.g. how about a fax sent from Murmanrybvod to a fishing vessel?), so we limit ourselves here to concluding that such incorporation at the level

of law does not seem necessary to spur further implementation efforts.

5 Added to this picture of a conscious effort to avoid implementation of its international fisheries commitments in the Barents Sea comes the fact that the original impetus behind the reorganisation process came from events in the Far Eastern fishery basin, where rumours of corrupt fishery inspectors were far more widespread than in the northern basin.

6 Another example, this time from the area of fisheries management, is the following: towards the end of the 1990s, it became increasingly difficult for Norwegian and Russian marine researchers to get permits from Russian authorities to conduct joint scientific cruises in the Russian part of the Barents Sea. From the Norwegian side, it was generally believed that some of the 'bad guys' (the 'power agencies') were behind the refusals. While we will not contest that this had an effect, we were once told by a Russian fisheries civil servant that the main obstacle was in fact the State Committee for Environmental Protection – by Norwegians generally perceived as a 'good guy' *par excellence* in Russian environmental politics. According to our source, the Committee felt obliged to increasingly spread its tentacles into new areas of governance in order to justify its existence.

References

Alexseev, M.A. (ed.) (1999), *Center–Periphery Conflict in Post-Soviet Russia*, St Martin's Press, New York.

AMAP (1997), *Arctic Pollution Issues: A State of the Arctic Environment Report*, Arctic Monitoring and Assessment Programme, Oslo.

AMAP (1998), *Arctic Pollution Issues: A State of the Arctic Environment Report*, Arctic Monitoring and Assessment Programme, Oslo.

Arctic Council Declaration (1996), Declaration on the Establishment of the Arctic Council (Ottawa, 19 September 1996), http://arctic-council/usgs.gov.

Arkhangelsk Regional Committee of State Statistics (1999), *Short Run Economical Indicators of Arkhangelsk Oblast*, Arkhangelsk.

Balton, D.A. (1996), 'Strengthening the law of the sea: The new agreement on straddling fish stocks and highly migratory fish stocks', *Ocean Development and International Law* 27, 121–51.

Benedick, R.E. (1991), *Ozone Diplomacy: New Directions in Safeguarding our Planet*, Harvard University Press, Cambridge, Massachusetts.

Bergman, R. (1997), 'Hazards from nuclear materials in the arctic region: do we know sufficient for assessing risks and deciding on priorities?', in D. Vidas (ed.), *Arctic Development and Environmental Challenges. Information Needs for Decision-Making and International Co-operation*, Scandinavian Seminar College, Copenhagen.

Bergman, R. and Baklanov, A. (1998), *Radioactive Sources of Main Radiological Concern*, Swedish Council for Planning and Coordination of Research/Swedish Defence Research Establishment, Stockholm.

Blakkisrud, H. (1997), *Den russiske føderasjonen i støpeskjeen. Etniske og territorielle utfordringer* (The Russian Federation in the Making: Ethnic and Territorial Challenges), Spartacus, Oslo.

Blakkisrud, H. (2001a), 'Federal reform in Russia: The case of Nenets Autonomous Okrug', in T.D. Clark and D.R. Kempton (eds), *Unity or*

Separation: Center–Periphery Relations in the Former Soviet Union, Praeger, Westport.

Blakkisrud, H. (2001b), 'The Russian regionalisation process: decentralisation by design or disintegration by default?', in G. Hønneland and H. Blakkisrud (eds), *Center–Periphery Relations in Russia: The Case of the Northwestern Regions*, Ashgate Publishing, Aldershot.

Blakkisrud, H. and Hønneland, G. (2001), 'Introduction', in G. Hønneland and H. Blakkisrud (eds), *Centre–Periphery Relations in Russia. The Case of the Northwestern Regions*, Ashgate Publishing, Aldershot.

Bond, A. (1996), 'The Russian copper industry and the Noril'sk joint-stock company in the mid-1990s', *Post-Soviet Geography and Economics* 37, 286–329.

Bond, A. and Levine, R.M. (2001), 'Noril'sk nickel and Russian platinum-group metals production', *Post-Soviet Geography and Economics* 42, 77–104.

Chayes, A. and Chayes, A.H. (1991), 'Compliance without enforcement: State behaviour under regulatory treaties', *Negotiation Journal* 7, 311–30.

Chayes, A. and Chayes, A.H. (1993), 'On compliance', *International Organization* 47, 175–205.

Chayes, A. and Chayes, A.H. (1995), *The New Sovereignty: Compliance with International Regulatory Agreements*, Harvard University Press, Cambridge, Massachusetts.

Churchill, R.R. (2001), 'Managing straddling fish stocks in the North-East Atlantic: A multiplicity of instruments and regime linkages – but how effective a management?', in O.S. Stokke (ed.), *Governing High Seas Fisheries*, Oxford University Press, Oxford.

Churchill, R.R. and Lowe, A.V. (1999), *The Law of the Sea*, Manchester University Press/Juris Publishing, Manchester.

Conolly, B. and List, M. (1996), 'Nuclear safety in Eastern Europe and the former Soviet Union', in R.O. Keohane and M.A. Levy (eds), *Institutions for Environmental Aid. Pitfalls and Promise*, MIT Press, Cambridge, Massachusetts and London.

Connolly, B., Gutner, T. and Bedarff, H. (1996), 'Organizational inertia and environmental assistance to Eastern Europe', in R.O. Keohane. and M.A. Levy (eds), *Institutions for Environmental Aid: Pitfalls and Promise*, MIT Press, Cambridge, Massachusetts and London.

Dahlström, M., Eskelinen, H. and Wiberg, U. (eds) (1995), *The East–West Interface in the European North*, Nordisk Samhällsgeografisk Tidskrift, Uppsala.

Darst, R.G. (1997), 'The internationalization of environmental protection in the ussr and its successor states', in M.A. Schreurs and E. Economy (eds), *The Internationalization of Environmental Protection*, Cambridge University Press, Cambridge.

Darst, R.G. (2001), *Smokestack Diplomacy: Cooperation and Conflict in East–West Environmental Politics*, MIT Press, Cambridge, Massachusetts and London.

Dellenbrant, J.Å. and Olsson, M.O. (eds) (1994), *The Barents Region. Security and Economic Development in the European North*, CERUM, Umeå.

Dellenbrant, J.Å. and Wiberg, U. (eds) (1997), *Euro-Arctic Curtains*, CERUM, Umeå.

Duchacek, I.D. (1987), *Comparative Federalism: The Territorial Dimension of Politics*, University Press of America, Lanham.

Fisher, D. (1997), *History of the International Atomic Energy Agency: The First Forty Years*, IAEA, Vienna.

Flikke, G. (ed.) (1998), *The Barents Region Revisited*, The Norwegian Institute of International Affairs, Oslo.

Food and Agriculture Organization (1993), Agreement to Promote Compliance with International Conservation and Management Measures by Fishing Vessels on the High Seas (FAO, 24 November 1993), *International Legal Materials* 33, 1994, 368–80.

Food and Agriculture Organization (1996), Food and Agriculture Organization, Code of Conduct for Responsible Fisheries (Rome, 28 September 1995), reproduced in G. Handl (ed.), *Yearbook of International Environmental Law, Vol. 6*, Clarendon Press, Oxford.

Freeland, C. (2000), *Sale of the Century: The Inside Story of the Second Russian Revolution*, Little, Brown and Company, London.

Goskomstat Rossii (1998), *Regiony Rossii* (Russia's Regions), Goskomstat Rossii, Moscow.

Government of the Russian Federation (1992), *Polozheniye o federalnom ekologicheskom fonde Rossiyskoy Federatsii* (Provision on the Federal Environmental Fund of the Russian Federation), confirmed by Presidential Decree No. 442 of 29 June 1992.

Government of the Russian Federation (1997a), *Ukaz Prezidenta RF ot 29 avgusta 1997 No. 950 'O merakh po obespecheniyu okhrany morskikh biologicheskikh resursov i gosudarstvennogo kontrolya v etoy sfere'* (Decree of the President of the Russian Federation of 29 August 1997 No. 950 'On Measures to Secure Protection of Marine Biological Resources and State Control in this Sphere'), 29 August.

Government of the Russian Federation (1997b), *Ob utverzhdenii polozheniya o litsenzirovaniya deyatelnosti v oblasti ispolzovaniya atomnoy energii* (On the Confirmation of the Provision on Licensing of Activities in the Use of Nuclear Energy), Order of the Government of the Russian Federation No. 865 of 14 June.

Government of the Russian Federation (1999), *O litsenzirovanii deyatelnosti po ispolzovaniyu radioaktivnykh materialov pri provedenii rabot po ispolzovaniyu atomnoy energii v oboronnykh tselyakh* (On Licensing of

Activities Connected to the Use of Radioactive Materials in Work on Use of Atomic Energy for Defence Purposes), Order of the Government of the Russian Federation No. 1007 of 4 September.

Government of the Russian Federation (2000), *Rasporyazheniye ot 9 fevralya 2000 g. No. 200-r* (Order of 9 February 2000 No. 200-r), the Government of the Russian Federation.

Gubanov, V.A. and Akhunov, V.D. (1995), 'Ministry of Atomic Energy of the Russian Federation (Minatom)', in *International Co-operation on Nuclear Waste Management in the Russian Federation*, International Atomic Energy Agency, Vienna.

Haas, P.M. (1990), *Saving the Mediterranean: The Politics of International Environmental Cooperation*, Columbia University Press, New York.

Haas, P., Keohane, R.O. and Levy, M.A. (1993), *Institutions for the Earth: Sources of Effective International Environmental Protection*, MIT Press, Cambridge, Massachusetts and London.

Hanf, K. (2000), 'The problem of long-range transport of air pollution and the acidification regime', in A. Underdal and K. Hanf (eds), *International Environmental Agreements and Domestic Politics: The Case of Acid Rain*, Ashgate Publishing, Aldershot.

Hanf, K. and Underdal, A. (1998), 'Domesticating international commitments: linking national and international decision-making', in A. Underdal (ed.), *The Politics of International Environmental Management*, Kluwer Academic Publishers, Dordrecht.

Hansen, E. and Tønnessen, A. (1998), *Environment and Living Conditions on the Kola Peninsula*, FAFO Institute for Applied Social Science, Oslo.

Hanson, P. (1994), *Regions, Local Power and Economic Change in Russia*, Royal Institute of International Affairs, London.

Hayashi, M. (1995), 'The 1995 agreement on the conservation and management of straddling and highly migratory fish stocks: Significance for the law of the sea convention', *Ocean and Coastal Management* 29, 51–69.

Hayashi, M. (1996), 'Enforcement by non-flag states on the high seas under the 1995 agreement on straddling stocks and highly migratory fish stocks', *The Georgetown International Environmental Law Review* 9, 1–36.

Hedenskog, J. (2000), *Mellan Nordpolen och Moskva: Murmansk oblast och relationen till centralmakten* (Between the North Pole and Moscow: Murmansk Oblast and its Relations to the Central Power), Defence Research Establishment, Stockholm.

Hønneland, G. (1998), 'Autonomy and regionalisation in the fisheries management of Northwestern Russia', *Marine Policy* 22, 57–65.

Hønneland, G. (2000a), *Coercive and Discursive Compliance Mechanisms in the Management of Natural Resources: A Case Study from the Barents Sea Fisheries*, Kluwer Academic Publishers, Dordrecht.

Hønneland, G. (2000b) 'Enforcement co-operation between Norway and Russia in the Barents Sea fisheries', *Ocean Development and International Law* 31, 249–67.

Hønneland, G. (2001), 'Centre–periphery tensions in the management of northwest Russian Fisheries', in G. Hønneland and H. Blakkisrud (eds), *Centre–Periphery Relations in Russia: The Case of the Northwestern Regions*, Ashgate Publishing, Aldershot.

Hønneland, G. and Blakkisrud, H. (eds) (2001), *Centre–Periphery Relations in Russia: The Case of the Northwestern Regions*, Ashgate Publishing, Aldershot.

Hønneland, G. and Jørgensen, A.K. (1998), 'Closed cities on the Kola Peninsula: From autonomy to integration?' *Polar Geography* 22, 231–48.

Hønneland, G. and Jørgensen, A.K. (1999a), *Integration vs. Autonomy: Civil–Military Relations on the Kola Peninsula*, Ashgate Publishing, Aldershot.

Hønneland, G. and Jørgensen, A.K. (1999b), 'A cross-border perspective on a North Russian gateway', *Post-Soviet Geography and Economics* 40, 44–61.

Hønneland, G., Jørgensen, A.K. and Kovacs, K. (1999), *Barents Sea Ecoregion Reconnaissance Report: A Report Commissioned by World Wide Fund for Nature*, The Fridtjof Nansen Institute, Lysaker.

Hønneland, G. and Moe, A. (2000), *Evaluation of the Norwegian Plan of Action for Nuclear Safety: Priorities, Organisation, Implementation*, Evaluation Report 7/2000, Royal Norwegian Ministry of Foreign Affairs, Oslo.

Hønneland, G. and Nilssen, F. (2000), 'Comanagement in Northwest Russian fisheries', *Society and Natural Resources* 13, 635–48.

Hønneland, G. and Nilssen, F. (2001), 'Quota allocation in Russia's Northern fishery basin: Principles and practice', *Ocean and Coastal Management* 44, 471–88.

International Atomic Energy Agency (1957), *IAEA Statute*, IAEA, Vienna.

International Atomic Energy Agency (1963), *The Vienna Convention on Civil Liability for Nuclear Damage* (Vienna, 21 May), IAEA, Vienna.

International Atomic Energy Agency (1974), *Nuclear Safety Standards* (Vienna), IAEA, Vienna.

International Atomic Energy Agency (1986a), *The Convention on Early Notification of a Nuclear Accident* (Vienna, 26 September), IAEA, Vienna.

International Atomic Energy Agency (1986b), *The Convention on Assistance in the Case of a Nuclear Accident or Radiological Emergency* (Vienna, 26 September), IAEA, Vienna.

International Atomic Energy Agency (1994), *The Convention on Nuclear Safety* (Vienna, 17 June), IAEA, Vienna.

International Atomic Energy Agency (1997), *The Joint Convention on the Safety of Radioactive Waste Management* (Vienna, September 1997), IAEA, Vienna.

International Maritime Organization (1972), The London Convention on the Prevention of Marine Pollution by Dumping of Waste and Other Matter, *International Legal Materials* 11, 1291ff.

Jönsson, C. and Tallberg, J. (1998), 'Compliance and post-agreement bargaining', *European Journal of International Relations* 4, 371–408.

Jørgensen, A.K. (1999), 'Norsk og russisk fiskerikontroll i Barentshavet – en sammenligning med hensyn til effektivitet' (Norwegian and Russian fisheries enforcement in the Barents Sea: A comparison with regard to effectiveness), MA thesis, Department of Political Science, University of Oslo, Oslo.

Jørgensen, A.K. (2001), 'The military sector: Federal responsibility – Regional concern', in G. Hønneland and H. Blakkisrud (eds), *Centre–Periphery Relations in Russia: The Case of the Northwestern Regions*, Ashgate Publishing, Aldershot.

Kaiser, R.J. (1994), *The Geography of Nationalism in Russia and the USSR*, Princeton University Press, Princeton.

Kotov, V. (1994), *Implementation and Effectiveness of International Environmental Regimes during the Process of Economic Transformation in Russia*, WP-94-123, International Institute for Applied System Analysis, Laxenburg.

Kotov, V. and Nikitina, E. (1996), 'To reduce, or to produce? Problems of implementation of the climate convention in Russia', in J.B. Poole and R. Guthrie (eds), *Verification Yearbook 1996*, Westview Press, Boulder, Colorado.

Kotov, V. and Nikitina, E. (1998a), 'Implementation and effectiveness of the acid rain regime in Russia', in D.G. Victor, K. Raustiala and E.B. Skolnikoff (eds), *The Implementation and Effectiveness of International Environmental Commitments. Theory and Practice*, MIT Press, Cambridge and London.

Kotov, V. and Nikitina, E. (1998b), 'Regime and enterprise: Norilsk nickel and transboundary air pollution', in D.G. Victor, K. Raustiala and E.B. Skolnikoff (eds), *The Implementation and Effectiveness of International Environmental Commitments: Theory and Practice*, MIT Press, Cambridge and London.

Levy, M.A. (1995), 'International cooperation to combat acid rain', *Green Globe Yearbook 1995*, Oxford University Press, Oxford.

List, M. and Rittberger, V. (1998), 'The role of intergovernmental organizations in the formation and evolution of international environmental regimes', in A. Underdal (ed.), *The Politics of International Environmental Management*, Kluwer Academic Publishers, Dordrecht.

Lønne, O.J., Sætre, R., Tikhonov, S., Gabrielsen, G.W., Loeng, H., Dahle, S. and Shevlyagin, K. (eds) (1997), *Status Report on the Marine Environment of the Barents Region. Report from the Working Group on the Marine Environment of the Barents Regions to the Joint Norwegian–Russian Commission on Environmental Co-operation*, Ministry of Environment, Oslo.

Makfol, M. and Petrov, N. (eds) (1998), *Politicheskiy almanakh Rossii 1997* (Political Almanac of Russia), Tsentr Karnegi, Moscow.

Maurseth, P.B. (1997), *Fra kald krig til økonomisk samarbeid – Perspektiver for handel og integrasjon mellom Norge og Russland i nord* (From Cold War to Economic Co-operation – Perspectives for Trade and Integration between Norway and Russia in the North), NUPI Report No. 216, NUPI, Oslo.

Maurseth, P.B. (2001), 'Russian regions in transition: centralisation through decentralisation?', in G. Hønneland and H. Blakkisrud (eds), *Centre–Periphery Relations in Russia: The Case of the Northwestern Regions*, Ashgate Publishing, Aldershot.

McAuley, A. (1997), 'The determinants of Russian federal–regional fiscal relations: Equity or political influence?' *Europe–Asia Studies* 49, 431–444.

McAuley, M. (1997), *Russia's Politics of Uncertainty*, Cambridge University Press, Cambridge.

Ministry of Atomic Energy (1997), *Polozheniye o Ministerstve Rossiyskoy Federatsii po atomnoy energii* (Provision on the Ministry of Atomic Energy of the Russian Federation), confirmed by Governmental Resolution No. 392 of 5 April 1997.

Ministry of the Environment (2001), *Avtale undertegnet om modernisering av nikkelverket i Petsjenga* (Agreement Signed on the Modernisation of the Nickel Smelter at Pechenga), the Ministry of the Environment, Oslo.

Ministry of Fisheries (1999), *Protocol from the 28th Session in the Joint Russian–Norwegian Fisheries Commission*, the Ministry of Fisheries, Oslo.

Ministry of Foreign Affairs (1993), *Declaration on Co-operation in the Barents Euro–Arctic Region* (Kirkenes, 11 January), the Ministry of Foreign Affairs, Oslo.

Ministry of Foreign Affairs (1995), *Plan of Action for the Implementation of Report No. 34 (1993–94) to the Storting on Nuclear Activities and Chemical Weapons in Areas Adjacent to Our Northern Borders*, the Ministry of Foreign Affairs, Oslo.

Ministry of Foreign Affairs (1996), *Declaration among the Department of Defense of the United States of America, the Royal Ministry of Defence of the Kingdom of Norway, and the Ministry of Defence of the Russian Federation on Arctic Military Environmental Co-operation* (Bergen, 26 September), the Ministry of Foreign Affairs, Oslo.

Ministry of Foreign Affairs (1998), *Agreement between the Government of the Kingdom of Norway and the Government of the Russian Federation on Environmental Co-operation with the Dismantling of Russian Nuclear Powered Submarines Withdrawn from the Navy's Service in the Northern Region, and the Enhancement of Nuclear and Radiation Safety* (Moscow, 26 May), the Ministry of Foreign Affairs, Oslo.

Ministry of Foreign Affairs (1999), *Declaration on Principles Regarding a Multilateral Nuclear Environmental Programme in the Russian Federation* (Bodø, 5 March), the Ministry of Foreign Affairs, Oslo.

Mitchell, R.B. (1994a), 'Regime design matters: International oil pollution and treaty compliance', *International Organization* 48, 425–58.

Mitchell, R.B. (1994b), *Intentional Oil Pollution at Sea: Environmental Policy and Treaty Compliance*, MIT Press, Cambridge, Massachusetts and London.

Mnookin, R.H. and Kornhauser, L. (1979), 'Bargaining in the shadow of the law: The case of divorce', *Yale Law Journal* 88, 950–97.

Morgenthau, H.J. (1978), *Politics among Nations: The Struggle for Power and Peace* (fifth edition), Alfred A. Knopf, New York.

Munton, D., Soroos, M., Nikitina, E. and Levy, M.A. (1999), 'Acid rain in Europe and North America', in O.R. Young (ed.), *The Effectiveness of International Environmental Regimes: Causal Connections and Behavioral Mechanisms*, MIT Press, Cambridge, Massachusetts and London.

Murmansk Oblast (1997a), Dogovor o razgranichenii predmetov vedeniya i polnomochiy mezhdu organami gosudarstvennoy vlasti Rossiyskoy Federatsii i organami gosudarstvennoy vlasti Murmanskoy oblasti (Agreement on the Delimitation of Subjects of Governance and Authorities between Agencies of the State Power of the Russian Federation and Agencies of State Power of Murmansk Oblast), signed in Moscow 30 November 1997, published in *Rossiyskiye vesti*, 25 December.

Murmansk Oblast (1997b), *O pribrezhnom promysle v Murmanskoy oblasti* (On Coastal Fisheries in Murmansk Oblast), Regional Law of Murmansk Oblast No. 91-01 of 30 December.

Murmansk Oblast (1997c), *O radiatsionnoy bezopasnosti naseleniya v Murmanskoy oblasti* (On the Radiation Safety of the Population of Murmansk Oblast), Regional Law of Murmansk Oblast No. 84-01, adopted by the Murmansk Regional Duma 30 October 1997, signed by the Governor 21 November.

Murmansk Oblast (1997d), *Ob oblastnom ekologicheskom fonde* (On the Regional Environmental Fund), Regional Law of Murmansk Oblast No. 60-02-ZMO of 3 June.

Murmansk Oblast (1998), *Soglasheniye mezhdu administratsiyey Murmanskoy oblasti i Ministerstvom Rossiyskoy Federatsii po atomnoy energii o vzaimnom sotrudnichestve v oblasti obrashcheniya s RAO i OYAT i razvitii atomnoy energetiki na territorii Murmanskoy oblasti* (Agreement between the Administration of Murmansk Oblast and the Ministry of Atomic Energy of the Russian Federation on Joint Co-operation in the Treatment of Radioactive Waste and Spent Nuclear Fuel and Development of Nuclear Energetics on the Territory of Murmansk Oblast), signed in Murmansk on 5 May.

Murmansk Oblast (2000), *Soglasheniye mezhdu administratsiyey Murmanskoy oblasti, Federalnymi organami ispolnitelnoy vlasti na territorii Murmanskoy oblasti, KNTS RAN, Severnym Flotom VMF MO RF i gosudarstvennymi predpriyatiyami po koordinatsii vzaimodeystviya v sfere yadernoy i radiatsionnoy bezopasnosti na territorii Murmanskoy oblasti No. 37-2/296* (Agreement between the Administration of Murmansk Oblast, Federal Bodies of the Executive Power on the Territory of Murmansk Oblast, Kola Science Centre of the Russian Academy of Science, the Northern Fleet of the Navy of the Russian Federation's Ministry of Defence and State Enterprises on the Co-ordination of Interaction in the Sphere of Nuclear and Radiation Safety on the Territory of Murmansk Oblast, No. 37-2/296), signed in Murmansk on 7 March.

Murmansk Regional Committee of State Statistics (1999), *Murmansk Region in Figures*, Murmansk.

Nikitina, E. (1991), 'New Soviet environmental policy: Approaches to global changes', *International Study Notes* 16, 3137.

Nikitina, E. (1995), *National Implementation of International Environmental Commitments: A Review of Soviet Literature*, WP-95-26, International Institute for Applied System Analysis, Laxenburg.

Nilsen, T., Kudrik, I. and Nikitin, A. (1996), *The Russian Northern Fleet: Sources of Radioactive Contamination*, Bellona Report No. 2, Bellona, Oslo.

Nilssen, F. and Hønneland, G. (2001), 'Institutional change and the problems of restructuring the Russian fishing industry', *Post-Communist Economies* 13, 313–30.

Northeast Atlantic Fisheries Commission (1982), Convention of Future Multilateral Cooperation in the North-East Atlantic Fisheries, *Official Journal of the European Communities*, 1981 L227/22.

Northwest Atlantic Fisheries Organization (1978), Convention on Future Multilateral Cooperation in the Northwest Atlantic Fisheries (Ottawa, 24 October 1978), *Official Journal of the European Communities*, No. L 378, 30 December.

OECD (1999), *Environmental Performance Reviews. Russian Federation*, Organisation for Economic Co-operation and Development, Centre for Co-operation with Non-Members, Paris.

Orlov, V.A. (1997), 'Perspectives of Russian decision-makers and problems of implementation', in J.M. Shields and W.C. Potter (eds), *Dismantling the Cold War: US and NIS Perspectives on the Nunn–Lugar Cooperative Threat Reduction Program*, MIT Press, Cambridge and London.

Pikayev, A.A. (1997), 'The CTR program and Russia: Is a new start possible? A Russian view', in J.M. Shields and W.C. Potter (eds), *Dismantling the Cold War: US and NIS Perspectives on the Nunn–Lugar Cooperative Threat Reduction Program*, MIT Press, Cambridge and London.

Raustiala, K. and Victor, D.G. (1998), 'Conclusions', in D.G. Victor, K. Raustiala and E.B. Skolnikoff (eds), *The Implementation and Effectiveness of International Environmental Commitments. Theory and Practice*, MIT Press, Cambridge and London.

Risnes, B. (2001), 'Relations between Moscow and the regions of Northwestern Russia – The legal aspect', in G. Hønneland and H. Blakkisrud (eds), *Centre–Periphery Relations in Russia. The Case of the Northwestern Regions*, Ashgate Publishing, Aldershot.

Russian Federation (1992), *O zakrytom administrativno-territorialnom obrazovanii* (On the Closed Administrative–Territorial Formation), Federal Law of the Russian Federation, No. 3298-1, signed by the Chairman of the Supreme Soviet 14 July.

Russian Federation (1993), *O sertifikatsii produktsii i uslug* (On the Certification of Production and Services), Federal Law of the Russian Federation, No. 5151-1, signed by the President 10 June.

Russian Federation (1995a), *Ob ispolzovanii atomnoy energii* (On the Use of Nuclear Energy), Federal Law of the Russian Federation, No. 170-FZ, adopted by the State Duma 20 October 1995, signed by the President 21 November.

Russian Federation (1995b), *O radiatsionnoy bezopasnosti naseleniya* (On the Radioation Safety of the Population), Federal Law of the Russian Federation, No. 3-FZ, adopted by the State Duma 5 December 1995, signed by the President 9 January 1996.

Russian Federation (1998), *Ob Isklyuchitelnoy Ekonomicheskoy Zone Rossiyskoy Federatsii* (On the Exclusive Economic Zone of the Russian Federation), Federal Law, adopted by the State Duma 18 November 1998 and by the Federation Council 2 December.

Russian Federation (2000), *Ob administrativnoy otvetstvennosti organizatsiy za narusheniye zakonodatelstva v oblasti ispolzovaniya atomnoy energii* (On the Administrative Liability of Organisations for the Violation of Legislation in the Use of Nuclear Energy), Federal Law of the Russian Federation, adopted by the State Duma 14 April, signed by the President 12 May.

Russian Soviet Federative Socialist Republic (1991), *Ob okhrane okruzhayushey prirodnoy sredy* (On the Protection of the Natural Environment), Republican Law of the Russian Soviet Federative Socialist Republic No. 2060-1 of 19 December.

Safranchuk, I. (2000a) (ed.), *Cooperative Threat Reduction Program: How Efficient?* PIR Centre, Moscow.

Safranchuk, I. (2000b), 'ESOA program in Russia: Results and problems of implementation', in I. Safranchuk (ed.), *Cooperative Threat Reduction Program: How Efficient?* PIR Centre, Moscow.

Sakwa, R. (1993), *Russian Politics and Society*, Routledge, London.

Sawhill, S. (2000), 'Cleaning-up the Arctic's cold war legacy: Nuclear waste and military environmental cooperation', *Cooperation and Conflict* 35, 5–36.

Sawhill, S. and Jørgensen, A.K. (2001), *Military Nuclear Waste and International Cooperation in Northwest Russia*, FNI Report 12/2001, The Fridtjof Nansen Institute, Lysaker.

Semenov, B. and Bonne, A. (1999), *Facilitating Radioactive Waste Management Co-operation with the Russian Federation*, paper presented at the Waste Management Conference, Tucson, USA, 28 February–4 March.

Shields, J.M. and Potter, W.C. (1997) (eds), *Dismantling the Cold War: US and NIS Perspectives on the Nunn–Lugar Cooperative Threat Reduction Program*, MIT Press, Cambridge and London.

Shlapentokh, V., Levita, R. and Loiberg, M. (1997), *From Submission to Rebellion. The Province versus the Center in Russia*, Westview Press, Boulder.

Skogan, J.K. (1986), *Sovjetunionens Nordflåte 1968–85* (The Soviet Union's Northern Fleet 1968–85), NUPI, Oslo.

Smith, G. (ed.) (1995), *Federalism: The Multiethnic Challenge*, Longman, London.

State Committee for Environmental Protection (1998), information leaflet, State Committee for Environmental Protection in Murmansk Oblast.

State Committee for Environmental Protection (2001), *Sostoyaniye prirodnoy okruzhayushey sredy Murmanskoy oblasti na Kolskom poluostrove v 2000 g.* (The State of the Natural Environment of Murmansk Oblast on the Kola Peninsula in 2000), State Committee for Environmental Protection in Murmansk Oblast.

State Committee for Fisheries (1999a), *Vremennoye polozheniye o raspredelenii kvot na vylov vodnykh biologicheskikh resursov vo vnutrennikh vodoyomakh, vnutnennikh morskikh moryakh, territorialnom more, na kontinentalnom shelfe, v isklyuchitelnoy ekonomicheskoy zone Rossiyskoy Federatsii, v zonakh inostrannykh gosudarstv i v rayonakh deystviya mezhdunarodnykh konventsiy po rybolovstvu* (Preliminary Provision on Quota Allocation of Catches of Aquatic Biological Resources in the Russian Federation's Rivers and Lakes, Internal Ocean Waters, Territorial Waters, the Continental Shelf and the Exclusive Economic Zone, as well as in Other Countries' Zones and in the International Convention Areas for Fishing), the State Committee for Fisheries of the Russian Federation, Moscow.

State Committee for Fisheries (1999b), *Polozheniye o vzaimodeystviye i koordinatsii deyatelnosti organov i voysk Federalnoy Pogranichnoy Sluzhby Rossiyskoy Federatsii i organov po okhrane, vosproizvodstvu rybnykh zapasov i regulirovaniyu rybolovstva Gosudarstvennogo komiteta Rossiyskoy Federatsii po rubolovstvu v sfere okhrany vodnykh biologicheskikh resursov* (Provision on Interaction and Co-ordination of the Activities of Bodies and Troops of the Federal Border Service of the Russian Federation and Bodies Responsible for Protection, Reproduction of Fish Stocks and Regulation of Fisheries in the State Committee for Fisheries of the Russian Federation in the Sphere of Protection of Biological Water Resources) (Moscow, 12 January), the Federal Border Service of the Russian Federation and the State Committee for Fisheries of the Russian Federation, Moscow.

Stavrakis, P.J., DeBardeleben, J. and Black, L. (eds) (1997), *Beyond the Monolith: The Emergence of Regionalism in Post-Soviet Russia*, Johns Hopkins University Press, Washington DC.

Stokke, O.S. (1998), 'Nuclear dumping in Arctic Seas: Russian implementation of the London Convention', in D.G. Victor, K. Raustiale and E.B. Skolnikoff (eds), *The Implementation and Effectiveness of International Environmental Commitments. Theory and Practice*, The MIT Press, Cambridge and London.

Stokke, O.S. (2000a), 'Subregional cooperation and protection of the Arctic marine environment: The Barents Sea', in D. Vidas (ed.), *Protecting the Polar Marine Environment. Law and Policy for Pollution Prevention*, Cambridge University Press, Cambridge.

Stokke, O.S. (2000b), 'Radioactive waste in the Barents and Kara Seas: Russian implementation of the global dumping regime', in D. Vidas (ed.), *Protecting the Polar Marine Environment. Law and Policy for Pollution Prevention*, Cambridge University Press, Cambridge.

Stokke, O.S. (ed.) (2001), *Governing High Seas Fisheries*, Oxford University Press, Oxford.

Stokke, O.S. and Tunander, O. (eds) (1994), *The Barents Region: Cooperation in Arctic Europe*, Sage Publications, London.

Stokke, O.S., Anderson, L.G. and Mirovitskaya, N. (1999), 'The Barents Sea fisheries', in O.R. Young (ed.), *The Effectiveness of International Environmental Regimes: Causal Connections and Behavioral Mechanisms*, MIT Press, Cambridge, Massachusetts and London.

Stortinget (1975), St prp nr 86 (1974–75) *Om samtykke til inngåelse av en avtale mellom Norge og Sovjetunionen om samarbeid innen fiskerinæringen* (Report to the Storting No. 86 (1974–75) On the Consensus to Conclude an Agreement between Norway and the Soviet Union on Co-operation in the Fishing Industry), Stortinget, Oslo.

Stortinget (1976), St prp nr 74 (1976–77) *Om samtykke til ratifikasjon av en avtale mellom Regjeringen i Kongeriket Norge og Regjeringen i Unionen av Sovjetiske Sosialistiske Republikker om gjensidige fiskeriforbindelser* (Report to the Storting No. 74 (1976–77) On the Consensus to Ratify an Agreement between the Government of the Kingdom of Norway and the Government of the Union of Soviet Socialist Republics on Mutual Fishery Relations), Stortinget, Oslo.

Stortinget (1994), *Report No. 34 (1993–94) to the Storting on Nuclear Activities and Chemical Weapons in Areas Adjacent to our Northern Borders*, Stortinget, Oslo.

Timerbaev, R. and Iorysh, A. (1999), 'International Co-operation in Nuclear Safety', in H.O. Bergesen, G. Parmann and Ø. Thommessen (eds), *Yearbook of International Co-operation on Environment and Development*, Earthscan Publications, London.

Underdal, A. (1992), 'The concept of regime "effectiveness"', *Cooperation and Conflict* 27, 227–40.

Underdal, A. and Hanf, K. (2000), *International Environmental Agreements and Domestic Politics: The Case of Acid Rain*, Ashgate Publishing, Aldershot.

UN Economic Commission for Europe (1979), *Convention on Long-Range Transboundary Air Pollution* (Geneva, 13 November), UN Economic Commission for Europe, Geneva.

UN Economic Commission for Europe (1988), *Protocol to the Convention on Long-Range Transboundary Air Pollution concerning the Control of Emissions of Nitrogen Oxides or their Transboundary Fluxes* (Sofia, 31 October), UN Economic Commission for Europe, Geneva.

UN Economic Commission for Europe (1991), *Protocol to the Convention on Long-Range Transboundary Air Pollution concerning the Control of Emissions of Volatile Organic Compounds or their Transboundary Fluxes* (Geneva, 18 November), UN Economic Commission for Europe, Geneva.

UN Economic Commission for Europe (1994), *Protocol to the Convention on Long-Range Transboundary Air Pollution on Further Reduction of Sulphur Emissions* (Oslo, 14 June), UN Economic Commission for Europe, Geneva.

UN Economic Commission for Europe (1998a), *Protocol to the Convention on Long-Range Transboundary Air Pollution on Heavy Metals* (Århus, 24 June), UN Economic Commission for Europe, Geneva.

UN Economic Commission for Europe (1998b), *Protocol to the Convention on Long-Range Transboundary Air Pollution on Persistent Organic Pollutants* (Århus, 24 June), UN Economic Commission for Europe, Geneva.

United Nations (1982), United Nations Convention on the Law of the Sea (Montego Bay, 10 December), UN Doc. A/CONF. 62/122, *International Legal Materials* 21, 1261.

United Nations (1995), Agreement for the Implementation of the Provisions of the United Nations Convention on the Law of the Sea of 10 December 1982 Relating to the Conservation and Management of Straddling Fish Stocks and Highly Migratory Fish Stocks (New York, 4 August), *International Legal Materials* 34,, 1547–80.

US Department of State (1992), Agreement between the United States of America and the Russian Federation Concerning the Safe and Secure Transportation, Storage and Destruction of Weapons and the Prevention of Weapons Proliferation (Washington, 17 June), *Treaties and Other International Acts Series*, US Department of State, Washington.

US Department of State (1993), Agreement between the United States of America and the Russian Federation Concerning Cooperation in the Elimination of Strategic Offensive Arms (Washington, 26 August), *Treaties and Other International Acts Series*, US Department of State, Washington.

VanderZwaag, D. (2000), 'Land-based marine pollution and the Arctic: Polarities between principles and practice', in D. Vidas (ed.), *Protecting the Polar Marine Environment: Law and Policy for Pollution Prevention*, Cambridge University Press, Cambridge.

Victor, D.G., Raustiala, K. and Skolnikoff, E.B. (1998a), *The Implementation and Effectiveness of International Environmental Commitments: Theory and Practice*, MIT Press, Cambridge, Massachusetts and London.

Victor, D.G., Raustiala, K. and Skolnikoff, E.B. (1998b), 'Introduction and overview', in D.G. Victor, K. Raustiala and E.B. Skolnikoff (eds), *The Implementation and Effectiveness of International Environmental Commitments: Theory and Practice*, The MIT Press, Cambridge and London.

Wæver, O. (1996), 'The rise and fall of the inter-paradigm debate', in S. Smith, K. Booth, and M. Zalewski (eds), *International Theory: Positivism and Beyond*, Cambridge University Press, Cambridge.

Weiss, E.B. and Jacobson, H.K. (eds) (1998), *Engaging Countries: Strengthening Compliance with International Environmental Accords*, MIT Press, Cambridge, Massachusetts and London.

Wettestad, J. (1999), *Designing Effective Environmental Regimes*, Edward Elgar, Cheltenham.

Whitefield, S. (1993), *Industrial Power and the Soviet State*, Clarendon Press, Oxford.

Yablokov, A.V., Karasev, V.K., Rumyanstsev, V.M., Kokeev, M.E., Petrov, O.Y., Lystsov, V.N., Emel'yanenkov, A.M. and Rubtsov, P.M. (1993), *Facts and Problems Related to Radioactive Waste Disposal in Seas Adjacent to the Territory of the Russian Federation*, Small World Publishers, Moscow.

Young, O. (1989), 'The politics of international regime formation: Managing natural resources and the environment', *International Organization* 43, 349–75.

Young, O. (1991), 'Political leadership and regime formation: On the development of institutions in international society', *International Organization* 45, 281–308.

Young, O. (1996), 'Institutional linkages in international society: Polar perspectives', *Global Governance* 2, 1–24.

Young, O.R. (ed.) (1999), *The Effectiveness of International Environmental Regimes. Causal Connections and Behavioral Mechanisms*, MIT Press, Cambridge, Massachusetts and London.

Young, O. and Osherenko, G. (eds) (1993), *Polar Politics: Creating International Environmental Regimes*, Cornell University Press, Ithaca.

Zimmermann, W., Nikitina, E. and Clem, J. (1998), 'The Soviet Union and the Russian Federation: A natural experiment in environmental compliance', in E.B. Weiss and H.K. Jacobson (eds), *Engaging Countries: Strengthening Compliance with International Environmental Accords*, MIT Press, Cambridge, Massachusetts and London.

Index